Wives and Wanderers in a New Guinea Highlands Society

WOMEN'S LIVES IN THE WAHGI VALLEY

Wives and Wanderers in a New Guinea Highlands Society

WOMEN'S LIVES IN THE WAHGI VALLEY

MARIE OLIVE REAY

EDITED BY FRANCESCA MERLAN
WITH ADDITIONAL INTRODUCTION
BY MARILYN STRATHERN

Australian
National
University

ANU PRESS

Australian
National
University

ANU PRESS

Published by ANU Press
The Australian National University
Acton ACT 2601, Australia
Email: anupress@anu.edu.au

Available to download for free at press.anu.edu.au

ISBN (print): 9781760464707
ISBN (online): 9781760464714

WorldCat (print): 1289471291
WorldCat (online): 1289469180

DOI: 10.22459/WWNGHS.2022

Cover design and layout by ANU Press. Cover photograph: Woman and pigs, Album 2
Reay 440/1194, Noel Butlin Archives.

This book is published under the aegis of the Humanities and Creative Arts Editorial
Board of ANU Press.

Contents

List of Illustrations   vii

Editor's Introduction   1
Francesca Merlan

Introduction   43
Marilyn Strathern

Preface   59

1. The World of a Woman   65
2. Carrying Leg   87
3. A Girl is Marked   111
4. A Rubbish Man Takes a Wife   133
5. Lothario Gains a Bride   143
6. The Amazonian Mood   159
7. Meri Tultul   173
8. Wandering Wives   175
9. A Woman of the Kugika   193
10. The Witch-Girl and the Shrew   209
11. True Cousin   211
12. One Family   221
13. Laik Bilong Man   225
14. 'Wandering Women' and 'Good Women'   251

Appendix A   257
Appendix B   259
Appendix C   265
Appendix D   269
Appendix E   285
Michael W. Young

Index   291

List of Illustrations

Photograph 1: Marie Reay   ix

Photograph 2: Marie Reay with colleagues from The Australian National University, 1955   4

Map 1: The Wahgi Valley and its location in Papua New Guinea, showing (most) place names mentioned in the text   8

Map 2: North and South Wahgi Census Divisions, showing tribal areas   11

Photograph 3: *Karim* leg (carrying leg) I—Kuma 1959   15

Photograph 4: *Karim* leg (carrying leg) II   16

Photograph 5: *Tanimbet*   17

Photograph 6: Girl bathed in pig grease   18

Photograph 7: Wahgi married woman   22

Photograph 8: Koma held by a male relative while being rebuked for running away to evade marriage, c. 1953–59   23

Photograph 9: Woman and pigs   67

Photograph 10: Two women and child   68

Photograph 11: Woman in garden   72

Photograph 12: Pig feast   84

Photograph 13: Wubalt festival (harvest feast featuring pandanus nuts)   84

Photograph 14: Feast with possible cult house   85

Photograph 15: Men wearing spirit boards   85

Photograph 1: Marie Reay

Source: Album 2 Reay 440/1194, Noel Butlin Archives

Editor's Introduction

Francesca Merlan

Editing and evaluating the work of Marie Olive Reay

The book before you was found in 2011, seven years after the death of its author, Marie Olive Reay, and about 50 years after she had made last amendments to the manuscript—probably around 1965. *Wives and Wanderers* presents a vivid, ethnographically based narrative of the lives of women of the Wahgi Valley, in the Central Highlands of Papua New Guinea. Reay explores the experiences of courting, attraction, love, marriage, and the combination of male dominance and barely restrained female resentment and rebelliousness which she found to be characteristic of this setting. Reay's attention was focused on what she saw as a radical discontinuity in the socialization of women in this part of New Guinea: a contrast between considerable freedom enjoyed by young women in the choice of male partners with whom to court before marriage, versus the sudden and dramatic deprivation of their freedom upon marriage. She saw marriage as a traumatic, often violence-laden experience in their lives.

Had it appeared earlier, *Wives and Wanderers* would have had a central place in the anthropological literature on Papua New Guinean societies, especially those of the Central Highlands. And it would have been the foundational, indeed the first, book on women's lives in that part of the world. But we must wonder about these hypotheticals.

First, we may ask why the work did not appear in Reay's lifetime? Reay was otherwise a fairly steady author; and she had worked on this manuscript for a long time. Some of the ethnography upon which it is based goes back to Reay's first fieldwork in the New Guinea Highlands, in the early 1950s. Why, then, did she not publish it? What considerations, perhaps hesitations, may have kept her from doing so? This Introduction offers some suggestions.

And second, though it lay unpublished so long, *Wives and Wanderers* remains amazingly contemporary. Through publication now, it may yet find a place in the anthropological literatures of Highlands Papua New Guinea, and of feminism, on grounds explored in this Editor's Introduction. At any rate, its continuing social relevance is not to be doubted. Though it is based on Reay's ethnographic documentation of gender relations near Minj in the Wahgi Valley in the 1950s and 1960s, much that it records remains characteristic today: its emphasis on male dominance and privilege, men's desires and efforts to marry multiply, women's responses and resistance to marriage arrangements, and the physical confrontation and violence involved in these relations.

Important changes have also taken place in the Highlands since Reay wrote this book. But this recently found work can still shed light on concerns long explored in the fulsome Melanesianist literature on gender relations, as well as upon gender issues recently articulated in new ways, such as the concern with gender-based violence in these societies. And consideration here of Reay's role as ethnographer, and her explorations as writer of this material on gender relations, will allow us to ask questions important to evaluating both anthropological and feminist literatures: In what ways may this have been a signal feminist work, and in what ways is it not quite apt to see it as such?

This Editor's Introduction will first tell the story of how this manuscript came to be found. Some detail will be provided for the reader on matters of content and editing that had to be taken into account in order to bring the manuscript to publication. It will then evaluate the work's place in the anthropological literature on Highlands Papua New Guinea, and feminist concerns in that literature. That exploration will include commentary on the work of Marie Reay as female anthropologist in a particular academic time and place, a writer, and a person who, in her academic and personal life, felt herself to be outside the ordinary.

Finding the book in the Reay Collection

We anthropologists at The Australian National University were to hold a conference, 'Anthropology's futures: looking forward from 60 Years of Anthropology at The Australian National University', in September 2011. A couple of months before that, I was rummaging through many boxes of the papers and effects of Marie Olive Reay in the basement of the Menzies Library at the university. This was part of a wider effort—initiated by Professor Kathryn Robinson—on the part of several of us at The Australian National University to find materials of interest from the files of our senior, mostly departed, colleagues, in order to assemble an historical display for the conference that would tell a story of 60 years of anthropology here.

For those unfamiliar with her, a brief introduction to Marie Reay is in order. Reay was an anthropologist whose ethnographic field sites were Australia and Highlands New Guinea. She conducted her first field research with Aboriginal communities in western New South Wales (Walgett, Bourke, Moree, Coonabarabran and others) in the 1940s, obtaining her first postgraduate degree for this from Sydney University in 1948. Later, in the early 1960s, she extended her fieldwork with Indigenous communities to Borroloola in the Northern Territory. In the meantime, from 1953, Reay became a doctoral student directed by first departmental chair Africanist S.F. Nadel, and supervised by Australianist anthropologist and public intellectual W.E.H. Stanner, in what was then called the Department of Anthropology and Sociology in the Research School of Pacific Studies at The Australian National University. She began field research in the Wahgi Valley in the Western Highlands of Papua New Guinea, with people she then referred to as Kuma. She completed her dissertation in 1957, and published it as a book in 1959: *The Kuma: Freedom and Conformity in the New Guinea Highlands*. She subsequently also researched and wrote extensively on elections, religion, political and social change in Papua New Guinea.

Reay was employed in the Research School of Pacific and Asian Studies at The Australian National University from 1959 to 1988, when she retired. She continued to do research and write for some years; she died in 2004. Anthropologist and colleague Michael Young wrote in an obituary (reproduced as Appendix E) that she was 'the first ethnographer to investigate in depth the position of women in a Highlands society'

3

(2005: 83). Over the course of her career she edited an influential collection on Aboriginal topics including social change (Reay 1964a), and published many articles. Marie also wrote non-academic prose and poetry, and maintained active correspondence with literary societies and writers and with her academic colleagues. She published her book on the Kuma early in her career, as well as numerous articles relating to New Guinea throughout it. But examination of her papers revealed considerable research material on New Guinea topics that had not yet been shaped into manuscript form (for example, major collections of myths, and of Wahgi shield designs); and much material that existed in manuscript form, but remained unpublished, including several articles, and the present work.

Photograph 2: Marie Reay with colleagues from The Australian National University, 1955

Top row left to right: Dr Peter Lawrence (Research Fellow), Mr C.A. Valentine (Fulbright Scholar), Dr Derek Freeman (Senior Fellow), Dr Adrian Mayer (Research Fellow), Mr Ron Penny (Research Fellow), Dr Walter Svoboda (Scholar) [note referred to as Dr Svoboda in annual report even though also a PhD candidate at the time]; Bottom row left to right: Miss Helen Woodger (Secretary), Dr W.E.H. Stanner (Reader), Mrs Fancy Lawrence (Departmental Assistant), Professor Fred Nadel (Head of Department), Miss Marie Reay (Scholar)

Source: Album 2 Reay 440/1194, Noel Butlin Archives

At the time that I began examining the Reay material, archivists at the Menzies Library, Margaret Shapley and the late Karina Taylor, were in the process of its documentation. Marie Reay had appointed her long-term friend and employee of the Department of Anthropology, Judith Wilson, as her executor. Though Wilson had initially thought she would be able to undertake curation of the collection upon Reay's death in 2004, a flood in 2007 damaged some of the files, and led her to think they would be safer if deposited in an institutional setting. She turned over the materials to the archive in the Menzies Library. When I began to search through them, it became obvious to me that the collection contained previously unknown manuscripts and required work beyond ordinary archiving to assemble them. I began sorting chapter versions of this book, and made an application to Wenner-Gren's Historical Archives Program to advance the work. The latter made it possible to employ an anthropologist to assist in putting together the various versions of papers and manuscripts and clarifying their status. The extensive collection has now been documented, archived and furnished with a Finder List (see Australian National University Archives: ANUA 440. 2013. Marie Reay collection (item list)).[1]

As this suggests, the rummaging turned out to be unexpectedly productive, in both of Reay's ethnographic fields. Going through box after box of Reay's Australianist materials from her 1940s fieldwork in northern New South Wales, I found copious fieldnotes of documentary interest from Walgett, Bourke, Moree, Brewarrina, Collarenebri, Mungindi, Boggabilla, Coonamble, Coonabarabran and Gulargambone, which still await, and would reward, detailed study. A copy of Reay's long-lost Sydney University Master's thesis of 1947 on kinship and communities in northern New South Wales came to light.

The many boxes of material from her long-term fieldwork in Papua New Guinea spanned a period from 1953 into the 1980s. During these years Reay made numerous fieldtrips to the Wahgi Valley (now within a newly configured province called Jiwaka, established in 2012). She was there so often that a contemporary and colleague, Jeremy Beckett, playfully called her 'Our Lady of Perpetual Fieldwork'.

---

1   Available at archivescollection.anu.edu.au/index.php/uipue. Note quotations that follow from these files all have the form 440- (Reay files) followed by item number.

In addition to a number of unpublished research papers and materials on New Guinea topics, from those boxes there also began to emerge various, numbered copies of chapters which were apparently parts of a book manuscript. Different versions of the book's chapter outline came to light. There was an early version with eight chapters, and later versions with fourteen, which guided the reconstruction of the scattered chapters, in all their variant drafts. Eventually enough chapters turned up so that it became clear it would be possible to reconstruct the book which you have before you.

The present manuscript thus represents a second book on Reay's original field site which she had nearly completed, in all likelihood by the mid-1960s, but—for reasons not directly stated in any of her notes—she never published. This publication therefore represents a large addition to Reay's known work, and is significant in several other ways on which there is further comment below.

Dating the manuscript

From Reay's fieldnotes, it is clear that she had a great deal to do with some of the major personalities in this book from the period of her first doctoral fieldwork 1953–55. Some letters and notes indicate that, while she had thought about and probably composed large sections of the book in the intervening ten years, on return to the area in 1963 she considered that the book was not ready for publication, and needed revision. She wrote a letter to this effect to administrator 'Pat' in Canberra on 30th March 1964.[2]

> We shall have to scrap plans for early publication of my book on the women here. The new material I have for it warrants a Part II (Ten Years Later), and it needs to be written up more carefully than I could hope to do in a hasty revision.

---

2   Pat O'Connor was originally appointed as Field Manager, New Guinea School Services (NGSS) which was the admin area that serviced the New Guinea Research Unit (NGRU). He reported to the Business Manager of the Research School of Pacific Studies (RSPacS) and the NGSS was part of the Business Manager's domain. After Independence, The Australian National University handed it over to Papua New Guinea and it became the Papua New Guinea Institute of Applied Social and Economic Research (IASER) and a local person was appointed as manager. Pat O'Connor came to the School, as Assistant to the Business Manager (of RSPacS and the Research School of Social Science [RSSS]) and then later he became Assistant Business Manager.

The addition of new materials evidently accounts for the large number of chapter outlines which were found in the Reay collection. She seems to have added approximately six chapters in the later period of the 1960s (and perhaps also re-worked earlier chapters).

The material as it was deposited and stored at the Menzies Library revealed no clear chronological ordering of chapter versions, or systematic filing of them by date. At least, by the time the materials were being searched and archived in 2011 there was no such definitive dating and ordering. Different versions of the same chapter were found in different boxes, and most boxes contained a diversity of materials (other papers, chapters of this book and another multi-chapter work in progress, and so on). Most of the chapters were typed and carbon copied; there were slightly different versions of a number of them. By going through them it was possible in many instances to definitively determine which version was the latest. This is because some typed chapter versions have corrections written on them in Reay's minute hand, and these corrections had been incorporated into later versions of the typescript.

A few of the chapter drafts or sections were dated; most were not. For instance, a section of what eventually was to become part of Chapter 8 ('Laik Bilong Man') entitled 'The Marriage of Buda and Gibbis' is dated 19/3/64; another section of the same chapter entitled 'The Marriage of Nere and Walump', 26/3/64. That these are so close together suggests that Reay was pulling together a 'current version' at that time. Those titles also seem to indicate that a change Reay made over some time, converting Wahgi names to English names of characters, was not complete by that date. In a few places, dates or times of events are mentioned in chapter versions (e.g. 'In October 1963 Konangil and his wife were talking together'—Konangil a person who considered Marie his 'sister', and whom she had known from her first fieldwork in 1953). The 14-chapter version presented here is, naturally, that which is the most complete and latest that could be assembled.

In conclusion, as of 1964, Reay decided that more revision was required, perhaps to account for change, in general or in the circumstances of particular persons, over the period of 10 years or so in which she seems to have worked on this manuscript. It remains unclear exactly what changes she might have thought of making; and even whether the difference between shorter (8-chapter) and longer (14-chapter) versions may have represented most of the changes she wanted to make. Her expressed sense of the need for revision is apparently part of the reason that she did not proceed to publish this work. But it was probably not the only one. It appears that she did not return to concerted work on the manuscript in the productive working years she had between the mid-1960s and her retirement.

Naming the people and titling the manuscript

In her original book (1959), Marie called the people she worked with 'Kuma'. She began, however, by stating that the people 'have no name for themselves' (Reay 1959: 1), as is indeed common in the region. People recognize the Wahgi River (see Map 1) as a boundary between those generally known as Danga (after the name of the largest grouping on the north side), and others living south of it known as Kuma (a colloquial contraction of Konumbuga, the name of the largest group on this side of the river). Both Danga and Kuma are part of a large regional grouping called Nangamp by their neighbours. These broad gentilics derive principally from the usage of others, outsiders; while segmentary groups are named.

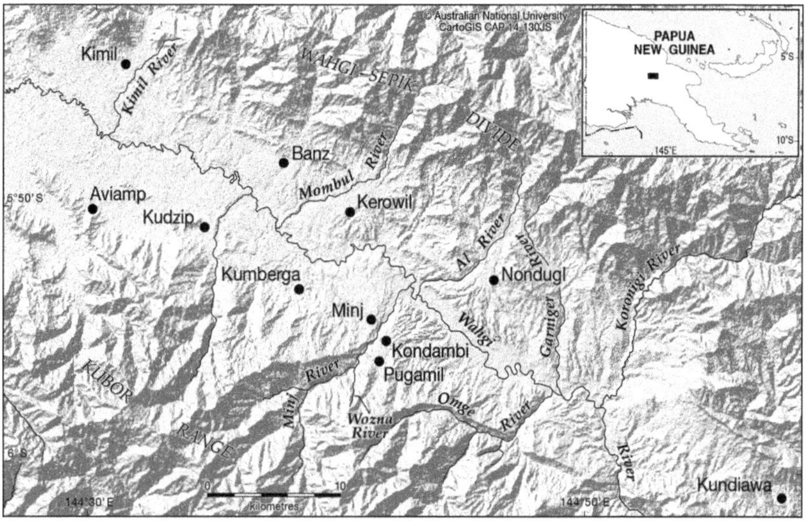

Map 1: The Wahgi Valley and its location in Papua New Guinea, showing (most) place names mentioned in the text

Source: CartoGIS, The Australian National University, CAP 14-130JS

People in the South Wahgi area tend to be identified either by this general, regionally based label, as Kuma (followed by a 'clan'-level name and perhaps a place where the group is located, e.g. Kuma-Kurupka of Kudjip); or by another similar term, as Damnge (followed by a clan-level name, e.g. Damnge-Kangilka). Marie worked with people around Olubus village (near Kondambi), an area in which the designation 'Kuma' was current, but was never the sole kind of identifier. In this later book she changed the general designation from Kuma to Minj Agamp, or 'people of Minj', a major town in the region and its administrative centre then.

From a brief passage in the Introduction, it seems that Marie understood Agamp as *akl-* 'east' plus *amp* 'woman'. This, however, is a false etymology, perhaps based on her incorrect identification of the stop consonant in this word.[3] The word she has adopted here, one which means 'people' in Minj and close dialects, is clearly [*akamp*], and does not contain a velar lateral such as occurs in the word [*akl*] 'east'. [*Akamp*] is not, however, the only word commonly used in these dialects to mean 'people'. As in most closely related dialects and languages, *yiamb* also means 'people', and is easily seen to consist of *Yi*=man + *amb*=woman 'men and women'. *Akamb* designates a large group of people, including men, women and children. *Akamp* is commonly combined with a place name, so that one may speak of Banz akamp 'people of Banz', or Minj Akamp, Nondugl Akamp, and so on. (Reay tended to use the spelling *agamp*, and I follow her in this in most contexts; but *agamp=akamp*.)

Titles found in her notes that Reay listed and seems to have considered at various times for this book include:

Women of the Wahgi: Sketches of a Male-Dominated Society

Women of the Wahgi ('good but not informative', seemingly a comment by Reay's colleague Ian Hogbin of Sydney University)

Wanderers in the Clouded Hills ('very pleasing but a little misleading; not all the women are wanderers', seemingly Reay's thought)

Women of the Clouded Hills ('better', Reay's comment?)

Wandering Women

Wantons and Wayfarers

---

3   I ascertained this by interviewing a Middle Wahgi speaker in 2013.

Women of the Kuma

Love Among the Kuma

Savage Passion

Dissent in Paradise

Sisters of Savages

Women Without Plumes

Women of the Wahgi Valley

The main title chosen for this volume contains elements that Reay seems to have preferred most consistently, and the W- alliteration she trialled in a variety of possible titles.

Her notes include a list of the persons who appear in the book, with their original names and then English versions of names, often quite florid translations of their original names, she had decided to use. There is also a key identifying the clan and other particulars of the characters in the book, which would make it possible to trace them and their descendants. That key has not been included in this edition.

Colleagues' knowledge of the manuscript

Some of Marie's near-contemporaries and academic colleagues, when asked, said they have vague recollections of Marie working on or mentioning a manuscript about women's life in the Wahgi Valley—but none of them recollects having seen it. The person to whom Marie clearly sent some version of the manuscript was Ian Hogbin, a senior anthropological colleague at Sydney University who had conducted fieldwork in the Solomon Islands and in Papua New Guinea (Beckett 1989). It is not clear what version of the manuscript he read, but he sent Reay two pages of comments, to which she responded. At that time the manuscript was titled *Waburamp* (Tok Pisin *wapra* 'prostitute' and *amp* 'woman', 'Loose Women'). In addition to small corrections, he made the following suggestions: he found the title 'meaningless' to an audience, and suggested instead 'Wandering Women of the New Guinea Highlands' or 'Rebellious Women in a Male-Dominated Society of New Guinea'. He felt the book should be preceded by a brief summary of Kuma social structure, focusing on marriage arrangements, preferences, prohibitions, payments, and relations with affines. He recommended a Dramatis Personae 'as in most of the longer Russian novels'. As things stood he said it was impossible to 'remember which person is which when they all have unfamiliar names'. (This may in fact have been what spurred Reay to translate all the names into English, to increase their recognizability.) Each chapter, Hogbin suggested, should be preceded by an introductory paragraph indicating the nature of the incidents to follow, and should also have a brief, final summarizing paragraph. The existing chapter headings, e.g. 'Lothario gains a bride' were, he felt, insufficiently indicative.

Map 2: North and South Wahgi Census Divisions, showing tribal areas

Courtesy of John Burton (1988) and deposited in library.anu.edu.au/record=b1780420 (North Wahgi Census Division) and library.anu.edu.au/record=b1780440 (South Wahgi Census Division)

Note: Groups in bold are referred to in the text.

Source: CartoGIS, The Australian National University, CAP 14-142JS

11

In a letter of response (also undated), Reay thanked him. She noted that titles like *Mambu* (the main title of a recent book by Kenelm Burridge, 1995[1960], subtitled *A Melanesian Millennium*) would also have to be called 'meaningless', but she found them intriguing. However, she noted she would be happy to call the book *Wandering Women*. She agreed on the matter of Dramatis Personae, and on the need for what she called a 'potted structural account' of marriage arrangements and related matters; and proposed that the polar stereotypes of 'good woman' and 'wanderer', which emerge as significant in the text, needed setting out at the beginning. If that were to be there, she was not so certain that each chapter would need a formal conclusion. She also responded to a number of other points concerning important phrases in the book: she was obviously concerned about the intelligibility of certain phrases common in Tok Pisin, such as *karim leg*, 'courting ceremony', for instance. Her letter to Hogbin concluded with a paragraph that does not seem to have ever made it into the manuscript, except perhaps in the form of one chapter that is incomplete (see further comment below on Chapter 7, which was to be titled Meri Tultul).

Following up on some of Hogbin's useful suggestions, this edition is accompanied by Map 1 showing main locations of Reay's field area; Map 2 which shows tribes that she mentions; and a few notes on marriage relations, below; as well as indicative photographs from her collection. (It is not clear which photographs she may have intended to use, so these have been selected to illustrate some main topics in the text.)

Women's structural position: Reay's and other views

Michael Young's remark cited above, that Reay was the first ethnographer to investigate women's life in Highlands society in depth, was made on the basis of work known at the time of her death in 2004. The present book manuscript, unknown then, represents her most concentrated ethnography in this area. Indeed, it now appears to have been the first full monograph on women's life in the Papua New Guinea Highlands. A stream of publications on women's lives and situation began in 1972 with Marilyn Strathern's *Women In Between*, based on ethnography of the nearby Mt Hagen region, ushering in a productive era of ethnography and gender theorization. Reay's depiction of women's situation in the Wahgi valley, and the themes in this book of 'wandering' and barely repressed rebelliousness under the strictures of marriage and marriage arrangement, directly and interestingly compare with ethnographies from parts of the Highlands, including older ones like Strathern's based on materials gathered much closer to the time of Reay's own fieldwork, and some written recently, several decades later.

Strathern's sense of issue regarding Hagen women, a view which became widely read, was expressed in her title *Women in Between*. Hagen, like the Wahgi Valley, is normatively patrivirilocal: women move on marriage to their husband's location, which is usually that of his father. Women are 'between' their families and groups of origin, and those of their husband. While strong ties to their places of origin are assumed of Hagen women, they are also always on their mettle to demonstrate their loyalty to their husband's place and kin. Each territorialized *haus man* or lineage into which a woman will marry also belongs to intermediate segmentary groups, and to a wider tribe and (in this region) tribe-pair. Women's marriages serve as the 'roads' of exchange relations between affines (people related through marriage), and also between the wider units to which the bride's and husband's lineage belong. At the time Strathern wrote, women as wives were among those people most likely to be suspected of incomplete integration into the group with which they were living, and of questionable loyalty. For this reason Strathern devotes considerable discussion to poisoning accusations frequently levelled against them: women are the archetypal suspects. Women accumulate insider status in the husband's home area over years, and through producing children and food for their marital households. These accomplishments are sources of their own senses of achievement and well-being, and through them, they 'come inside' and belong within the husband's locale.

Balancing a certain marginality of Hagen women as wives is a strong appreciation of the relationships between affines and groups that their marriages instantiate; and the according of recognition to women as persons within this framework. Thus, while marriages are arranged, and strongly haggled over between husband's and wife's kin, the intended bride is asked whether she will 'go' in marriage: she is given this initial say. Her sense of commitment is important, as kin on both sides realize, and as Strathern observed. As she describes it, a woman's sense of worth is strongly linked to her appreciation of a sufficiency of bridewealth having been given by the groom's kindred for her. The overall dynamics of marriage negotiation and realization seem different in some respects from those described by Reay for the Wahgi and exemplified from real-life examples in this book.

One of the apparent differences, which figures largely in the present manuscript, is the emphasis in the Wahgi material on courtship rituals, and the freedom which young girls had to choose courting partners. Courtship then, as Reay described it, consisted in young girls and their chosen partners engaging in *karim leg* (literally, 'carrying leg'). Girl and partner sit with legs extended, hers locked between his, so they can talk and nestle together in close contact—but supposedly not go too far, as *karim leg* was not simply a matter of private flirtation but also a public spectacle, visible to others, all aware of whom a girl had chosen. Older, including married, men preened themselves and were flattered to be chosen as courting partners. Reay's photo collection also shows couples engaging in *tanim het*, in which couples sit close, turning their heads and pressing noses and faces together.

Of course, here as elsewhere in the Central Highlands, men might aspire to have more than one wife. For a young unmarried girl, courting demonstrated her capacity to choose, to be valued, and to confirm the desirability of the men they chose. There was more to it than that: girls could choose, but were also regularly dispatched by their families to engage in courting. They were to be returned home 'bathed' in pig oil and decorated with feathers, ornaments and valuables for the girl's family, not for her alone. But still, there was a strong element of choice, flirtation and the girl's desire to captivate a particular partner. For that reason, courtship as depicted by Reay was also an activity that could provoke jealousy, fights between women over men, and between men and women in other combinations—with wifely jealousy a common inflammatory issue. It could be a source of contention if choices were thwarted, denied, interfered with, as well as realized.

Main aspects of courtship that Reay emphasizes are the passions involved, the contention it can cause, and very importantly also, its abrupt termination and the end of any kind of free choice for girls. Once married, girls were no longer to flirt or court. Men, of course, might continue to do so. Chapters in this book illustrate some of the resulting situations.

Photograph 3: *Karim* **leg (carrying leg) I—Kuma 1959**
Source: Album 6 Reay 440/1198, Noel Butlin Archives

Photograph 4: *Karim* leg (carrying leg) II
Source: Album 6 Reay 440/1198, Noel Butlin Archives

Girls' freedom is transformed into constraint. They must then, as wives, cope with men's continuing drive to marry other wives, and to continue to be seen as attractive. Women are not to make themselves attractive to other men. Husbands and other relatives readily mete out violence to women not considered to be toeing the line. Men regularly coerce and force their wives. There are many episodes recorded from life here in which husbands capture their 'wayward' wives, lock them into the house, subjugate them with sexual and other physical violence, exercise male dominance and privilege. But wives resist, display physical courage, readiness to defend themselves as well as to attack and to fight with men—and also display anger and resignation on occasions when they can do no more.

Photograph 5: *Tanimhet*
Source: Album 6 Reay 440/1198, Noel Butlin Archives

Reay's view of women's position differs from Strathern's. In her thesis and book (Reay 1959), Reay recognized that women are identified in terms of the clan of their father and, after marriage, that of their husband. But in a wide sense, she took the view that 'the association of women with particular clans can in no case be characterized as fully effective "membership"' (Reay 1959: 44). By this she meant that women did not have the ability to exercise the rights and obligations of clan membership as men do. It would be more apt, she suggested, to regard women themselves as transferrable 'property' of the clans with which they are identified, as 'assets' the clans 'possess' rather than constituent members of them (Reay 1959: 45).

Photograph 6: Girl bathed in pig grease
Source: Album 6 Reay 440/1198, Noel Butlin Archives

She identified principles of clanship and equivalent exchange as importantly constitutive at many levels among the Minj Agamp, describing the levels of segmentary structure (Reay 1959: 25–56), and the overall strong association of a given 'parish', or residential location, with a particular clan, and in terms of a strongly agnatic ideology (i.e. one which presumes continuing relatedness in the male line, despite the actual presence of numbers of non-agnates, and the vagueness of actual genealogical connections at many levels). Equivalent exchange refers to a strongly held ideology that a woman should be returned for a woman received in marriage, sometimes in the form of 'sister exchange', but also on the basis of other arrangements. Reay found insistence on equivalent gain to balance loss to be a general societal principle, operative both in marriage arrangements and in other forms of exchange.

Reay expressed a sense of the structural centrality of the disposition of women in marriage for the social order. In a draft proposal for another book on the place of women among the Minj Agamp which Marie evidently intended to write (see also further), but in a style rather different from the present one, she wrote:

> At present it is proposed to advance the hypothesis that what appears to be a serious discontinuity in the socialization of the women is explicable in terms of the value placed upon the enjoyment of sexual relations between men and unmarried girls, and [that] this discontinuity is normally prevented from having permanently disruptive effects on female personality and on society by the integrative operation of another major value, that of exact equivalence, through the economic arrangements associated with marriage.

Indeed, Reay's conclusions in the present volume are more consistent with the thinking revealed in the draft outline we have just examined, than they are an interpretive examination of the lively ethnographic material it presents.

Clearly, Reay had the view that there were profound tensions in this Highlands social order, but that there was at least partial structural balancing of them. Her book *The Kuma* (Reay 1959) had described these tensions, and their association with (especially, but not only) female suicide, and the un-doing of social arrangements which occurred as a cargo cult swept through the area at the time of early European presence—occasioning, for example, breaching of the strictures of clan exogamy and other bounds of conformity. One of her continuing concerns, however, was not simply with the management of structural tensions, but with the freedom of persons, particularly women who appeared to her so coerced, confined and punished.[4] She concludes the present volume by suggesting that if Wahgi marriage depended on the consent of both parties, women could no longer be exchanged to satisfy obligations between men and groups. If Papua New Guineans attain liberty and equality such that women may choose whom they marry, and even *if* they marry—and Reay regards this as the granting of a fundamental human right—this will involve 'not merely the dispersal of ignorance and ill will but also the dissolution of Kuma society' in its dependence upon exchanges of women, pigs and wealth. Reay's ethnographic work was thus closely attentive to what she saw as patent inequalities in the Kuma form of life, and a related question of freedom, especially, but not only, for women in this society.[5]

Overall, Reay harboured a view of women in the Wahgi as subject to regular disparagement and male violence. Pacific anthropologist Martha Macintyre held many conversations with Reay while at The Australian National University in the 1980s.[6] From these conversations she concluded that Reay saw male–female relations, especially in regard to sex and work, as fraught with tension and violence. Reay narrated the following fieldwork episode to Macintyre as having been formative of her attitudes: Reay was walking on a path and came across a group of young Kuma men standing around a woman in labour. The young men were laughing and ridiculing the woman by imitating her screams. The baby's feet had emerged and the woman was in agony. Marie asked them to

---

4   Reay had earlier conducted research in Australia at the Cootamundra Girls' Home for indigenous girls under direction from A.P. Elkin. From this research, too, Reay had taken away a view of restraint and oppression exacting a particular toll on indigenous girls and women in the Australian context.

5   Reay (1964b) reviewed Ronald M. Berndt's book *Excess and Restraint: Social Control among a New Guinea Mountain People* (1962), finding that, in its emphases on violence, sex and repression, it was 'stimulating and controversial'; but, she also implied, somewhat unbelievable in certain respects which, she thought, might reflect male fantasy. To students she recommended reading the book; to Berndt, more fieldwork that might add up to a more fully researched and contemporary view.

6   Macintyre was a PhD student enrolled at The Australian National University from 1979–83, and was involved in a departmental working group on gender in 1983–84, also keeping up contacts with the Department and Reay thereafter. A working group on Language in Cultural Context was convened in the department in the years 1980–82. A following one on Gender Relations in the Southwestern Pacific in 1983–85, in which Macintyre participated, was organized and convened by Roger Keesing, Michael Young, and Marie Reay. In 1986 Martha Macintyre held three long interviews with Marie Reay about her life and career, one of which she recorded. I thank her for reading and commenting on this Introduction, and for her permission to cite this anecdote and her sense of Reay's views.

help carry her back to the village. They refused on the grounds that the woman was polluting in that state. Marie ran and got two women to help her, but the woman and the baby died. Reay was the first anthropologist that Macintyre heard talk about the extent and regularity of violence towards women.

These emphases lead me to connect Reay's portrayal of Highlands life, both in her 1959 book and in this one, with the (early) work of Lisette Josephides (1975), the more recent work of Holly Wardlow (2006), and ongoing research and writing on gender relations, domestic and gendered violence, and their association with HIV/AIDS (Hammar 2010; Jolly, Stewart and Brewer 2012) under the recent, and increasingly mobile, conditions of life in Papua New Guinea.

Josephides (1975) focused her analysis of Kewa (Southern Highlands), ostensibly a society with no hereditary offices and no formalized inequalities among men, upon the 'production' of inequality through male control of women's labour. Like Reay, Josephides saw Kewa attributes of the 'group' as those associated with maleness, with women having no place in male descriptions of group identity. She identified transaction as the male political activity *par excellence*, and the female role as a dependent one, despite its centrality in production and reproduction.

Perhaps most astonishing are the close affinities between Reay's distinction between 'wives' and 'wanderers', and Wardlow's (2006) characterization of the clearer emergence and definition in the last couple of decades of a category of 'wayward women' among the Huli. Wardlow's is an account of women who, with recent mining activity and greater mobility, become 'passenger women', accepting money for sex. The present manuscript gives us another comparator case of women's chafing against constraints from an earlier period and another part of the Highlands. I would argue the comparison suggests the structural potential in-built within a range of Highlands societies for women who conform to expectations to be regarded as wifely, and women who do not, to have little room to move, and to be categorized by kin and others as the 'wanderers', the (sexually and otherwise) wayward women, of Reay's (and Wardlow's) accounts.

Photograph 7: Wahgi married woman
Source: Album 6 Reay 440/1198, Noel Butlin Archives

Photograph 8: Koma held by a male relative while being rebuked for running away to evade marriage, c. 1953–59

Source: Album 6 Reay 440/1198, Noel Butlin Archives

How did Reay think about change with respect to these topics that most concerned her? In this manuscript she clearly expresses the view that Australian administrative presence had changed things, in the direction of reducing violence meted out to women, and making Wahgi men aware of risks they would run of being thrown in jail if they treated women as brutally as they might otherwise have done.[7] By the time of Reay's fieldwork colonial government stations, courts and jails had been established, and these and administrative attitudes and process served to deter some male violence. Reay depicts people in the Wahgi, both men and women, as realizing that the Australian administration required them to consider *laik bilong meri* 'what a woman wants', as a relevant (and probably new) category; as well as *laik bilong man* 'what a man wants'. The common novel element in these phrases is expression of an individual's will and choice. Notwithstanding any deterrent effect of administrative presence, the depiction of what we now call gender-based violence is stark in this book. Today, this is more a concern here and in other parts of the Highlands than ever before. There is greater awareness in Papua New Guinea and on the part of outside observers how high are levels of domestic and other gender-based violence. One may even conclude that some aspects of ongoing social change both contribute to, and militate against, these high levels. Christian religiosity has burgeoned, and Christian sectarianism has become more diverse, throughout the Highlands. Residential change has been such that husbands and wives now mostly live together (whereas formerly they lived in separate houses in this and many other regions, separateness typically bolstered by ideas and practices of female pollution). Alcohol has become much more accessible, as have guns. Access to money is increasingly important, and social relations are increasingly monetized, in most places, even as obvious inequalities in wealth also increase. Yet in Jiwaka in particular (as the province in which Reay researched is now called), there is now a number of strong female political leaders, and there is greater access for girls and women to education and jobs.

Reay did not live to see any of these things in their current form. Yet she was alert to the question of women's gaining position and power—clearly something extraordinary in her day. She titled one of the proposed chapters of this book Meri Tultul, and was fascinated to try to find out how a woman of Kudjip she had heard of had come to be an

---

7   According to Martha Macintyre, Reay thought that some cases of alleged Kuma female suicide were disguised homicides.

administrative official. (See Chapter 7 in which the one paragraph she seems to have written about this topic is reproduced.) Unfortunately she was never able to pursue the investigation at Kudjip.

This manuscript would have been the first full-length ethnography of women's lives had it appeared; and in its exploration of the contradiction Reay saw between early freedom and subsequent marital constraint for women connects directly with current emphases on gender, violence and social change. Its publication now provides an unexpected window onto gender relations, and gender-based violence, in an earlier period. As a background piece it can stimulate attempts to understand what has remained the same, and what has changed and inflected gender relations in new ways.

Experimental ethnographic writing

A second landmark quality of this manuscript is the experiment it represented in ethnographic writing, for Reay personally as well as in terms of dominant contemporary standards. Two modes are manifest over a long period in Reay's writing on Wahgi women. The first is grounded in certain social structural and psychic problems she saw as inherent in the courting, marriage and related gendered and gendering practices of the Wahgi Agamp, and expressed in conventional, academic descriptive and analytical terms. The second, which she trialled in this book, is closely ethnographic and seemingly very much grounded in the verbal as well as other forms of social action concerning women that she observed. It is lively and dramaturgical. The reader has the impression of experiencing the unfolding of events. Reay seems to have given fairly separate expression to these two modes in her published as well as unpublished work, and not woven ethnography and explicit theory into the same pieces of writing in a more integrated way.

Let us take some examples of the first, more usual, academic style. This style characterizes her first book on the Kuma (1959), and some later work on women's life too. In 1966, about the time she may have finished the current version of *Wives and Wanderers*, Reay published a paper called 'Women in Transitional Society'. A chapter in a volume called *New Guinea on the Threshold* (independence came in 1975), Reay's paper underscored the extent to which Papua New Guinea was 'originally a man's world', and described women's 'anomalous place in a set of social, economic, and ceremonial transactions carried out by men, namely the payments connected with marriage' (1966:166). Reay considered the conflicting values involved in bridewealth (complicated by Australian officials construing marriage as a relation between the partners, and failing to understand its group-connecting dimensions). She described new kinds of roles and training becoming available to women (as nurses, teachers, in social welfare work, as well as in volunteer religious and training associations); and with expected change, predicted a strong role for women as culture carriers, 'transmitting awareness of the past' (1966: 184) as part of the adjustment of Papua New Guineans to changing conditions. She also mentions the need, given the favouring by formal and informal courts of the principle of *laik bilong meri*, for recognition of a complementary principle, *laik bilong man* ('what a man wants'), which would allow younger men to defer marriage in the interests of their further education or for other such reasons.

Reay's documents include an (undated) draft outline of what was no doubt intended to be a book-length manuscript titled 'The Socialization of Women in Relation to the Institution of Marriage and the Value System of Wahgi Society' (440-383). The draft outline of the work consists of thirty chapters. Coverage of women's life was evidently intended to be comprehensively related to all major domains of Wahgi life, illuminating social structure and psychic life. Chapters were: Social Grouping; Patterns of Work and Ownership; Kinship; Authority Structure; Sorcery and Witchcraft; Warfare; Food Exchanges; Ceremonial; Aesthetic Expression; Economic Roles; Kinship Roles; Roles in Ceremony; Stages in the Life Cycle; Breast Feeding; Sphincter Control; Explicit Controls During Childhood; Initiation; Sexual Behaviour During Childhood and Adolescence; Adoption; Spirits and Nonda (Mushroom, Toadstool— Reay wrote extensively about the hallucinogenic use of mushrooms); Mediums; Witches; *Amp Wabure* (Loose Women); Exchange of Women; Betrothal; The Event of Marriage; Marriage Payments; Divorce; The Widow; The Remarried Woman.

More revealing are the brief statements of problem and conclusion that accompany the draft outline. Reay summarised the book's problem as follows:

> Marriage in Wahgi society presents special problems of adjustment for the woman, because by the time she is given in marriage the process of socialization is rarely complete. The event of marriage

is generally a violent, almost traumatic experience for the bride in this society and, although she is already aware that this kind of marriage does take place, it is contrary to her own expectations. It will be demonstrated that, viewed within the life cycle of the woman, the event of marriage is a fully institutionalized rite de passage which is itself a part of the socialization process, if 'socialization' can be defined as the structuring of the mature social ego. An attempt will be made to explain, in terms of the value system of Wahgi society, what appears to be a radical discontinuity in the socialization of women, this sudden negation at marriage of expectations which are thoroughly consistent with the modus vivendi of the unmarried girl. I shall try to relate this to the equally startling reversal at marriage of the male's essentially passive role in sexual relationships.

Much of this is also the content of the present volume. But this manuscript is written in a lively, theatrical style. This was obviously an experiment with a new genre for Reay, compared with her other academic work including the published *Kuma* book, and the above planned volume. The statement of the tensions she saw for women—radical discontinuity, the negation of freedom and expectations—are the same. But the presentation is very different. The present work is most directly grounded in her ethnographic observation, and foregrounds personalities, their actions and struggles with each other. The larger structural issues are present but backgrounded, emerging in particular sections and especially in conclusion, where Reay also does not hesitate to be both moralizing and predictive. The projective psychological testing that her notes and documents reveal her to have practiced (see Reay 1959: 95 for indications that this was encouraged by S.F. Nadel) is not mentioned explicitly in this book, but was a method associated with Reay's interest in personal equilibrium and disequilibrium. She makes it clear that, when they are disciplined, constrained and even violently assaulted, women show themselves to be persons full of will and fight (and thus in no way does she present them as victims). Yet the vivid ethnography shows the extent of their structural disadvantage, and thus operates in the service of theoretical conceptualization (Lutz 1995).

It is important to locate Reay in relation to other stylistic experimentation arising around this time from ethnographic experience, some of it originating from New Guinea, and perhaps known in some form to her (although how much remains unclear). Most notable among such efforts would be Kenneth E. ('Mick') Read's vibrant story of his two years' field research in the Eastern Highlands, *The High Valley* (1965). Read characterized this work as autobiographical and necessarily personal, but also as an important antidote to the 'antiseptic' quality of so much anthropological writing. Indeed, his moving account of the betrothal and marriage of a young girl, Tarova (Read 1965: 172–211), is multi-perspectival, grounded in sympathy with the girl herself, also offering great insight into the acts and feelings of men and women involved, and a convinced but tempered sense of the structural inequalities involved in marriage here, especially of such a young girl as Tarova. Doubtless Reay came to know this book, and must have perceived its relation to her own work. Read's work is, as he noted in several places, deliberately 'subjective', and he was indeed very much a subject in his own book, to an extent that Reay is not in the work before us.[8] Her most subjective published statement is found in Reay (1992).

The present book complemented another dimension of Reay's life, a lasting interest in literature and writing of poetry. Her letters and papers reveal how closely she followed new literary work, especially in Australia, and particularly poetry; and that she entered various poetry and writing competitions. For this book she compiled a dramatis personae of her characters, and gave them all vivid, translated English names, obviously thinking of the stories that comprise these chapters in theatrical terms. Ian Hogbin apparently encouraged her to do this. He seems to have found the style appealing. But it is not clear how other academic readers might have reacted. Although this must remain speculation, it seems possible that Reay hesitated in finalizing this manuscript because of the way she had formulated it: somewhere between an ethnographic account and a literary work. (Strathern, this volume, characterizes this as 'highly creative non-fiction'.) There were then relatively few companion efforts—many fewer than began to emerge with a more explicit set of alternative styles a decade and more later in the 1980s and 1990s, a large number of them feminist.

---

8   Read studied with Ian Hogbin in Sydney. Hogbin and Reay clearly had a friendlier and more trusting collegial relation than she had with many others. She also admired his writing greatly, and they shared a love of literature. Hogbin was homosexual and Marie lesbian, while Read expressed homosexual interest in relation to a New Guinean companion somewhat more explicitly in a work that followed *The High Valley* (Read 1986: 11–12). Read also had a wife, Monica, and a son. His long-term interest in homosexuality was expressed professionally, in fieldwork in a gay bar throughout the 1970s, and in his serving as the first President of the Anthropological Research Group on Homosexuality (later renamed Society for Lesbian and Gay Anthropology).

It seems telling that, despite having worked on this manuscript for ten years and more, beginning with her earliest fieldwork and incorporating some of its observations, Reay also continued to think in terms of a more academically written account of women's lives, cited above, 'The Socialization of Women in Relation to the Institution of Marriage and the Value System of Wahgi Society'. These concerns about style of presentation, and the implications, may have been what caused her to turn away from this project after the mid-1960s. It is also worth noting that another partial book manuscript found in her documents was, like this one, in more experience-near style.

Because Reay explored this more dramaturgical style of writing for a long period of time, it is of interest to examine one of the chapters of the present book to illustrate the relation between the closely observed fieldnotes from which it is drawn, and the final version of the chapter.

From 1954 there are copious fieldnotes concerning a girl named Muru who is a main subject of Chapter 9 of the final manuscript, 'A Woman of the Kugika' (for some detail on this clan, see Reay 1959: 31). From different periods of note-taking it is clear that Reay kept up with Muru over a period of at least, and probably more than, thirty years—for in one biographical sketch document concerning Muru, which Reay obviously intended for publication, she notes that Muru was a neighbour of hers during a fieldwork period of 1983. By the finalization of Chapter 9, Muru had become 'Cass', and her mother, originally Mai, had become 'Vine'.

The basics of Cass[Muru]'s situation are quickly told in synoptic form, but synopsis is interspersed below with short passages showing how Reay represented the situation in this book. Cass[Muru]'s mother Vine[Mai] was brought home as a widow by a Kugika clansman (originally Tai, later re-named Raggiana), from a bout of warfare in the north of the valley. With her Vine[Mai] brought her small daughter, Cass[Muru], and Raggiana[Tai] raised the child in his household. Vine[Mai] and Raggiana[Tai] later had a son, a brother to Cass[Muru]. When the time came Raggiana[Tai] first gave Cass[Muru] in marriage to a man of Konumbuga Taukanim, a 'brother' clan (for some detail on Konumbuga, ibid.).

In Chapter 9 of this book, Reay expands on what this situation represented for Cass[Muru] according to commonplace Kuma norms, emphasizing Cass[Muru]'s feelings concerning her marriage, and then upon her husband's death:

> ... Raggiana [Cass[Muru]'s stepfather] gave Cass to the Konumbuga Taukanim in exchange for one of them [for another woman]. ... But Cass's husband died before she had become reconciled to being married to him, and some of the Taukanim wives ... resented her presence among them. She pleaded with her stepfather to take her back instead of leaving her to be appropriated by another Taukanim man ...

After her husband's death, Cass[Muru]'s stepfather instead gave her to a man, Bird[Kai], of his own clan, Kugika Koimamkup. This was of course considered acceptable because Cass[Muru] was adopted and not originally of Kugika. Reay makes it clear, though, that Cass[Muru] 'did not go willingly' to this new husband, Bird[Kai]. Cass[Muru] had two children with Bird[Kai]. Both died and the parents wrapped them in burial shrouds and decorated them with valuables. Cass[Muru]'s feelings were evidently violently assaulted when she discovered one day that her husband had come and removed the valuables, presumably for further use.

This situation is graphically reproduced in this book, through her recounting of field experience and conversation. Reay says of Cass[Muru] in this book:

> One day she showed me, at one side of her unused cooking grove, an old house which had once been inhabited but was not beyond repair ... 'My children', Cass told me. 'We put them in there'... Cass tore away some of the cobwebs and removed the cross-bars. We could see, just inside, the dim shapes of two bundles wrapped in mouldy bark cloth and lap-lap material, lying side by side. 'They just fell sick and died' Cass told me flatly. Then she began to relate, with a sudden surge of anger, something Bird had done.

What Bird[Kai] had done was to strip the children's bodies of their valuables. Reay goes on in Chapter 9 to articulate the significance of this, especially for the parents, mother and father; and the 'horror' Cass[Muru] expressed to her in recounting the pillage.

Cass[Muru]'s relations with Bird[Kai] worsened, and she began to seek support for a separation from him. She found some on the part of her real paternal relatives, who said they regarded her marriage to Bird[Kai] as incomplete because they had never received any portion of bridewealth. Raggiana[Tai]'s own clan, on the other hand, regarded him and not her paternal relatives as perfectly entitled to any such payments because he had brought Cass[Muru] back with her mother and provided for her.

Cass[Muru] went to the Government Station to try to get help in separating from her husband, but was at least thought to have become involved with one or more men there, and came to be seen by her own relatives, including her brother, as a 'wandering woman', a harlot. She evidently did have an affair with a native policeman from Chimbu, who later on tried to make a case for having the resulting son handed over to him. While all this was going on, Bird[Kai]—her husband—continued to try to get her back by various means, including assaulting her, penning her up in a house, and so on. When Cass[Muru] defended herself and retaliated by alleging in public that he had tried to force her to perform fellatio—regarded as anomalous, crude and degrading—Bird[Kai]'s co-clansmen moved to the view that a decision about the marriage should be left to the Court of Native Affairs, which duly dissolved it in 1955. Many other matters of the marriage—payments, allocation of the pigs Cass[Muru] tended, and so on—remained unresolved for a long time, as Bird[Kai] continued to try to force Cass[Muru] to come back despite the Court's ruling. Many further relationships in Cass[Muru]'s life—with her mother's co-wives as well as her own, her brother, and so on—of course continued in their complexity beyond the 'divorce'. Cass[Muru]'s expressed desire to go to live with the Chimbu policeman was opposed by her brother, who also vetoed Reay's offering her any help to travel to him. Ten years after the divorce, by 1964, Cass[Muru]'s brother, who had a daughter but no son of his own, was acting as father to her son by the Chimbu man and was determined that the son grow up as a member of Kugika clan.

A life story as complex as this could of course serve to illustrate a great range of issues. In the conclusion of Chapter 9, Reay extricates herself from the immediacy of the story and explicitly focuses on issues in a more evaluative way:

> Cass's life would have been different in many details if the Australians had not come to the Wahgi Valley and established control there during her lifetime. Her separation from Bird would have been even more tenuous an arrangement than it was if she had not had the support of the Court of Native Affairs and of her family's friends among the interpreters and native police.

In this context, Reay seems to treat the role of the Court as positive. This episode illustrates Reay's conviction that some instability, as well as some possible benefits for women, had been introduced into marriage relations by the insistence of *kiaps* and government that *laik bilong meri* (what the woman wants) should be given consideration. In the book there are several mentions of men's concerns about dealing with women as they would have formerly done because of fears of government interference, and the possibility that women might complain. The story also shows that a woman's struggle to free herself from a marriage may quickly lead to her being regarded as a 'wanderer', a harlot, often—as in Cass[Muru]'s case— by some of 'her' people, like her brother, who have an interest in the condition of her marriage. It illustrates, in short, the structural imbalance characteristic of women's lives: that a woman's deviation from patterns of marriage and behaviour approved by kin and affines caused their view to oscillate quickly to one of her as a 'wanderer'.

Reay also mentions another point several times: that despite all provocations Bird[Kai] offered her, Cass[Muru] never publicly referred to his having stripped their children's corpses of the valuables they had placed with them. Cass[Muru] told Reay that this might have led to Bird[Kai]'s being jailed: it would presumably have been felt to be even more repellent than her public revelation of sexual indecency. And, Reay concludes, Cass[Muru] did not refrain from revealing the theft out of a sense of identification with her husband, but rather because she identified with Kugika as a result of her adoption and long-term association with the clan into which her mother had married. She was more a 'woman of the Kugika' in that sense, than through her own marriage into it, which had been a history of tribulation.

Reay's fieldnotes (Australian National University Archives: ANUA 440. 2013. Marie Reay collection (item list): 440: 373-001) reveal her recordings of many of the events of Cass[Muru]'s case in real time, for instance:[9]

> 24.2.54 Muru[Cass] was walking back from Minj along the Big Road when she met a manki-masta [house boy] from Minj who had followed her. He asked her where she was going and she answered that she was going home. He laughed and said, "You're going to your lover, not to your house" & dragged her into the bushes & had sex. Int. with her. A police boy saw them and they ran away. Muru went to Kai[Bird] and told him what had happened. Much discussion between Kai and another Koimamkup man & Tagba, who came up while they were talking. Kombuk II [a native medical assistant; Kombuk was also the name of Muru's brother, hence the II] said that Muru did not call out

---

9   As do her letters from the field. See Appendix D as an example of a personal letter which illustrates how she conveyed the field events she was observing to friends and household in Canberra.

when the manki-masta grabbed her—Kombuk's house is close to the place and he wd [sic] have heard her. The men concluded that Muru had gone with the manki-masta willingly & had only told Kai about it because the police man had seen what had happened and might tell Kai anyway. Kai grabbed the lap-lap & scarf Muru wore on her head, & tore her pubic bilum. He tried to tear off her beads but she protected them. Kai said angrily that it was clear that Muru had a lover because whenever she went to Minj she decorated herself with beads & scarf & lap-lap. He argued that if she didn't have a lover she wdn't [sic] bother decorating herself … etc.

27.10.54 In the afternoon, KAI[Bird] went down to the Minj River to wait for Muru[Cass] to return from Minj. He hid in the pit-pit near the water. Muru came from Minj with TUAN (WAU's brother) and KOBIA (Konumbuga). KAI tried to throw her in the water, but the Konumbuga men held him off while Muru escaped. KAI took Muru to his women's house and told her to cook him some food. She refused and tried to run away. They chased, and eventually Muru came to Kondambi [the settlement where Reay was living]. KAI stopped hitting and pulling her when he became aware that a crowd had gathered at Kondambi to watch them. Muru came up to Kondambi near KAI's house, when Andamung was taking into the house some kumu [ond kumu?] she had mumed [sic; mumued, cooked in a ground oven]. Rain was coming. KAI called out to Andamung to take Muru's belongings to his women's house. Andamung pretended not to hear him. Rain came, and KAI went to his own house.

28.10.54 Last night, Muru slept with KAI's wife Komdilj and intended to go to Minj today to stay with Kobilj-Kerewa's wife. Onim asked me whether I had any news of Muru today and wanted to know whether Muru was still all right or whether KAI had killed her.

At many places in Chapter 9 as briefly illustrated above Reay recounts, in conversational form, what happened at times between Bird[Kai] and Cass[Muru]. For example, Cass[Muru] went to visit her brother without her husband's permission. He beat her on return, and then, as reported in Chapter 9, said something to her which reveals something of the presuppositions he acted on in beating his wife, and threatening to kill her brother:

'You can't go over there again. If you go to see your brothers, they will give you to another man, but you are married to me and I won't stand for it.'

Reay's detailed fieldnotes provided the content of the chapter's narrative. Clearly the events were observed by Reay day by day, and she also recorded what was said about developments, usually attributing the remarks to particular people. Portions of her fieldnotes consist entirely of attributed remarks and conversations, reflecting the importance of conversation, speech-making and represented (or reported) speech in the lives of these Highlanders. Even if we assume that her command of the local language grew with time, it seems likely she would have had considerable assistance from one or more helpers in documenting these events and remarks each day, particularly during the early years of her fieldwork. Marie mentions having had field assistants, and also the regular companionship of younger people, e.g, a young boy (of perhaps 12 or so) upon whom she could depend to run errands.[10] It is clear that Cass[Muru] herself contributed in some part to Reay's language learning, for she writes of her in her notes:

> Muru was my 'sister', since her stepfather's brother had 'adopted' me as his 'daughter' … Muru tried to teach me her language, not by listing things which could be identified, as the other women did, but by patiently making me understand things she wanted to tell me. I believe a kind of sympathy grew up between us … (Australian National University Archives: ANUA 440. 2013. Marie Reay collection (item list): 440: 373-001)

So the chapters of this book as they stand largely represent Reay's narrativization of women's life stories from her fieldnotes, which were probably constructed in part by assistance Reay got in recording conversations and commentaries, as well as from her own on-going observations. This mode of writing and representation was, as already suggested, clearly experimental in some ways for Reay herself. In its theatricality, its focus upon characters, action, and talk, it clearly differed from the canons of academic writing she had employed in her thesis, and in other work which she continued to produce after she had apparently left this project in limbo. However, she did less with the other proposed, more academically styled, book on Wahgi women.

---

10   Both Reay and a boy like this were presumably fluent in Tok Pisin, and he could have translated from the local language whatever may have been unclear to her. See Reay 1992: 147 on language proficiency and 1992: 163 on field assistants.

Reay in context: Colonial, academic, personal

Reay was unusual in having shifted to fieldwork in Papua New Guinea from fieldwork with south-eastern Aboriginal groups, long since pacified in a basic sense, and resident on reserves on the fringes of country towns as marginalized people in Australia. While there were or had been some female ethnographers of Aboriginal Australia (including Ursula McConnell, Grace Sitlington, Ruth Fink Latukefu, Faye Gale, Catherine Berndt, and lone female social workers such as Olive Pink; subsequently, Nancy Munn and Diane Barwick), there were relatively few ethnographers working in Papua New Guinea in Reay's early research period, and most of the others were men: Peter Lawrence, Mervyn Meggitt (who likewise went from Aboriginal Australia to PhD work in New Guinea), Mick Read, Richard Salisbury, Ralph Bulmer, among others.[11]

Exceptions to the dearth of women in Papua New Guinea were path-breaking Hortense Powdermaker, who worked in New Ireland in the 1920s; Camilla Wedgwood, who worked in Manam 1932–34, Phyllis Kaberry, who did fieldwork both in Australia (1934–35) and in the Sepik region of Papua New Guinea (1939–40); and Paula Brown, who did research in roughly the same time period as Reay in Chimbu. The major period of Papua New Guinean ethnography, with a greater diversity of both male and female ethnographers, was yet to come (though the first anthropological pair, Margaret Mead and Reo Fortune, preceded Ronald and Catherine Berndt, who worked in the Eastern Highlands from 1951–53, by about 15 years; and Marilyn and Andrew Strathern by three decades). But, crucially, during the period of increasing anthropological research in New Guinea from the 1950s when Reay began her work, Australia made its presence as colonial power felt in many parts of the country, and in the Highlands at least, was met with considerable enthusiasm.

A certain colonial privilege was assumed and enjoyed by most of these ethnographers, men and women. Some, such as Peter Lawrence (whose most famous work remains *Road Belong Cargo*, a study of cargoistic movements on the northern Rai coast of New Guinea), used to tell

---

11   During this time, under A.P. Elkin at Sydney, unmarried women were discouraged from going to Papua New Guinea and remote Australia. Elkin preferred them to conduct fieldwork instead in 'settled' Australia (J.R. Beckett, pers. comm.)

anecdotes about the period, evoking a picture of the anthropologist's privilege in summoning 'natives' to interview on the verandah (though this was not necessarily all their fieldwork amounted to), and in visiting the Australian plantocracy.[12] Marie Reay, too, enjoyed some of these privileges. It is clear that she had good access to the District Officer; that she had use of a car and driver; and that she had young male assistants who did her housekeeping, and some who also gathered daily news, reported on court cases and other activities, and also translated for her and helped her transcribe. There was more readily accessible local Australian administrative presence (for instance at Minj), than there has been since.

However, this does not mean that female researchers were treated without prejudice (Reay 1992: 142–143). Michael Young (2005: 83) notes that the Wahgi 'god-administrator' disapproved of female anthropologists, especially those who broke the 'White Women's Protection Law by wearing shorts'—which Reay did. 'Modified Bombay Bloomers', Reay called them, capacious khaki shorts of which she wrote that they 'looked terrible' and would certainly 'discourage any sexual passion that happened to be present' (Reay 1992: 166). Like female anthropologists elsewhere— Elsie Clews Parsons with her groundbreaking, later-controversial *Pueblo Indian Religion* (1939), for example—Reay was treated by New Guineans as an honorary male in that she was regularly present at otherwise gender-restricted ceremonies and events (see Reay 1992: 154 on 'white woman's privilege').

Reay used to refer to her time in Papua New Guinea as 'meadow work', making a humorous contrast with the more ordinary anthropologist's 'fieldwork'. She obviously enjoyed her time in Papua New Guinea. She was a contemporary of Mervyn Meggitt, D'Arcy Ryan, Ralph Bulmer, Mick Read, Robert Glasse and other anthropologists, and was a person to whom a number of new aspiring fieldworkers turned, including Marilyn Strathern and, later, Michael O'Hanlon, for information and suggestions about research in the Highlands. Her responses, from letters and records, appear to have often been rather astringent.

---

12   For the record, I knew Peter Lawrence in periods from the late 1970s until towards the end of his life in 1987, and had the opportunity to hear many stories from him about different styles and episodes of fieldwork, which (to his credit) he rarely repeated, but always seemed to have a large store of new ones.

In contrast to her absorption in fieldwork, Reay's academic situations, and especially her appointment at The Australian National University, tried her, particularly in latter years. In his obituary, anthropologist Michael Young (2005: 83) remarks that Reay observed a succession of male departmental chairs and different styles of academic leadership. 'As a graduate student she had been exploited by Elkin, bullied by Nadel, and patronized by Stanner, so she took a dim view of god-professors in general, and tended to remain aloof from departmental politics', he writes (ibid.; see Reay 1992: 138–139). From personal acquaintance with Marie when I was at The Australian National University in 1981 as a visiting junior academic, and from conversations in the late 1990s when I and my family visited her in her home on the central coast of New South Wales, I can attest that, at least for some of her working years, she felt persecuted under particular departmental chairmanship. She said that she was closely monitored by Professor and departmental head Derek Freeman, who often gave her up to ten directives and notes a day about her duties, and (at some point) denied her the right of supervising postgraduate students (though she clearly did supervise a number of students, including Pacific and New Guinean scholars Grant McCall, Daryl Feil, Wayne Warry and Epeli Hau'ofa).[13] She also, perhaps in conjunction with this, had some periods of mental instability and recurrent depression in later years.

Reay remained bitter about the treatment meted out to her to the end of her life. Probably not often mentioned outright, but certainly well known, was the fact that Marie was lesbian. She lived at some distance, with a female companion in a small town about 30 kilometres from Canberra, rather secluded from most university contacts. However, in some ways she was flamboyant rather than reclusive. For a period of time she drove a little, bright red sportscar. And as Young (2005: 83) notes, she was socially active in many ways outside the university: she was a Justice of the Peace for many years, took an active role in developing Australian anthropological organizations, including the Institute of Aboriginal Studies from its founding in 1964, in literary affairs, and in cultivating relationships with friends and family. In her declining years she lived with

---

13   Freeman's stated reason for this was that she was not 'in the paradigm' of sociobiology to which he had become converted. Lest her report seem incredible, it seems apt to say here that, when I came as newly appointed professor to The Australian National University in latter 1995 and was also clearly seen not to be in the paradigm, I was repeatedly sent reading material, and telephoned, by Professor Freeman, until I demanded that he cease both activities, on pain of my taking measures.

her sister on the New South Wales coast north of Sydney, mainly hoping (she remarked sardonically) to outlive certain academics who had made her life difficult in Canberra.

Was Reay a feminist in the sense of having a particular interest in women's lives, or liberation? Yes, in some ways, in my opinion; but not in others, almost despite herself. She focused in her Wahgi ethnographic work on certain topics, as revealed in the archiving of her material: mushroom madness; ritual; folk tales; design, the structure of Kuma segmentary groups, various manifestations of principles ordering the wider society, and questions of conformity, constraint and freedom. Through it all, her focus on women's lives, and the inequalities they lived with, came to shape a good part of what she did. This was not through prior decision or commitment on her part; in fact, the reality of women's lives, and their work, seems not to have appealed to her, nor to have particularly evoked her sympathy or personal interest: she regarded it as tedious. She evidently found much more interesting the conduct of court cases, and politics, including developing electoral politics in Papua New Guinea. She was personally in sympathy with some individuals, following their ups and downs closely, and offering them help and rewards as seemed right to her: as mentioned above, she recorded in her notes her willingness to take Cass[Muru] to Chimbu to fulfil her desire to see her Chimbu partner again—a plan vetoed by Cass[Muru]'s brother's vehement opposition. Her letters and notes reveal her plans and preparations to bring New Guinean visitors to Canberra. But despite this not having been her main interest, she attended ethnographically to the courtship and marital careers of Wahgi women over a long period. For it became apparent to her that the disposition of women was structurally central to Kuma society, and she clearly felt strongly about this. She was fascinated by the contrast between the freedom accorded to young girls to choose and pursue courting parties; and the vast limitation of their freedom that came about with marriage. She recorded unflinchingly the considerable amount of violence through which women were kept in line in Kuma society. This connected with a strong feeling she had concerning personal freedom, her view of women's fate as denial of freedom to them, and her view of Wahgi society as riven by powerful tensions.

Reay seems to have drawn back somewhat from the Gender Relations in the Southwestern Pacific working group which convened at The Australian National University 1983–85, and brought many scholars together there—despite the fact that she had originally been involved in its planning. In conversation with Martha Macintyre, Reay expressed some dissent from what she saw as the preoccupations of this group. She took the view that its feminist orientation could only generate a partial and unrealistically rosy view of women's lives in Papua New Guinea. She objected to views that she felt tended to detract from an understanding of inequality and power difference in male-female relations in Papua New Guinea (see Reay 1992: 161).

In concluding this book Reay suggests that should women be treated more fairly and equally, and be enabled to have more control over their own lives—and she believes that this should happen—the society of the Minj Agamp as we know it would become unrecognisable, and its major structures would be significantly altered. While much change has occurred in the meantime, it is difficult to say that the social order has become radically altered or unrecognisable. Nor have women become 'free' in the way Reay considered desirable. It is speculative, but all things considered, Reay may have shared some sense of oppression with them, especially in light of persecution she suffered in her academic situation, but perhaps also more generally.

Such sensibilities as these, however, did not make of her an easy personality. She had high academic standards. She was evidently an acute observer and admirable ethnographer, and left behind copious valuable field materials. An excellent and exacting writer herself, she could be an acerbic critic of other people's expression. Michael Young (2005: 83) remarks that she could be intimidating and abrasive to students and junior colleagues, though moderating her sharpness with sly, dry humour. She could be kind and generously attentive to students, recalls Wayne Warry, whom she visited in Port Moresby and in the field, in Chimbu Province. Many academics such as myself, who shared a corridor and many interests with her, found her at the best of times to be a sharp, receptive though sometimes slightly testy interlocutor and critic. If her not publishing this book in her lifetime was an exercise of the same critical sense against herself, I think that was unfortunate. The book is hereby available and readers can judge for themselves its place in feminist, anthropological, and specifically Melanesianist literatures.

Acknowledgements

My thanks to Jeremy Beckett, Michael Young and Martha Macintyre for comments on drafts of this Introduction, and helpful information they provided concerning Reay and the university scene in Reay's time as they knew it; Judith Wilson and Wayne Warry for their recollections of Reay; James Weiner and Margaret Jolly for reading a draft; Alan Rumsey for useful editorial suggestions; John Burton for permission to reproduce his North and South Wahgi Census Division maps and information on tribal distributions; ANU Head Archivist Maggie Shapley, and the late Karina Taylor; anonymous referees for ANU Press; and Zazie Bowen and Ria van de Zandt for their invaluable contributions to readying this volume for publication. Wenner-Gren's Historical Archives Program is gratefully acknowledged for having supported the archival work that was necessary to assemble this manuscript.

References

Australian National University Archives: ANUA 440. 2013. Marie Reay collection (item list), available at archivescollection.anu.edu.au/index.php/uipue (accessed 26 February 2014).

Beckett, Jeremy 1989. *Conversations with Ian Hogbin.* Sydney: University of Sydney.

Berndt, Ronald M. 1962. *Excess and Restraint: Social Control Among a New Guinea Mountain People.* Chicago: University of Chicago Press.

Burridge, Kenelm 1995[1960]. *Mambu: A Melanesian Millennium.* Princeton, NJ: Princeton University Press.

Hammar, Lawrence 2010. 'From Gift to Commodity … and Back Again: Form and Fluidity of Sexual Networking in Papua New Guinea', in Vicki Luker and Sinclair Dinnen (eds), *Civic Insecurity: Law, Order and HIV in Papua New Guinea.* Canberra: ANU E Press. doi.org/10.22459/CI.12.2010.04.

Josephides, Lisette 1975. *The Production of Inequality: Gender and Exchange among the Kewa.* New York and London: Tavistock.

Jolly, Margaret, Christine Stewart and Carolyn Brewer 2012. *Engendering Violence in Papua New Guinea.* Canberra: ANU E Press. doi.org/10.22459/EVPNG.07.2012.

Lutz, Catherine 1995. 'The gender of theory', in Ruth Behar and Deborah Gordon (eds), *Women Writing Culture/Culture Writing Women*. Berkeley: University of California Press, pp. 249–266.

Parsons, Elsie Clews 1939. *Pueblo Indian Religion*. Chicago: University of Chicago.

Read, Kenneth E. 1965. *The High Valley*. New York: Charles Scribner's Sons.

Read, Kenneth E. 1986. *Return to the High Valley: Coming Full Circle*. Berkeley: University of California Press.

Reay, Marie 1959. *The Kuma: Freedom and Conformity in the New Guinea Highlands*. Carlton, Vic.: Melbourne University Press.

Reay, Marie O. 1964a. *Aborigines Now: New Perspective in the Study of Aboriginal Communities*. Sydney: Angus and Robertson.

Reay, Marie O. 1964b. 'Review of Ronald M. Berndt, Excess and restraint: social control among a New Guinea Mountain people', *Oceania*, 35(2): 149–154.

Reay, Marie 1966. 'Women in transitional society', in E.K. Fiske (ed.), *New Guinea on the Threshold: Aspects of Social, Political, and Economic Development*. Canberra: Australian National University Press, pp. 166–184.

Reay, Marie 1992. 'An innocent in the Garden of Eden', in Terence Hays (ed.), *Ethnographic Presents: Pioneering Anthropologists in the Papua New Guinea Highlands*. Berkeley: University of California Press, pp. 137–166.

Strathern, Marilyn 1972. *Women in Between: Female Roles in a Male World: Mount Hagen, New Guinea*. London: Seminar Press.

Wardlow, Holly 2006. *Wayward Women: Sexuality and Agency in a New Guinea Society*. Berkeley, Los Angeles and London: University of California Press.

Young, Michael 2005. 'Obituary: Marie Olive Reay, born Maitland, NSW, died Booragul, NSW, 16 September 2004, aged 82', *The Asia Pacific Journal of Anthropology*, 6(1): 81–84.

Introduction

Marilyn Strathern

This is a remarkable publication by any account. What has been so skilfully unearthed and edited by Francesca Merlan is a vivid first-hand description of conditions in the New Guinea Highlands encountered early on in the short decades between the establishment of the post-war administration and Papua New Guinea's independence. Its historical value is immense, and no small portion of that comes from the directness and immediacy of Marie Reay's presentation, which appears such a short step from original fieldnotes. Therein, as the reader discovers, lies part of the author's craft. For she has compiled a work from a very specific viewpoint. On more than one occasion she was to remark that she had not gone to the Highlands to work on what subsequently was known as gender relations, and this account does not fit easily into the field of women-focused gender studies that followed her own early forays. Rather, the writing here was directly motivated by what she observed of the way women were treated.[1] The message is powerful. Sixty years on from her first observations in the mid-1950s, I imagine that *Wives and Wanderers* will turn out to be of great comparative interest to contemporary debates in Papua New Guinea about the role of violence in men's and women's affairs.

Reay must have been the first solo woman anthropologist to undertake ethnographic work in the Highlands, and as Merlan makes clear in her Editor's Introduction is certainly celebrated as the first to take up an interest in women's issues. We might conclude from the emphatic claim in her own authorial preface, namely '[B]eing a woman myself, I try to show in this book that the women of the Minj Agamp are people in their

---

1 'Predominantly interested in religion, politics, and a few other things, I came to the study of gender relations by the accident of working in a place where women were exploited, oppressed, and cruelly treated' [Statement, see footnote 3, probably 1983].

own right …' (see Preface), that there was an axiomatic connection here. However that would be to lose a vital component of the story. Reay will not have been the only one of her generation to betray something of an ambivalence when it came to writing on women.

While not claiming to have plumbed this ambivalence, I signal the need to appreciate the complexity of her situation as an academic in the 1950s and 1960s. Although she uses a vocabulary ('people in their own right') that was to characterize the emergent feminist anthropology of the 1970s, part of the spiritedness of her stance may well have sprung directly from her own initial struggles, rebellion even, to be taken seriously as an anthropologist. The double-bind was that to take her (only) as a 'woman' was not to take her seriously.[2] It is not irrelevant that a colleague who had known her for many decades should have remarked of the three senior men who overshadowed her years as a graduate student that they had exploited, bullied and patronized her in turn (Young 2005: 83). So there were occasions too when, far from joining cause with those interested in a focus on women's affairs, she instead spoke of her work *as an anthropologist*. As an anthropologist, she was interested in a spectrum of social activities, in the whole society, to adopt the argot of the period. The spectrum included what she herself put under the rubrics of religion and politics; indeed it may have been especially by her work in these areas that she would have wanted (at one stage at least) to be most remembered. Gender relations, she once stated, 'do not substitute for other aspects of social relations in ethnographic elucidation … [although they do] usefully supplement them'.[3] As Merlan reminds us, she was writing such supplements, notably 'Women in transitional society' (Reay 1966), at the same time as this account.

Interesting as the exercise would be, it would be less than true to Reay's own independence of mind to introduce this book in terms of what it might have meant to the world of scholarship—then and since—had it been published in (say) the late 1960s. One has to respect the fact that she chose not to publish it herself. As the reader will discover, the author

---

2   I put it this way to re-capture something of the tenor of the time. This was also how she recollected it herself, years later, a point I return to below.

3   From her statement to the Gender Relations Research Group that she convened along with Roger Keesing and Michael Young in 1983–84 at The Australian National University (the group's project was called 'Gender relations in the southwestern Pacific: ideology, politics and production'). What of my own recollections of Marie Reay may have coloured this Introduction date both from this period, and from earlier periods of residence in Canberra (1969–72 and 1965).

did not place it in relation to other works of the time (Merlan notes the lack of references; the book did not physically exist on the same shelves), and to place it thus now would be to foreclose other courses of reflection on it. After all, if one thinks of the history of Melanesian ethnography,[4] who knows what its intervention might have meant if it had appeared instead in the mid-1970s, or in the later 1980s. At the (supposed) point of publication, Reay might have provided such a contextualization herself, yet it would have been out of character with how she had presented the account in the draft we have now. What she wrote simply did not fall into any of the ethnographic genres of those times. If anything it might have been closer to the poetry that we know she was also writing. I don't have access to what her poems were like, but take the genre in its broadest sense as allowing highly creative non-fiction. Meaningfully, her world of poetry was not one she introduced into the anthropological arena.[5]

Reay had already contributed a major ethnography in the conventional sense (*The Kuma*, 1959a), and one that was subsequently to be a pivot of much comparative work by others. In *Women and Wanderers* analysis remains very largely off stage (apart from its introductory chapter, there are some expository context-setting passages), and the pride of place is given to descriptions of people's doings, as they apparently occurred, in story-like form. Nonetheless there was a theoretical reason for presenting Minj (Reay's preferred name for Kuma in this volume) men and women in this way through these stories. Do not be mistaken: this book has a specific argument. There is far more to it than a rehearsal of the kind of spectacular detail—and here it is indeed spectacular detail—that is often referred to as ethnographic 'richness'. Yet to put it that way is to follow the curious marginalizing of detail that anthropologists sometimes indulge in, as though readers of ethnographies can take richness for granted. It would be a shame to do that here. So before we come to the argument, let me first comment on one dimension of the text's effectiveness.

---

4   The historical record was of concern to Reay. Had she contributed, as she at one point was planning, to the volume *Dealing with Inequality* (Strathern 1987) (which sprang from the 1983–84 project [see footnote 1]), it would have been in the form of an afterword entitled 'A historical commentary on the ethnography of gender (Highlands New Guinea)'. I may add that from Minj, where she was living at the time, she had taken the trouble to comment on several of the individual chapters.

5   However Michael Young mentions her as a graceful writer of short stories as well (2005: 84), and she certainly wrote creative non-fiction in prose form for her anthropological colleagues. One such work was a 'reconstructive fantasy' of some of 'the conditions in which patriliny could transform to matriliny'. Called 'Myth and matriliny', and entailing adaptations of myths from Foi, Kuma and Tubetube (draft paper, Australian National University Archives: ANUA 440. 2013. Marie Reay collection (item list)), she presents it herself as 'short short story'.

Immediacy: The genre

Much ethnography is seemingly written of the moment. Yet the moment in which the ethnographer writes is also turned to the ends of exposition, and conveying a sense of immediacy has to compete with that. The trade-off between immediacy and reflection, between what is observed and what is analysed, seems inevitable. This was certainly true of the kind of ethnographic reporting that came out of the Highlands of Papua New Guinea in the 1960s and 1970s, including Reay's own monograph. Ethnographers made greater or lesser attempts at conveying atmosphere, mood, ethos, in order to convey in turn some of the original immediacy of the impressions made on them. Reay does it here without making herself the obvious channel of such an experience. What we have in the present volume is neither an ethnography in the strict sense of the term nor the original fieldnotes and diaries that were conventionally taken then as the most immediate form of writing. Rather, we have a re-creation, possibly something bordering on a 'reconstructive fantasy' (see footnote 3), which is simultaneously the outcome of reflection (implying analysis) and able to convey the immediacy of living in a Minj Agamp world. The last point can be made by saying what genre this is not.

The subject matter concerns 'women' (as conveyed by the title(s)); the vehicles of narration are events. Thus while the narratives are indeed as much about women, and their doings and thoughts, as about men, the writerly device that carries the narratives is story-telling, taking the reader through longer or shorter sequences of events. The stories all have female protagonists. Accepting that they are designed to show us something of women's lives, an anthropologist would probably suggest that everything will turn on the kind of context the narrator chooses for his or her characters. Reay seemingly downplayed contextualization; in any case, other work meant that the larger framework of Minj 'society' could be taken as read. Here we are only told enough about what has been going on, or about women's relationships with others, to make sense of the particular events being described. Then again, although there are some wonderful pen portraits, none of the accounts is comparable to a life-history or biography. Instead we are presented with stretches of happenings and occurrences as they happened or occurred to named individuals ('all true cases' (see Chapter 1)). Now the narration of events as they follow or loop back on one another would have been familiar to analytical models of the time that took a 'case study' form. Yet these narratives are not extended case studies either. As much as they follow particular individuals in their relations with other, they also switch from this person's experiences to that person's, and only incidentally do they speak of background or future outcomes. These abbreviated contextualizations hardly have the revelatory coherence expected of a case study. Indeed, they as much echo a practice Reay herself brilliantly depicts: how Minj men are adept at finding a 'context' for creating a dispute or pursuing a claim in whatever history of prior events serves the purpose. They explain events by other events.

I am both exaggerating and being more explicit than Reay ever is. Yet the point is that I think she is being true to a particular tenor of life. She expressed it formally when (in a retrospective reflection) she referred to social relationships as the building blocks for social structure precisely because relationships had an inherent dynamism (Reay 1992: 139). Although this could be said of anywhere, perhaps in this style of narration she has caught a particular edge to the abruptness of people's incursions into one another's lives. In these narratives Minj Agamp often seem caught off guard by the actions of others or have to impress their will through what may seem over-determined or impetuous or wayward action. This is seemingly matched by the starkness with which Reay narrates people's attitudes and intentions. The stories would not be stories if they did not have speaking characters, yet in the events presented here what is spoken is often very brief and direct and without nuance. Perhaps it is relevant that much of the dialogue concerns cross-sex interactions. (We are not given either the kind of allusive rhetoric or involuted gossip that men and women might conceivably have directed to those of their own sex, nor the subtleties she refers to at the beginning of her Preface.) What is certainly relevant is that the stories told here deal with facets of men's and women's relationships with one another. More specifically, the different topics revolve largely around the disposition of women (in marriage) between men, and women's subsequent protests.

On this it is worth emphasizing what the Editor also underlines, for Reay came back to it again and again in her writings, and it is practically the first observation she talked about in her retrospective piece: how much she had been much struck by the practice of wife-takers forcibly seizing or kidnapping ('pulling') their brides. Whether from the men's point of view a woman was being 'taken', or as also happened, peacefully 'given', being coerced to marry accompanied a violent abruptness written into every woman's life. Plainly the transformation from girl into wife was not unexpected as a practice, because it was everyone's (woman-speaking) fate, but it could be unexpected as an event, in the here and now, in the way it happened, in this manner rather than that manner. Seizure was designed to ride rough-shod over the woman's feelings, whether or not her kin were in connivance. And other events followed: the way young women were seized or otherwise handed over had all kinds of repercussions, including, as we shall see, how the reputation of being a wanderer was acquired.

This aspect of Agamp life is seemingly well served by relating events that show men and women impinging on one another's actions, motives, values. At the same time the concept of 'event', as I have been using it, seems to summon too abstract a sense of (naturalized) space-time; maybe that of (interpersonal) 'encounter' serves better. It was not her term but, in a paper that came out in the same year as her monograph (Reay 1959b), Reay had talked of encounters staged between men and women. The dramatic one-day fighting games, which typified what she spoke of as conflict between the sexes, were interestingly open-ended. Indeed one might think of them as experimental probings of what the effect of such interchanges might be, how far each side could push the other, what either would be provoked to reveal to the other. Drawing from this, one might say that an element in any 'encounter' is its unpredictability: people try to guess what will happen, watch how others behave, see how this or that person will react. The dynamic of the relationship makes outcomes for a moment unknown.

It is in producing a narrative of encounters that Reay exploits the genre of story-telling. It enables her to capture quick changes from moment to moment, to follow sequences of actions as well as words, imagine people's thoughts and feelings, and conjure what they said from what she remembered or noted or had heard from countless situations similar to that being described. The result is obviously not a novel, and seems far from the kind of semi-fiction that allows *events* to be re-arranged.[6] Of course I do not know for sure, but part of the intention seems to have been a fidelity to the unfolding of events themselves: it is the encounters that carry the message. If this is true, it is presaged in the delicacy with which she introduces the names of her characters. English names (fiction) they are not, even though they are in English (creative non-fiction).[7]

---

6   As when the focus is on the characters.
7   They are translated, with some linguistic flourishes of her own, from the vernacular. In 'The politics of a witch-killing' (Reay 1976) she uses regular English names (Joe, Malcolm, etc.).

Reflection: The argument

This book captures a poignant moment in the colonial experience of the people of the Wahgi Valley. Like the analysis, the colonists are off stage too, yet the effect of their presence is pervasive. It is there in the demeanour of women, in the hesitations of men, in the sequence of 'local leaders' (*luluai*[8] and *tultul*[9] to councillors), and is crystallized from time to time in references to the kiap's court (Court of Native Affairs). One constant refrain when a pig ceremonial was impending was the threat of imprisonment that came with Government officers' disapproval of certain practices. This is argument by stealth, so to speak, since in other writing Reay was quite explicit about the incursions of kiaps' views on the nature of bride wealth (imagining it as placing a value on a woman's head, as a purchase would) and on the need to base marriage on a bride's willingness to go to a particular man (as though marriage concerned the bride and groom above their clans and subclans). Indeed the unpublished outline of a longer work (see footnote 15), as Merlan describes it in the Editor's Introduction, clearly laid out an argument that could be applied to the present volume; Merlan draws attention to the explicit note on which *Wives and Wanderers* ends.

Perhaps it was the recency and impact of Government intervention, and anticipation of more changes to come, that led Reay to speculate not only on the future of Minj Agamp but on their past. Drawing on archaeological materials available at the time (they were to be drastically altered by subsequent study in ways she could not have foreseen), she imagines earlier conditions of oppression. She ponders on the changes that might have come about with the introduction of pigs and sweet potato, as she understood them to have been, just as she ponders on what *laik bilong meri* (again, see Editor's Introduction) might mean for the future flourishing of Minj society. She was of her own time, anthropologically speaking, in her grasp of 'society' as an entity to be studied. However inflected by its historical location, it had an analysable coherence, one in which men's affairs were important. So although the story-lines follow women, which gives them some centrality, when men

---

8   A village or tribal chief appointed by the government. Originally it meant a leader in battle (Mihalic 1971: 125).
9   The assistant village chief appointed by the government; he is second in command in a village or area. Originally he was the messenger for the *luluai*. Sometimes also he served as interpreter (Mihalic 1971: 199).

come into a story there is no particular attempt to describe them (the men) from a woman's perspective—they appear as the author knows them from their own spheres of action. For all that she takes up a 'woman's viewpoint' (see Chapter 1), then, it is a view that attends specifically to various 'fields' of women's lives and to their protests about their situation. The present volume does not invite us to take a woman's perspective on (say) male arenas of public activity.[10]

Reay is quite clear that those arenas were only viable because of what women made possible—the form of men's politics and ritual would not have occurred without it. She shows the underpinnings of male activity both through the work women did (this is part of her opening argument about Wahgi prehistory, but is not further documented here), and through their being principal vehicles for men's alliances. This is a message that is drummed home again and again. Yet it is all very well concluding in abstract terms that men depend on women for their relations with other men, or that men's interests always came first. That is not the form in which such realities appear to the actors. Reay's argument on this score is presented concretely and vividly in the movement of the stories. The effect of laying out encounters (events) conveys the remorseless repetition of actions, the moment at which the blow is dealt, the haphazard routine careless rough handling of being 'pulled', and just how women stage their protests.

For all that the dynamics of an 'encounter' introduces an uncertainty as to how any particular episode will end, the stories, one after another, also convey certain predictabilities of outcome. There were only so many possibilities open to the way in which marriages were set up, the very notion of marriage implying the moment at which diverse men—the prospective groom, a former betrothed, the girl's fathers, brothers and mother's brothers, along with the subclans of these men—would reveal their interests in the girl. This set the scene for men's anxieties, whether in relation to the prospective bride, in relation to the men on whom they had claims, or in relation to their competitors. Nonetheless, negotiations between in-laws, not to speak of losing and gaining with rivals, was all part of what men expected from one another. Of the bride who was the object of their efforts, these stories equally tell of how often they would be

---

10 See the section in Reay (1959a: 181) called 'Women's interpretation of male values'. Nonetheless, had the volume been published in the (later) 1960s, it would have long preceded later claims that there had been no serious attention paid to women's spheres of actions.

faced with the outcome of other men's actions in quite another register—men succumbing to girls' desires as 'courting' partners. For girls (not the men), becoming a wife put an end to that.

Minj stereotypes of the good and bad wife that Reay describes (elaborated in 1959a) were not just judgements on the differing characters of women; they expressed, from the perspective of 'good' wives and their menfolk, expectations about what marriage meant to the subclans negotiating it. Reay's emphasis in this volume, and she makes it evident, rests on those who protest at their fate. They seemingly had little positive language through which to express themselves, beyond playing on the fact of their own desires for this or that person.[11] However they were prone to being the objects of considerable negative stereotyping. The possibility of a young woman being stigmatized as a 'wandering woman' does not seem to have been far below the surface of marriage negotiations, even though the number of Minj women whose whole lives acted out that stereotype were very few. It came to the surface as soon as a woman showed she was resisting what her menfolk had planned for her.

Without the words (or wealth) with which to put her case, a young woman could nonetheless demonstrate something of her position through her actions. She could run away from the husband marked for her. However, there were only two places to run to—back home to her own kin or to another man. For women who wanted to avoid the reputation of being a 'wanderer' this was a double-bind. While going off to another man courted the reputation of someone prepared to go from man to man, going back to the kin who had organized her marriage in the first place was not necessarily any escape either. Moreover, if sending her back again did not work then *they* would send her off to another man, and in some cases there were whole strings of such attempts. In other words, men's obligations to other men created the 'wandering woman' pattern as they passed their kinswoman from this person to that person.[12] They were not

---

11 Non-marriage was not a viable alternative, although Reay imagined this might change in the future.

12 In some cases a prospective husband did this, for another in his subclan, to a woman he did not want as a wife for himself. Reay also records a fascinating conversation in which two men ponder on the fact that it would be very difficult for older men to find (more) wives if women did not (and thus to the men's advantage) run away from their husbands (Chapter 8)! Such expectations no doubt fed into the picture men built up of women's waywardness, not knowing what was in their mind (see Chapter 8).

necessarily going against a girl's specific desire for different partners: there appear to be examples here of girls not really knowing what they want, apart from wanting to make a protest.

This, we might say, is a Minj version of the kind of double-bind gender situations in which women have found themselves in other contexts.[13] These situations have taken different forms, and might have been generated by different issues, but in numerous societies of the old New Guinea Highlands women seemed to have borne the brunt of men's ambitions and men's dependence on them. None of this is to mitigate the force of women's own actions and the events they set in train, and quite emphatically Reay does not want us to forget this side of things. At the same time, the stories in this book show—and it is an argument we can take away from them—just how at a particular point in their lives Minj women have often had no recourse but to act in ways that jeopardize their future prospects.

Coda

Reay had not just been struck by the practice of 'pulling' brides, she was upset by the often brutal way in which girls were dragged off, and conveyed her reaction to the people around her. I wonder if recounting some of the events she witnessed brought writerly relief. I wonder too if this is not where we encounter something of her ambivalence. For as far as her main publications were concerned, she was not going to argue from a woman's perspective in order to re-write the sociology.[14] Sorry as she might be for women's slave-like status, that of itself did not make them into central anthropological subjects. At times she voiced the opinion that

---

13 Across the Highlands was also the more general double-bind women experienced when caught between kin and spouse: the same people (her husbands, brothers) whose interests a woman should ideally promote, and to whom she could appeal, were those who were also prepared to pursue *their* interests in her at her expense. Women being scapegoated for troubles between male affines was part of the phenomenon.

14 Though she was prepared to write on the 'status of women' in Papua New Guinea at large, and had views on what it might really take to improve their lot, in Minj [Kuma] as well as more widely (e.g. 1966).

much of what women did was dull. 'I had no intention', she recollects (Reay 1992: 158), 'of giving a derogatory picture of Kuma [Minj] society by focusing on the slave population'.[15]

Her extreme language ('slave population') belonged to the early era of investigations in the Highlands that had led to the model of 'sexual antagonism' between men and women. The myriad conflicts played out in these stories are testimony to some of the circumstances that lay behind that. This is not the moment to take stock of the anthropological debates that ensued. However, in the light of issues current in today's Papua New Guinea to do with domestic violence, largely men's violence against women, it may be the place to reflect on certain dimensions of Minj society in the 1950s and 1960s. Reay herself had no compunction about drawing on her Minj material in order to depict life in the Papua New Guinea Highlands at a large.[16] But for all the features that Minj Agamp shared with their neighbours, there were many they did not or, better put, combined at that point in time in their own particular way. The effects of such combinations run throughout these narratives. A significant point, then, on which the book would be interesting for current concerns over violence is its reminder of an anthropological truth. While, on the one hand, it is important to identify a common (and in this case depressingly widespread) phenomenon, on the other hand, one of the anthropologist's jobs is to observe the micro-processes at work. Such processes simultaneously point to general enabling factors and render them with exquisite[17] local distinctiveness. We need both eyes on what is happening.

One or two aspects of Minj society illuminate the then conditions of possibility for the plight of young girls at the moment of marriage, which could so easily turn them into archetypes of wandering women, and which affected their options for action. Reay considered these aspects in various (published and unpublished) contexts, and they recall the kinds

---

15 As Merlan has discovered, she must have had something of a change of heart later, with her plans for a full-length work. This comment was her recollected reaction to the suggestion that she might write her PhD thesis on women.

16 This is not to imply that she was not interested in anthropological comparison. Additionally, at various points she specifically contrasted Minj Agamp with their neighbours, including comments made by Minj folk on the differences.

17 An epithet in English that can refer to pain as well as pleasure. I write 'local' as to time or place; this does not equate with what is indigenous or traditional—Reay consistently drew attention to changing historical conditions.

of topics that anthropologists of the time were discussing.[18] Men in Minj of the time seem to have got themselves into the position of competing with one another over the disposal of women in ways that complexified everyone's lives.

First, Minj women were in a position to protest at their marital circumstances precisely because they had had experience of a life before marriage in which it was they who had been encouraged to take the initiative in relation to men. The abrupt reversal of affairs was to be depicted by Reay as a kind of initiation for girls, though superficially it had very different contours from boys' harsh (at one point she describes it as 'brutal') subjugation. It is worth remembering that the practice and violence of initiation varied widely across Highlands societies. The 'breaking in' (see Chapter 1) of adolescent girls in Minj specifically involved men being assertive ('pulling' brides) where once it had been the girls who were assertive. This is of course an explicit theme of the present book.

Secondly, Minj society was among those where men's relations with other men included diverse possibilities for their subclan making claims on one another's womenfolk, summed up in the adage of 'sister exchange' (by no means universally the case in the Highlands). There were many roads to such arrangements. Thus one man (subclan) might claim another (subclan)'s daughters or sisters, either in order to marry the woman himself, or to bestow her on other men who in turn had claims on him. In kinship terms these were variously thoughts of as rights to one's (one's father's/subclan's) cross-cousins, or on the subclan to which a 'father's sister' had earlier gone in marriage, or over an in-law's 'sister'.[19] Chains of obligations, expectations and disappointments in these matters threaded their way through men's affairs. As Reay observed elsewhere (1975–76: 92), and in objection to simplistic models of woman-exchange between two groups, Minj [men] 'are thus able to disperse the activity of wife-giving into a process involving three or more wife-givers in the arrangement

---

18   It hardly need be said that many other issues come into play as well, especially to do with the aftermath of pacification such as increasing wealth in circulation (see, for example, Merlan and Rumsey 1991: 25–26), and a wider field of contacts over which men could pursue their claims.

19   However, they may also 'give them [sisters, daughters] to affines or non-agnatic cognates who present them to clansmen who need wives' (Reay 1975–76: 91), so that even 'marriages with spouses who lack precise genealogical specification' (loc. cit.) would nonetheless be the outcome of debt relations between men across several different clans. Reay also makes it clear that the principal perspective is not that of the prospective spouses but of the senior relatives with women to bestow and claim (that is, of the wife-givers and wife-takers, to use the anthropological idiom of the time).

of a single marriage'. Trying to forestall later trouble by giving early betrothal payments to assert a claim on a particular individual, as men did especially over the first girl born to a relative obliged to help him, did not mean that when the time came she was necessarily willing to go to him (see Chapter 1).

A third observation is that the rationale for the way in which men thus sorted out their affairs through women was not confined to marriage; women were 'given' to repay debts with other origins and rationales, such as liability for a death, as is mentioned in these pages (see Chapter 14) (and see Reay 1992: 146). It would have to be a specially heavy debt, but such occasions contribute to the impression that Minj men seemed concerned less with women's part in the break-up of marriages (as might be the emphasis in other societies) than with getting women to go where they wanted in the first place.

This in turn, fourthly, may have affected the degree of support that a woman's kin gave her, if she were mistreated or sought refuge with them, at different moments in her life. Minj men sought wives from their friends and allies in war, and from temporary enemies (who might be intermittently friendly and hostile), but not, as in some parts of the Highlands, from permanent enemies. Allies were men who had close and multiple interests in one another's affairs. The focus in these stories is the way in which marriage is instigated, and as we have seen that was the very moment in time at which the interests neither of her parents or brothers nor, for that matter, of her usually benign mother's kin necessarily coincided with her own. Their persona was now that of 'wife-giver' to their allies.

Finally, while the marriage payments were as everywhere part of a nexus of life-cycle reciprocities between affines, given other kinds of obligations that were being met, such payments seem to have had an ambiguous place in the way Minj Agamp instigated conjugal relations. Of special note is the fact that, driven by a fear of waywardness on women's part (suppose the woman ran away!), or anticipating possible laziness or childlessness, men often delayed making such payments until the birth of the first child (Reay 1959a: 100; and see Chapter 1).[20] Men's scepticism thus created a period of uncertainty in which a new wife was so to speak put under a 'test' of fidelity before either her in-laws or her kin found themselves

---

20   Outside the hyperactive period of a clan's Pig Ceremonial (see Chapter 1).

fully committed to the union through wealth exchange. This was by no means true of all bride wealth-giving societies in the Highlands. In Minj, waiting to see whether or not a woman would become a wanderer publicly reiterated the possibility that it might happen to anyone.

This is but the beginning of a list of issues on which Reay wrote in other venues. She did not shrink from pointing to the predicaments and problems that people pose for one another, and in some manner always will. Here in this volume, and the numerous stories it tells of a period in Minj lives, we witness the kinds of encounters that sharpened her observation of such a home truth. The anthropological record is considerably the better for it.

Acknowledgements

This is a rather belated tribute to Marie Reay's work. She was a very present figure in my early efforts at understanding Highlands societies, and the Kuma (Minj Agamp) a significant point of comparison; I appreciate the opportunity to make my debt explicit. Needless to say the opportunity would not have come without Francesca's Merlan's brilliant initiative, as well as Judith Wilson's initial care and Ria van de Zandt's formidable input to the present volume.

As to our interactions, I have a few carbon copies of letters from an intermittent correspondence with Marie in the 1970s–1980s, which remind me what warm terms we came to be on. That was not how it began—the first letter I received from her is cherished in my memory for the double rebuff, both to my presumption to be a scholar (it began 'in your undated letter about your proposed fieldwork in the Mt Hagen area …') and the limitations on women being subjects of study. Reay's letter to me was sent in 1963, in response to an introductory letter from myself. Reay was making an implicit contrast with my proposed study as I had sketched it in my introductory letter to her, as to be conducted at the same time as field research of Andrew Strathern, 'roughly along the male-female divide', and with reference to 'aspects of female status in Hagen'. Said Reay in her initial response to me: 'My own study has emphasized the position of women simply because this happens to be crucial to Kuma society, not because of the sex of the investigator or any special interest of my own'.

References

Australian National University Archives: ANUA 440. 2013. Marie Reay collection (item list), available at archivescollection.anu.edu.au/index.php/uipue (accessed 26 February 2014).

Merlan, Francesca and Alan Rumsey 1991. *Ku Waru: Language and Segmentary Politics in the Western Nebilyer Valley, Papua New Guinea.* Cambridge and New York: Cambridge University Press.

Mihalic, F. 1971. *The Jacaranda Dictionary and Grammar of Melanesian Pidgin.* Milton, Qld: The Jacaranda Press.

Reay, Marie 1959a. *The Kuma: Freedom and Conformity in the New Guinea Highlands.* Carlton, Vic.: Melbourne University Press.

Reay, Marie 1959b. 'Two kinds of ritual conflict', *Oceania,* 29: 290–296.

Reay, Marie 1966. 'Women in transitional society', in E.K. Fiske (ed.), *New Guinea on the Threshold: Aspects of Social, Political, and Economic Development.* Canberra: Australian National University Press, pp. 166–184.

Reay, Marie 1975–76. 'When a group of men takes a husband: A review article', *Anthropological Forum,* 4(1): 77–96.

Reay, Marie 1976. 'The politics of a witch-killing', *Oceania,* 47(1): 1–20.

Reay, Marie 1992. 'An innocent in the Garden of Eden', in Terence Hays (ed.), *Ethnographic Presents: Pioneering Anthropologists in the Papua New Guinea Highlands.* Berkeley: University of California Press, pp. 137–166.

Strathern, Marilyn (ed.) 1987. *Dealing with Inequality. Analysing Gender Relations in Melanesia and Beyond.* Cambridge: Cambridge University Press.

Young, Michael 2005. 'Obituary: Marie Olive Reay, born Maitland, NSW, died Booragul, NSW, 16 September 2004, aged 82', *The Asia Pacific Journal of Anthropology,* 6(1): 81–84.

Preface

Sticks and stones may break my bones
But names can never hurt me.

The incidents recounted in this book happened to real people, but I have too much respect for them as persons to label them with the names by which they are commonly known, and often readily identifiable, in their own land. They have been kind enough to allow me to observe, hear about, and record behaviour which they themselves have often known to be scurrilous, immoral, and sometimes illegal in the eyes of Australian immigrants and expatriates. This kindness was made possible initially by Mr Jack Emanuel (Acting District Officer at Minj at the time of my arrival in 1953) explaining to their leaders that my work was to find out about and understand what I could of the ways of the local people. In the days when the *kiap*'s word was law, he instructed the leaders that they and their people must help me in this work. Their initial difficulty in regarding the task of learning the ways of a particular people as 'work' was overcome when I explained to them that I was not simply doing this for my own interest but was paid by a *bigpela masta istap long Canberra*. The *bigpela masta* was modelled largely on the late Professor S.F. Nadel,[1] the head of the department in which I was collecting material for a doctoral thesis; but his image was expanded to include some aspects of The Australian National University's relations, as an educational institution, with one of its research scholars and also to account for my reactions, which I could not refrain from expressing verbally at times, to communications from my particular supervisor of studies. The people among whom I lived and worked had no means of knowing that the demands of impending

---

1   Siegfried Frederick Nadel (24 April 1903 – 14 January 1956), known as Fred Nadel, was an Austrian-born anthropologist, who specialized in African ethnography. In 1950 he was appointed to the Inaugural Chair in Anthropology at The Australian National University, also shortly becoming Dean of the Research School of Pacific Studies. He died unexpectedly at the age of 53 of a coronary thrombosis after only a short time in residence in Canberra.

thesis-writing loomed larger in my mind than the demands of a particular professor of Anthropology and Sociology in my insistence on precision in detail, accurate dating of past events, and such matters.

I hope that the people among whom I worked and propose to work further will eventually be literate enough in both English and their own vernacular to read this book and judge for themselves what it contributes to an understanding of a particular period in their life. The language that is their own (and which I call Minj Agamp Yu)[2] is rich in overtone. It is a marvellous language for punning, in which they themselves delight. Possibly the best puns are those using words with different connotations in Minj Agamp Yu and Pidgin. Playing on words that have at least three distinct meanings (in one language or another, or both, and also in one or more of the secret vocabularies in either tongue) is not unusual. When they grasp the subtleties of English they will probably be responsible for the most complex and semantically exciting puns ever devised.

Many of the names I have given for the characters in this series of sketches are simple, direct translations of the vernacular names into their English equivalents. English versions of some names are derived logically from their verbal components, but these are often ambiguous and some names are not directly associated by the people themselves with the particular derivations that can be identified. The system of naming these people follow is so different from our own that an occasional name may startle or mystify a reader, so a word of explanation may be in order. The people of the Middle Wahgi tend to use the total resources of their language in bestowing personal names. Most names refer directly or indirectly to some incident or saying that took place about the time of a person's birth;[3] but when a person dies his name is often perpetuated by being 'changed' or substituted for the name by which a young relative has been known up to this time. Thus the name may refer to an incident or saying from the time of birth of some long forgotten ancestor, and sometimes the incident or saying is not even known precisely to the parent who bestows the name. It seems quite probable that personal names for which no meaning can be found may have been derived in this way and corrupted later, over the generations, until they have no apparent semantic content at

---

2   See Editor's Introduction regarding Akamp; yu 'language'.
3   As elsewhere in the Central Highlands; see Merlan, Francesca and Alan Rumsey 1991. *Ku Waru: Language and Segmentary Politics in the Western Nebilyer Valley, Papua New Guinea.* Cambridge and New York: Cambridge University Press, pp. 236–238.

all. The names I give in Chapter 3 as Ko I and Ko II are common female names beginning with Ko, one ending with the word for 'no' and the other ending with a second person singular verb form.

Trees, flowers, weapons, and the elements of ceremony are commonly found names. With all the resources of language to choose from, some givers of names have selected parts of speech (particularly participles and second personal singular verbs). Place names serve as personal names; natural and manufactured objects are common. Biological processes yield names which are used in conversation without shame or embarrassment, and when a man's name is found to be Defecating or Vomit this does not allege anything about his personal habits. A woman is called Love (which should be understood in a strictly physical sense) simply because her father came upon a public petting party soon after her birth. Another is called Harlot because she was with her mother in the birth-hut when a potential prostitute arrived in the territory of her father's clan.

The man whose name I have translated as Defecating had that name bestowed on him as a child, but in adulthood he is addressed and referred to by a double-barrelled name which I have had to translate for brevity as Defecating In-Law. The second part of the name is not a direct translation of 'affinal relative' [relative by marriage], it is a common term of address for men who maintain two places of residence and alternate between them. One or two men in each clan are addressed by this term. The only alternative places of residence a man ever has are the territories of his own patrilineal clan and that of his wife's clan, so it is by virtue of being an 'in-law' to the men of the latter clan that he receives this designation. This clan has almost invariably at least one other man with the same bestowed name as the affine, so the special term of address is a distinguishing device.

Readers who are acquainted with my earlier book, *The Kuma* (Melbourne University Press for ANU, 1959),[4] will recognize that the people I call Minj Agamp[5] here are the same people as I called Kuma then. I considered but rejected retaining the earlier designation for consistency. Certainly in 1953–55 the people living north of the Wahgi River referred to the southerners collectively, when they had to do so, as

---

4 See Reay, Marie 1959. *The Kuma: Freedom and Conformity in the New Guinea Highlands.* Carlton, Vic.: Melbourne University Press.
5 Minj people. Reay uses 'Minj Agamp' and 'Minj people' alternately in this book.

'Kuma'; but by 1963 they had dropped this practice. The establishment of distinct local government councils north and south of the river, making the entire southern region the 'Minj Council area', provided the northerners with a handy label for the southerners as a whole—the Minj people (Minj Agamp in the vernacular). Considering the real barrier to communications the wide and swiftly flowing Wahgi River constituted before it was effectively bridged in the mid-1950s, and the nature of the pre-European contacts between north and south, it seems certain that the 1953–55 collective name 'Kuma' was just as much an introduced label as the later 'Minj' designation. It was a less effective label. The name 'kuma' is an abbreviation of Konumbuga, the name of the largest clan south of the Wahgi. It signified primarily the name of the phratry[6] centred about the Minj River, a phratry which included Konumbuga clan and was distinguished as the 'real' Kuma whenever it was necessary to make it clear that this phratry alone was referred to, and not the people of the south as a whole. The people called 'Kuma' in 1953–55 constituted a unit for patrol officers who made separate census patrols on foot on either side of the river, and also for an anthropologist trying to find a reasonable unit of less intensive study than the intimate clan-community; but the local people themselves had no other real occasion for seeing all people situated south of the river as a unit. The northerners exchanged wives and trading partners with particular clans in the south but had no occasion for developing a special term for southerners as such until they and the southerners were being censused.

Konumbuga, which has always been in modern times the most numerous and eminent clan in the south of the Middle Wahgi, was exceptionally successful in warfare and had more enemies of long standing among individual clans than any other group. A clan in the Middle Wahgi would read an unforgiveable insult into any attempt to subsume it for scientific or any other purposes under a name that is a simple abbreviation of the name of its traditional enemy, and I hope that any future member of the Minj Agamp who is able to read my earlier book will view with tolerance an anthropologist's effort to integrate into her mode of classification the fashion of a particular era in which her first fieldwork in the region was done.

---

6   A term used in anthropology to refer to larger units which interact in ritual, marriage or other affairs, sometimes also called a 'super-clan' unit.

Agamp means 'people'. Etymologically it is plainly derived from the words 'eastern woman'[7] (or women), and I do not want to be dogmatic about why it should have been derived in that way. It seems likely that it may express a migration from the direction of Mount Hagen in earlier times. And part of the answer will doubtless be that Minj Agamp Yu (the language whose speakers call it the only 'true speech') is essentially the language of a male speaker, so that any term for 'people in general' (including both male and female) would need to specify not both male and female but simply some idea of 'women as well as ourselves'. Being a woman myself, I try to show in this book that the women of the Minj Agamp are people in their own right and not simply specific adjuncts to a male-dominated society.

---

7   As discussed in the Editor's Introduction, the form cited does not relate to the word for 'east', which contains a velar lateral [*akl*]. This one is [*akamp*]. Reay seems to have incorrectly identified the consonant.

1

The World of a Woman

The Wahgi River meanders through a fertile green basin in the Central Highlands of New Guinea. The Minj people (called after the government station and the sub-district in the Western Highlands which it serves) inhabit the part of the valley that lies south of the river. They build their dwellings on wooded spurs that reach out towards the centre of the valley basin and in narrow side-valleys formed by tributaries that rise in the Kubor Mountains and flow into the Wahgi. The valley is bounded by mountains, the Kubors in the south and the Wahgi-Sepik Divide in the north. Minj men venture beyond these mountains to trade and, in modern times, to accompany the occasional patrol by Distårict Administration, Malaria Control, or missionary officials; but the life of their womenfolk takes place within the confines of the Wahgi Valley itself and the Middle Wahgi region in particular.

Each married woman has her own house, still typically a long low building designed to accommodate the pigs that are in her care. She herself sleeps in a tiny back room, where the only access to her quarters is between rows of pig stalls. Traditionally the pigs and the taboos associated with them served to chaperone the woman in the absence of her husband. Pigs were thought to be sensitive to the smell of human semen and to sicken and die in response to it. The Minj people so valued pigs that, improbably as it may seem to peoples with a different idea of these animals, a man's respect for his clan's aspirations to protect and increase its supply of pigs acted as a brake on any tendency he might have to be intimate with his wife in her house rather than his own or to seek to enter the houses of other men's wives in order to obtain illicit satisfactions. A central hearth dominates the living room of the woman's house, though she cooks most meals for her domestic group in the cooking grove outside the house in fine weather.

A distinct devaluation of pigs in recent years led to a few essays in constructing separate buildings (mostly now abandoned) for animals, an increase in adultery, and an increase also in the extent to which men are prepared to sleep with their wives inside 'women's houses' which accommodate pigs. A speech delivered by an English-speaking mission schoolboy at the opening of the successful House of Assembly candidate's European-style house in March 1964 made slighting references to the unenlightened tradition that led 'everyone' to sleep 'in the same houses as pigs'. It was clear that he had no conception of the way women and pigs protected each other in former times.

The concern of these people for pigs dominated their life. Pigs and women were men's pretexts for fighting in the old days. This obsession has given way, among those who live near the Government Station, to anxiety about money; but any attempt to understand how they are adapting to the demands of modern living must take account of their traditional relationship with pigs, which continues among people who live far from the Station. They ate pork mostly on ritual occasions: at marriage and death payments and also at the climax of the Pig Ceremonial their own clans and those of their maternal and affinal relatives[1] held; pigs that sickened and died were the only ones eaten informally at home. In their traditional theology, Bolim The Great Spirit who was propitiated in order to ensure fertility in the clan's women was matched by Geru the Great Spirit who was propitiated in order to ensure fertility and well-being in the clan's pigs. Geru's house, built anew for each Pig Ceremonial, was the site of those parts of the boys' initiation that could not be conducted in the bush. Dead parents had to be propitiated with the sacrifice of pigs, and when the sacrifice failed to alleviate the sickness or misfortune blamed on the ghosts a medium might reveal during a séance that the ghosts had been angered further by the sacrifice of the wrong pig. Each pig had a personal name and when the time came for its owner to slaughter it the woman who had cared for it grieved as for a beloved person.

---

1 In-laws.

Photograph 9: Woman and pigs
Source: Album 2 Reay 440/1194, Noel Butlin Archives

Photograph 10: Two women and child
Source: Album 2 Reay 440/1194, Noel Butlin Archives

Pigs as well as people depended traditionally on the sweet potato for the bulk of their food. The culture of the Middle Wahgi at the time of European penetration of the Highlands in the early 1930s was shaped largely from the way a lively and sensible people, who nevertheless had a strong magical bent, adapted their needs to these two major resources, pigs and sweet potatoes. And yet it seems likely that pigs, which we know were not indigenous to Papua New Guinea, did not arrive in this part of the Highlands till the eighteenth century. And we now know that the sweet potato has been in Papua New Guinea no more than 350 years. This means that the 'traditional' culture of the Middle Wahgi must be recent.

Indeed there is much to suggest to an ethnographer that this culture is so recent that if we could document the past as thoroughly as we can document the present we would find that it was simply a phase in cultural adaptation and development. The task of reconstructing that past is too great a challenge to be ignored, though much of our reconstruction must at present be speculative. An intriguing feature of recent Middle Wahgi culture is the people's failure to make practical use of the volcanic stone mortars and pestles which abound in the area but which they treated as antiquities of uncertain origin. It was as if these objects had been made and used by a different people who had inhabited the valley in earlier times and had abandoned them there when a more energetic people arrived and dispersed them. It seemed unlikely that a superior technology could be supplanted so easily; why did the present-day people, who are quick to adopt new skills when these are useful to them, not take to using the pestles and mortars? The answer, that these objects could not have appeared to be of use to them, still left much unexplained. The Bulmers' archaeological research (1964a, 1964b)[2] suggests that the modern people's guess that the artefacts must have been made by their own ancestors (the 'ancestral spirits') is almost certainly right.

The Minj people's own view of the past gives a look of newness to their culture. They see their oral history in two periods. The recent past is simply a series of events in the changing relationships between clans that have existed during the lifetimes of their fathers and grandfathers. The verbal record of these events is a kind of social history or, more precisely, a political history dealing with the two topics of warfare and group segmentation. There seems

2 See Bulmer, R.E. 1964a. 'Prehistoric stone implements from theNew Guinea Highlands', *Oceania* 34: 246–268; Bulmer, R.E. 1964b. 'Radiocarbon dates from the New Guinea Highlands', *Journal of the Polynesian Society* 73: 327–328.

to be no reason why we should doubt the authenticity of the main facts that make up this record. But the facts, as I think we can say they are unless we do encounter evidence for doubt, are undated. Some important events of this recent history, which occurred before Minj people living in 1953–55 were born, could have taken place during the lifetime of their grandfathers or of much earlier ancestors. The time when one's grandfather was a young man seems a long time ago when there is no firm record of that time or any earlier period. We shall probably never know how much is missing from the verbal record; but, viewing the events in sequence and allowing for the time that must have elapsed between some of them, the whole period of recent history could have taken place in 200 years.

The period before 'recent history' is preserved in snatches of legend. These purport to recount the origins of some facets of the present-day world: how human beings came to inhabit the valley, how certain useful plants came into being, and how some social institutions happened to form. The myths are generally recounted as stories, not as facts, by these pragmatic people; and few, if any, would be prepared to swear that they are true. I suggest that they may be true in essence through expressing in symbols what must have actually occurred in earlier times. As archaeological and ethno-botanical findings gain in precision, we can hope to interpret more accurately the historical meaning of the origin myths.

Kumberag, near Kugmil (west of Minj), seems to have been the first settled habitat of a people who had formerly been semi-nomadic food-gatherers. Legend has it that the first man and woman 'came up out of the ground like bean-plants' at this site. I suggest that this is simply an elliptical way of saying that they were already accustomed to travelling about the area when they settled at Kumberag, as against any possibility that they might have migrated there at this time from some other part of the Highlands. The legend specified 'like *bean-plants*', which come up as recognizably beans; so the first Minj people were recognizably Minj people when they arrived at Kumberag. The people at Kumberag were joined by the male ancestor of the oldest phratry, an ignorant primitive who walked out of the bush where he had been foraging like a wild pig—that is, gathering and hunting. They taught him civilized speech, the art of house-building, and the other skills of settled social life before he went to another site and founded a strong clan with his wives and his sons. The image 'like a wild pig' is recurrent in Minj Yu (the Minj language). Men say they would like to act like wild pigs—brawling among themselves, and snatching women and food as they want them—but renounce this wish because of the demands of living together in groups. One clan has a legend that it is descended from a pig; this suggests that the myths of origin may not themselves be very old. All the myths of origin are consistent with, and some can be interpreted as contributing directly to, a view of the Minj people's early ancestors as food-gatherers and hunters.

These must have been the people who made and used the pestles and mortars. The early women probably carried these implements in the net bags of the kind that still dangle from their descendants' heads; these bags would seem to be more serviceable for carrying chattels on the march than for transporting loads of sweet potatoes from garden to residence. What the early Minj people ground in these mortars is not certain. From the possibilities Bulmer lists when considering (1964b) hunting and gathering in the Highlands generally, the oak-like Castanopsis nuts would seem the most likely. But I would posit that the early Minj people may have ground the tiny Nothofagus beechnuts. This would make sense of an otherwise incomprehensible reference modern Minj people make to a certain fungus (possibly a kind of Hydnum) as 'the Nothofagus of the ancestors', though they themselves have no explanation of the symbolism involved. Grinding the Nothofagus beechnuts would be inconvenient and time-consuming, and so might readily stimulate a change to a settled mode of life as soon as the early Minj people found that tending gardens of tubers would be more efficient than gathering nuts. The discovery of a suitable tuber and its potentialities under cultivation would then explain why the stone mortars were not judged to be useful enough to be retained till modern times. It is hard to imagine what tuber could have induced the Minj people to adopt a settled life before the introduction of the sweet potato. Yams and taro are present, but the Minj methods of cultivating the particular varieties available could not have supported a population of any size. A wild Pueraria is present, but I have noticed it growing only on sites where cultivation would have been inconvenient and there is no tradition that it was ever cultivated. The sweet potato alone is quick-growing enough and easy enough to grow to account for such a dramatic change, and until more definite evidence of a pre-sweet potato agriculture can be produced I am inclined to posit that the Minj people have not been practising agriculture longer than 300 years or so. The sharp distinction contemporary Minj people draw between living 'like wild pigs' and living 'together' in communities of scattered homesteads suggests that the change may have indeed been dramatic, even planned, rather than a long acquisition of increasingly settled habits, and that the change may even have been as recent as I am suggesting here.

Photograph 11: Woman in garden
Source: Album 2 Reay 440/1194, Noel Butlin Archives

It is possible that the change from a gathering economy to a settled agricultural one precipitated, accompanied, or even brought about a similarly dramatic change in the relation between the sexes. The prime motive for adopting a settled life would probably have been to facilitate the defence of expanding bands. The name for 'people in general' (Agamp), which includes the word for 'woman' but not that for 'man',[3] expresses men's dependence on the opposite sex,[4] but women must have been a distinct liability to their menfolk during skirmishes that took place wherever they happened to be during their wanderings. If my surmise that the stone mortars were used for grinding Nothofagus beechnuts is correct, the men could have used the imposition of this arduous and time-consuming task on the women as a means of 'getting back at' them for being necessary and burdensome to them. This would put men in two minds about the adoption of agriculture, for they might see it as a necessary step for their own protection from their enemies but an unfortunate opportunity for women to be emancipated from their drudgery.

Agriculture did not in fact emancipate the women from their drudgery, and the world of the Minj people was still a man's world when I was with them during 1953–55. The men haggled over the women, pigs, and material valuables that passed from clan to clan in a complex network of exchanges. The balance in these exchanges was important in the lives of the men; and women, pigs, and material valuables were male obsessions. The valuables they haggled over were the plumes and shell ornaments that formed their betrothal, marriage, and death payments and decorated their bodies when they were dancing.

'Women' they said contemptuously 'are nothing'. Females were simply the creatures who cared for a man's pigs and gardens, who bore and nourished a man's children and so contributed to the wealth and strength of his own and his forefathers' clan. They had no part to play in really important decisions—whether to go to war, whether to hold ceremonies, and whether to give a particular bride to this clan or to that.

---

3 See Editor's Introduction.

4 I suggest that when the male ancestor of Kuma phratry (standing for people who were still roving food-gatherers) had to learn 'civilized language' (*Yu wi*, true speech) at Kumberag after simply 'grunting like a pig', the change in his (their) language took the form of vocabulary expansion, formalization of verbal etiquette, and such matters which could have seemed crucial to the speakers but need not have involved radical structural alteration of the language.

The Government had banned warfare. It had also banned personal violence. Formerly a man could drive an arrow into the thigh of his reluctant bride to ensure that she would not run away from him, but, although this practice still continued in side-valleys away from the Government Station, he would now be liable to go to jail if he were caught. The custom of the Minj people allowed a man to establish his right to a particular bride by giving her family (her parents, her brothers, and her father's clan brothers) a betrothal payment, regardless of her wishes. When he wanted to press his claim and take her to his home, he often had to take her by force. This, too, was against the white man's law.

One consequence of this curbing of violence was that the women of the Wahgi Valley were not so easily intimidated as they may have been before pacification. Still living in a man's world, they tended their pigs and gardens as before. But they rebelled openly against the arrangements the men made for them. Few girls suffered to be led unprotestingly to bridegrooms their families had chosen for them. Few women submitted without complaining when their husbands took new wives. I found the Minj people a quarrelsome lot who liked to settle their differences in public with florid verbosity, and the things they disputed about most were women and pigs.

Much of this book deals with women's protests, all true cases recorded as they happened during 1953–55, supplemented with further marriage disputes recorded in 1963–64 and with some information elicited retrospectively about the intervening period. I summarized the social institutions of the Minj people in my earlier book. Here, by presenting slices of Minj life, I want to show what kind of people the women of the Wahgi really are.

The men of Minj classified women in terms of two stereotypes of female behaviour—'wandering women' and 'good women'. Their opinion of women in general was so low that they thought that all would be 'wanderers' if they had a chance, but the behaviour of most women fell somewhere between the two extremes and much closer to that of the 'good women', the male ideal of what a woman ought to have been and rarely was, than to that of the 'wandering women', a label the men applied very readily to any who fluctuated from the ideal in any way. The idea of a 'wandering woman' embraces two Minj concepts—that of a woman who sought escape from the bonds of married life by running away to a clan that was a traditional enemy of her husband's, and that of a women who wandered perpetually from clan to clan and was unable to settle down to raise children and pigs in one place. I translate the two distinct vernacular concepts by a single term because the enemy's woman arriving in a clan's territory was treated as warriors might treat the spoils of war, even after formal warfare had ceased, and her having been the enemy's chattel justified the man treating her as if she had been unbroken to the ways of constancy and regular work. When it became clear that an occasional woman could not settle down, the men interpreted this as meaning that her insatiable lust had driven her to break the bonds they had woven for her and wander always in search of new sexual adventures. The men of Minj had a high regard for their social institutions but a low opinion of basic human nature. They admitted freely that they themselves would be 'like wild pigs'—greedy, selfish, and perpetually brawling—if they did not have their traditional rules of living to guide them. They averred that women, in the absence of social restraint, would have been irresponsible, lazy, and, above all, sexually insatiable. On this theory, which the men held, a 'wandering woman' was a woman who was not constrained by the ordinary demands of social living to curb her inner nature. When a women showed any signs of becoming a 'wandering woman' (and the men were quick to read such signs), the stigma of this label made it hard for her to maintain ordinary social relationships: the other women despised her for refusing to conform with the pattern they themselves tried to follow, and the men treated her as a common prostitute who was unable to demand a fee. The image of the 'wandering woman' was a powerful deterrent to women who felt inclined to stray from their allotted path, but it was not a wholly effective deterrent. Many women set out to see how far they could go in trying to circumvent the plans the men had made for them without actually acquiring the dreaded reputation with the uncompromising label.

The contrast with Australian Aboriginal women, with whom I have also worked, is startling. Aboriginal women also lived in a male-dominated society, but they accepted and even welcomed male dominance because it suited them to do so. While the men were preoccupied with the esoterica of initiation and ceremonial life—affairs of little consequence in the eyes of the women—the women themselves, freed from male surveillance, were able to enjoy the company of their peers and lead full and interesting lives of their own. Aboriginal sex life in the regions where I have worked seems to follow a clear pattern of dominance and submission between the respective sexes, with tenderness typically unrelated to sexual experience, and this pattern seems to have suited Aboriginal women well. The women of the Minj region, however, had not progressed beyond rebellion. They would have agreed with Radcliffe Brown's statement, which he made partly in jest, that marriage was fundamentally 'an act of hostility'. Their men had to achieve dominance, not simply take it for granted, in the sexual act, and the women themselves had to fight for the right to submit to them by putting up a losing struggle.[5] An individual woman could come to a habit of submission after being married for some time, but relatively few seemed to do so. Although she herself was required to be faithful to the one man, her husband could avail himself of any opportunities the unmarried girls offered him and the favours of the adolescent girls brought him great prestige. A man who was successful in winning them was likely to neglect his wife, a woman who was his by definition and did not have to be sought to bring him prestige, and turn to her simply when he wanted to use her as a means of getting progeny. Often he neglected her long before she had an opportunity to demonstrate to him that she could be tamed into becoming a satisfactory sex partner for him.

Female anthropologists, because they have been Europeans dealing with native peoples subject to European domination, have often been able to penetrate the secrets of native men who have been used to hiding vast areas of ritual and other experience from their female associates. The work of Margaret Mead, Laura Bohannan, Kathleen Gough, and others shows this plainly. Male anthropologists, on the other hand, have been handicapped by a history of European men's sexual interest in native women; many have told me that they could not interview a native woman privately because the natives, including the woman herself, expected them to seduce her. But there have been many more male anthropologists than female anthropologists, and few male researchers have had wives who are anthropologists too. This means that anthropology has been too often a study by men of men, with a total neglect of the native women's viewpoint and an unconscious acceptance by male anthropologists of an outlook that subsumes male dominance in fields where it is not particularly natural or appropriate.

There is probably a good deal of truth in the popular assumption that the suppression of women in countries where their general status is low has come about through ignorance and ill will on the part of men.

---

5   See Appendix A.

In the predominantly male culture of Minj, the suppression of women was crucial for the existence of the major institutions. Here was a society that depended upon the unreasonable quelling of female aspirations for its very continuance. Outside interference with one important element in the suppression of women—the breaking in of wild young fillies at adolescent marriage—has brought the Minj people to a cultural crisis at least comparable to the one they may have experienced when they gave up roving in the bush and settled down to tend their gardens.

Unmarried girls had an easy life in the early 1950s, for they had no pigs to tend and no pressing obligation to help their mothers in the gardens. Their 'work' was to attend certain ceremonies, held at night, which provided occasions for men and girls of intermarrying clans to meet. I have referred to these as 'courting ceremonies' because they introduced a youth to the field of girls from which his marriage partners would come, but they had little to do with individual courtship. The girls would gather in the house of a clansman whose wife belonged to the same clan as the visiting men. The visitors sat in a circle with their backs to the central fire, and the young hostesses formed an outer circle facing them. The men began a nasal singing while they and the girls swayed their bodies. The songs were simple, with a meaningless refrain after each line. They sang of birds and flowers, trees and rivers of different places and the girls who lived there. A favourite form of the song named another clan and proclaimed, 'Their girls have pretty noses, but the girls of this place also know how to turn their heads'. 'Turning their heads' was the main action of the courting ceremony. Both men and girls turned their heads from side to side as their bodies wove about. The faces of the men were intent and those of the girls dreamy as they moved in time to the hypnotic rhythm of the songs (see Photograph 5). A girl's face would come closer to that of one of the men beside her, and she would press her nose to his. They continued to turn their heads,[6] using their joined noses as a pivot and pressing their cheeks together several times. Then the girl would draw away from the man, continuing to weave her body from side to side. She could repeat the action of rubbing noses and pressing cheeks with the same partner or with the man on the other side; she could continue to sway provocatively towards each in turn without coming into

---

6   This practice, common in many parts of the Central Highlands, is referred to as *tanim het* in Tok Pisin.

contact with either; or she could rest awhile and quietly smoke a cigar. After a time, the men would change places and resume the actions with different partners.

When a man had built a new 'women's house' to accommodate the pigs in the care of a particular wife, young girls were again in demand for a house-opening ceremony. The girls of the wife's clan were invited to take over the house for an evening before she moved her pigs into it. Youths of the host clan cluttered the living room, with some forced to stand outside the door, while the girls sat in the individual pig stalls. A master of ceremonies called the names of particular men the girls had whispered to him and these men walked proudly into the section of the house where the girls waited. Much merriment resulted from the men's blundering efforts to find the right pig-stalls in the dark. Every man whose name had been called had been summoned by a particular girl to 'carry leg'[7] with her. This practice is described in Chapter 2.

After evenings of the first kind, the visiting men had to sleep in the house where the ceremony had taken place and sleeping arrangements ensured that no serious impropriety could take place after the fire was out and people were asleep. After evenings of both kinds, the visitors had to invite their hosts to a return ceremony held in their own clan territory. All friendly, intermarrying clans held such ceremonies. A man could not ask a girl to press her nose to his and show that she had chosen him as a partner. Nor could he ask her to have his name called to join her in the pig-stall of the new house. One who was never chosen simply gave up attending courting ceremonies of both kinds. One who was often chosen gained much prestige on account of his popularity with girls. Married men were not debarred from attending, and many did so, but these were always men who were confident that the girls would invite them to participate fully in the evening's entertainment.

There was no limit to the number of wives a man might have if he could afford the marriage payments for them. There were few polygynists at a particular time, but nearly every man would have been one if all the

---

7 Tok Pisin *karim lek*. Mihalic (Mihalic, F. 1971. *The Jacaranda Dictionary and Grammar of Melanesian Pidgin*. Milton, Qld: The Jacaranda Press, p. 107) defines the practice as a Middle Wahgi courtship practice where a girl sits on a boy's lap or alongside a boy, with both her legs across one of his thighs. Both parties rub noses for hours.

wives he had ever had had stayed with him. A married man might have affairs with young girls who went to courting ceremonies, but a married woman's interest in other men counted as adultery.

The women did not accept this situation with docility. They preferred their husbands to be monogamous, and tried to drive away any extra wives who came. The wife of a man who went to a courting ceremony sometimes derided him, jeering that he thought he was still a good-looking youth. A woman finding her husband with a girl might attack him angrily.

Women were plainly jealous of their husbands' right to be as promiscuous as they themselves had been before marriage—not necessarily because they had insatiable sexual appetites but because they resented being treated as possessions or chattels of the men when this constituted a reversal of their positions of apparent power over the other sex during adolescence. Driving away co-wives as a man acquired them enabled a woman to keep her husband to herself; she could not effectively prevent him from obeying any invitations he might receive from girls to associate with them casually, but so long as no question arose of his marrying one of them she could demonstrate that she had some kind of power over him: in a sense, she could see him as a permanent possession of her own, much as the casual lovers of her adolescence had been temporary possessions she could discard at will. Women were jealous, too, of the particular co-wives who came to share their husbands, though such jealousy was only apparent towards co-wives from other clans than their own. Part of the trauma of marriage was the removal of the girl from her clan brothers and age-mates and her enforced residence in a community of strangers. She was able to help her clan brothers after marriage by encouraging her husband to make gifts to them and by nagging him to fulfil his material obligations towards them promptly; but once he gained a new wife from some other clan his obligations towards his affines were divided and the first wife's efforts on behalf of her brothers and her clan had to compete with the identical efforts of another woman representing different interests.

Once a woman married, she was no longer eligible to attend courting ceremonies. The ceremony of marriage itself was usually delayed until the woman was resigned to the loss of her single status; often, indeed, until she was clearly going to bear her husband's child. Marriages contracted during a clan's Pig Ceremonial, however, tended to be celebrated quickly because of the contribution the ceremony made to the general display of wealth at that time. At this ceremony, whenever it happened to be performed, the woman's brothers had to hand her over formally to her husband's group and receive the marriage payment in exchange. They would have already visited the husband and inspected the payment, haggling over individual items and discussing which had to be 'backed' by a return gift of equivalent goods.

The day before the 'marriage' ceremony, the bride's brothers killed a pig and cooked it to exchange for the pork the husband's group would bring. That night the girl's mother held a separate ceremony to cleanse and warm the skin of the bride. She built a great fire inside her house and drew a curtain of dried leaves across the doorway to trap the heat. The women of the subclan sat around the fire, singing songs similar to those of the courting ceremonies. The bride knelt before the fire and roasted herself until the sweat poured from her skin. Her skin had to be 'hot' to prepare her for marriage. (Ideally the same ceremony had been held before the bridegroom had taken her to his home, but girls could rarely be persuaded to participate willingly. Consequently some mothers alleged that their daughters' recalcitrance at the beginning of marriage was only to be expected when their skins were not 'hot' enough.) The women wiped the girl's skin with soft leaves, for the heat of the fire had to cleanse her skin and prepare her to be decorated the next day. The singing would continue far in to the night. This ceremony was primarily the business of women, but men and boys could be present to help them with the singing. It was a good opportunity for people not given to bathing to cleanse themselves as well as the bride.

The next day, the people of the bride's subclan gathered in the cooking grove to decorate her. Her mother took a gourd of pigs' grease from the house and rubbed it on the girl's skin to make her shine. Fluffy new bunches of cords, gifts from the wives of her father's clansmen, were brought and fastened over her old garments. The crescent-shaped goldlip pearlshell she wore at her throat was taken away to be polished by one of these women with leaves dipped in water, and then it was fastened around her throat again with several others. The women placed on her head an openwork skull cap, freshly netted, and in the spaces between the knots the men stuck feathers in the girl's springy black hair. They decorated her as for a big dance. She wore delicate earrings made of pieces of tree-kangaroo fur; a round white shell, looking like a slice of onion, hung from her nose; the glittering tail feather of an Enamel (King of Saxony) Bird of Paradise curved upward from each nostril (see Photograph 6).

The bridegroom and his relatives arrived. One of the men carried the marriage payment, borne aloft on a bamboo banner fixed to a pole. Shell ornaments of various kinds covered both sides of the banner, and Bird of Paradise plumes waved in a row along the top and, in a large payment, around the edges. He planted the pole upright in the ground. The women of the party followed, laden with string bags full of pork, and great flaps of pork-fat were folded over their heads. They spread banana leaves on the ground and piled the pork on top of them.

The relatives of the bride brought her forward and an orator of her subclan made a speech. The men stood in two lines, and she had to pass between them (as along the aisle of a church) holding a hatchet, or sometimes a bush knife, upright in her hand. The pose with the raised hatchet was a ritual stance, and none of the Minj Agamp could explain it to me. The hatchet was to become the property of the bridegroom, but it seemed to me that the unconscious symbolism of the bride's pose had to do with her hostility towards the marriage and that she would have required little provocation to bring the hatchet down on her intended partner's head if he were standing nearby. In fact he remained in the background and had no particular role to play in the ceremony. One of the bride's male relatives took her free hand and gave it to a man of the bridegroom's group who was to have some measure of responsibility for her in her new community. The women who were married to the bridegroom's patrilateral[8] relatives embraced her, uttering joyous cries of welcome and inviting her to be a 'sister' or 'daughter' to them.

Now it was time for both parties to exchange pork. The bride's brothers and subclan brothers held slabs of fat while she and the women already married into the bridegroom's group bit off tiny pieces. She herself did not eat the pork-fat but simply savoured the salty flavour and spat out the pieces, which children and other persons with no particular priorities in tasting pork on this occasion retrieved. The men of the bride-groom's group then held the flaps of pork-fat they themselves had contributed and let the bride's mother and other women of that group taste it. Then the men tasted it also. The formality over, the people of the two groups chattered happily together, often nibbling vegetable snacks they exchanged informally between them, until the bridegroom's relatives took the bride back to their home. The women of each group carried home the meat the other group had brought, to divide it later.

---

8   That is, the groom's relatives on his father's side.

Marriage among the Minj Agamp was essentially a transaction between groups. One patriclan[9] had given a bride to another patriclan for one of its members. The units that actually took part in the transaction were subclans, but they did this explicitly on behalf of their clans. The men intended her for a particular man of that clan, but the bridegroom had no part in the marriage ceremony. The bride's relatives handed her to another man, who was to watch her interests now that she was married. He would receive part of the first pig she reared for her husband. If she left to return to her parents and brothers, this man would bring her back. Later, if her husband's relatives ever accused her of illicit magical practices, this man would defend her.

The 'marriage' ceremony was repeated later when she had borne a child, for her husband was required to make a further payment to her clan for each child she bore, but by delaying the presentation of the initial marriage payment as long as possible an astute bridegroom could stave off the demands of predatory in-laws by complaining that he had just recently given them a substantial payment, and the relations between ostensibly friendly clans were complicated by lasting indebtedness. He was required to make yet another payment when she died and when a woman had outlived her husband their son owed this payment to his maternal uncles. A husband's clan had to pay more plumes and ornaments to her brothers when each of her children died. These payments went on beyond the lifetime of the individual parties to any marriage.

A man had a further motive in delaying the ceremony at which his marriage payment was handed to the bride's clansmen. Only when he knew that she was going to bear his child could he be certain that she would not leave him and go to another man. Men could and did use physical violence to intimidate their wives into staying with them in the old days, but this was increasingly hard to get away with in 1953–55. In a legend purporting to recount the origin of marriage, two women shot little arrows into a man's thigh to prevent him from leaving them. The bridegroom in the Minj area used to do this to a bride who tried to run away. If she persisted in her efforts to escape, he might drive a stake through her foot and tether her to his house. These cruelties had disappeared in 1953–55 excepting in the more remote places, but women's reluctance to enter the marriages arranged for them remained. They did not want to give up the freedom and status of their years of attending courting ceremonies, and they had no immediate interest in raising pigs and children.

---

9   A clan recruited through men, i.e. where a man's children belong to his clan, but his sisters to her husband's clan.

At the time of my first arrival, three clans—Konumbuga, Kugika, and Tangilka—were preparing for the Pig Ceremonial. Traditionally a clan would hold this important festival at long intervals, ideally the time casuarina trees planted on the ceremonial grounds take to mature. Kugika clan had held its Pig Ceremonial fifteen years previously. Intervals between the festivals held by some of the other clans suggested that the accession of new wealth with the arrival of Europeans was shortening the interval a clan needed to build up its stock of pigs. The festival required many months of preparation, more months of dancing and display, and finally the climax came in a series of spectacular ceremonies and a mass slaughter of pigs. The central idea of the Pig Ceremonial was fertility—fertility in the clan's women, pigs, and gardens—and the consequent aggrandisement of the clan as an important, large, and wealthy group of patrilineally related males (see photographs 12, 13, 14 and 15 of ceremonies and festivals taken by Reay).

The Kugika men danced proudly on the ceremonial ground at Kondambi while their wives stood apart and watched the spectacle with wonder, admiration, and often obvious envy. The women themselves wore their drab working clothes—a bunch of greasy cords dangling from the waist at back and front. The splendid plumes and glittering shell ornaments were not for them, and they had no part in the men's dancing. Little girls and adolescents could deck themselves in plumes and shells and take part, but married women had to be content with watching.

Marriage was the dividing line between the good time and the hard time for women of the Minj Agamp. Beforehand, they selected their own partners at courting ceremonies and summoned men to be their companions in more intimate encounters. Afterwards, their life was dominated by the necessity of caring for gardens and pigs, of bearing and rearing children, of contributing to the wealth and strength of their husbands' clan. Everything suddenly became a chore. No bells rang at a Minj marriage service, but if they had done so they would have tolled for departed freedom and suppressed sexuality. Marriage was the time when a woman's own interests had to be suddenly subordinated to those of a man—of a man who was neither lover nor brother, neither a clansman with whom she had already learned to identify herself nor a tender companion whose interests could easily become her own.

Photograph 12: Pig feast
Source: Album 6 Reay 440/1198, Noel Butlin Archives

Photograph 13: Wubalt festival (harvest feast featuring pandanus nuts)
Source: Album 6 Reay 440/1198, Noel Butlin Archives

Photograph 14: Feast with possible cult house
Source: Album 6 Reay 440/1198, Noel Butlin Archives

Photograph 15: Men wearing spirit boards
Source: Album 6 Reay 440/1198, Noel Butlin Archives

2

Carrying Leg

The Minj Agamp do not 'make love'; in their own language they 'give love'. Giving love, in a strictly physical sense, was of continual interest to them. A man had to give love to his wife or wives in order to obtain children, and he also had to give it to any of the unmarried girls who solicited him. The female life cycle was divided sharply from the onset of puberty into concupiscent adolescence and then severe married chastity, with no gradual preparation for this sudden change. The rules of social living forbade a man to give love to another man's wife, and there were drastic penalties, no longer enforceable in the 1950s, for an adulteress and a lover who was not her husband. On the other hand, a man who had a reputation of being sexually attractive was much admired. He achieved such a reputation when the young girls sought him and fought each other for the fleeting possession of him. He would strut about like a cock in a barnyard, trying to attract them. He would arrange a gaudy plumed head-dress on his carefully dressed hair; urge his mother and clan mothers to weave fresh fluffy aprons for him; hang crescents of goldlip [pearl]shell[1] at his throat and attach little wads of tree kangaroo fur to his ears; and he would tuck sprays of aromatic plants into his woven cane armbands and his leafy bustle, hoping that their love magic would work. But he himself could make no explicit advance to the girls; if one of them wanted him, she could summon him. No man ever disobeyed such a summons.

The most popular way of giving love was 'carrying leg': in Minj Agamp Yu, 'making a bridge of legs'. The man would sit on the grass beside the girl who had summoned him and stretch out his legs before him.

---

1 An important wealth item in many parts of the Highlands, now superseded by money in most.

She rested both her legs on one of his, and this was the signal for him to lock them between his own by crossing his ankles. They used to hold hands and talk softly. What they said to each other was private and rarely overheard by other couples sitting nearby. Perhaps they were planning to meet each other after dark in the bushes at the bottom of somebody's garden; or perhaps they were complimenting each other on the way their skins gleamed with pigs' grease or pandanus oil.

When the men of Kugika clan cleared their ceremonial ground at Kondambi in preparation for their Pig Ceremonial, they left a patch of grass for the young people to occupy while carrying leg. There was enough grass under the tall casuarinas to accommodate about twenty couples. It was ostensibly for parties of young people, but every mature man, even if he had grey in his beard, hoped that the splendour of his regalia for the dances would dazzle the girls of other clans so that he too would be summoned to lock ankles and hold hands in public and demonstrate that he was still attractive.

Two Stay was nearly 40, but he had decorated himself with particular care one day early in the festival. Red, yellow, and black plumes shimmered upwards from his forehead, and a crescent-shaped pearlshell following the line of his jaw partly hid his thick black beard. The men of the clan, helped by their adolescent daughters and all the children who were old enough to pound a hand drum, had begun to dance early. Forming phalanxes corresponding to their subclans, they bent their knees and their heels stamped the dust in time to their drumbeats. The drumming and loud singing could be heard for miles around. Many people from neighbouring clans, hearing the festive sound, came to watch the spectacle and comment approvingly on the gorgeous and valuable adornments of the dancers.

Suddenly a girl dashed from the crowd of spectators and snatched a hand drum from a handsome young dancer, forcing him to follow her in order to retrieve it. The other men grinned as they continued to dance, for they knew that she had learned this bold ruse from watching the pig festivals held by people living north of the Wahgi. The local girls preferred more subtle ways of summoning partners to carry leg. During one of the pauses in the dancing, while the men stood around in groups, talking and smoking and parading their plumes, Two Stay was gratified to find a little Ngeni-Muruka boy approaching him to deliver the message that a certain girl of his clan was waiting near the patch of grass. Two Stay went to her at once, and soon they were sitting close together in company with several other couples and whispering to each other.

'Look at Two Stay carrying leg with the Ngeniga girl!' one of his clansmen said to me. 'A few plumes, and a man looks half his age. The girls think so, anyway.'

'But what will Apron say when she hears about it?' whispered one of the women, naming Two Stay's wife. 'I shall go and tell her.'

Apron was not present at the dancing. Her baby had been ill, so she was sitting huddled over a meagre fire inside her hut across a creek from the ceremonial ground. She came at once, with her baby astride her hip, as soon as she received the women's news. A good woman, who behaved as a wife should, did not complain when her husband carried leg but acted as if she were proud of his being successful and attractive. Apron, however, was not a particularly good woman by Minj standards. She was a jealous wife. Like many men who could afford no more than one wife, Two Stay was hen-pecked. But this was no time for whittling away his self-confidence by prolonged nagging until he gave in to her wishes. Apron strode purposefully on to the crowded ceremonial ground, her eyes glowing with anger. It was inconsiderate of her husband, she said, to be playing around with girls while their baby was still recovering from an illness. The baby himself, jogging along astride her hip, sucked his fingers for comfort, too young to realize his mother's purpose but accustomed to her changing moods and sensitive to her displeasure.

Apron halted a few feet away from Two Stay and his pretty young companion. They stared at her speechlessly. They had stopped holding hands, but the girl's legs were still locked between the man's ankles. Apron seemed surprised that they did not spring apart and run away when she confronted them. She wrenched the baby from her hip, and his dark eyes grew wide with alarm.

'You want my man?' Apron cried. 'All right, you can carry the baby too!'

She threw the startled infant on to the Ngeniga girl's lap. The girl let him roll to the ground as she jumped up in fright and rushed away. Two Stay's clansmen and their wives were crowding round, eager to watch a man's reaction to his wife's interference. He scrambled to his feet, grasped her wrist, and struggled with her. But Apron was a robust woman, and her outraged feelings gave her added strength whereas Two Stay was hindered by his surprise and embarrassment.

'You told me once,' she screamed so that everyone could hear 'that if I ever found you with a girl I could give her the baby'.

The crowd laughed uproariously at this revelation from the intimacies of marriage, and Two Stay looked sheepish. He hit out at Apron, but she evaded him so he appealed to the other men to help him. He addressed some of the men of his own subclan by name, but they folded their arms and stood well back.

'It is a private quarrel between husband and wife,' they muttered. 'A man has to settle that himself.'

Two Stay looked about him helplessly. At last a young man, Dog, shouldered his way to the edge of the crowd.

'The members of a man's group support him in any quarrel with outsiders,' he said proudly, stating a maxim all his hearers knew to be true, 'but when he quarrels with his wife that is judged to be a private matter and he has to settle it himself. Two Stay's subclan, Burikup, is only a little group. His subclan brothers will not help him, because they do not like to interfere between a man and his wife. I am Koimamkup. We Koimamkup are strong men. We do not let our wives interfere with our pleasures. Men should be able to carry leg when they want to, without their wives preventing them. I will help you, Two Stay.'

Dog strode forward and grabbed Apron by the wrists. She wriggled in his grasp, but she was not strong enough to shake him off.

'Now beat her!' Dog cried to her husband. 'I will hold her for you.'

Two Stay struck his wife soundly again and again— on the shoulder, on the chest, on the back, on the hip, on the buttocks, wherever his hand was able to touch the body that still twisted in Dog's grasp. The women in the crowd watched earnestly for awhile, knowing that they too would be treated in this way if they were bold enough to interfere with their husbands' right to carry leg. Two Stay's brother's wife had picked up Apron's baby and was rocking him gently on her shoulder. But soon the crowd drifted away. The phalanxes of plumed men re-formed to resume the dancing. Two Stay was to exhausted to join them, and he contented himself with strutting about the edges of the ceremonial ground, satisfied that he had won a point.

Apron fled, as soon as Dog released her, to have a good cry in the privacy of her house. She told me later that she had achieved her purpose, which was to separate Two Stay and the Ngeniga girl. Taking a beating was a small price to pay.

* * * *

The ceremonial village of Kondambi was deserted, for it was the weekly day of Government work for Kugika clan. I used to spend this day at home, for the absence of the Kugika gave me an opportunity to put my notes in order and write letters for the weekly mail. But the weather was perfect and I needed little incentive to go outdoors. Hearing faint voices, I strolled out on to the ceremonial ground to investigate. The rectangular ground was lined with long-houses belonging to different groups within the clan. Burikup, the smallest subclan, had a single long-house. Koimamkup, a larger group, also had a single long-house, but most of the Koimamkup people had built their long-houses at Bomung, a smaller ceremonial village half a mile away from Kondambi. The dominant subclan, Penkup, had four long-houses. Penkup, like the other subclans, consisted of three named subdivisions. Damba subdivision had a long-house of its own, and Kumnga subdivision had another. The two wealthiest and most important men of the clan, the brothers Raggiana and Big Insect, belonged to Penkup Baiman subdivision, and each of the brothers had built a separate long-house for himself and his immediate followers.

The voices came from the Penkup Kumnga long-house. They belonged to Ko I, a Penkup Kumnga girl, and Ko II, a Konumbuga girl whose maternal uncle had adopted her and kept her with the Kugika. The two girls were 14 or 15 years old, age-mates who had both been attending courting ceremonies for more than a year. Both of them had the large eyes, flat noses, and full lips the Minj Agamp admired in people of both sexes. Ko II was lean and supple; it was easy to visualize her trudging to the gardens in ten years' time, with the weight of an infant pulling the loop of her net bag taut across her forehead and another child toddling beside her. But Ko I had that extra attribute of Minj beauty which she was likely to lose early, possibly before the birth of her first child: a rounded plumpness that showed a wholesome bulge above her strained cummerbund of woven cane and on either side of the woven cane bands that clasped her upper arms like broad tourniquets. Ko I was a favourite of the headman or *luluai*, Big Insect, for he delighted in the prospect of the large marriage payment the Kugika would receive for such a luscious bride. The Minj Agamp did not expect unmarried girls to work hard, and when Ko I complained that she had a headache after staying up all night at a courting ceremony the *luluai* told her to take Ko II as a companion and go home to rest.

I never found Minj teenagers stimulating companions, because they seemed empty-headed, all the time preoccupied with the dreary nonsense of petting and courting ceremonies. But I was curious to know how the two girls would idle away their day while their mothers and their less fortunate sisters were engaged in trimming grass on the Government Station, so I greeted them from the doorway of the Kumnga long-house.

'You have come, White Woman!' Ko I returned my greeting. 'Sit with us awhile.'

She patted the floor beside her, and I scrambled inside. Like the floors of the dwelling houses, this one was carpeted with dried grass and rubbish consisting largely of the spongy cores of sucked sugarcane which people discard where they sit as they take refreshment. Ko II had brushed away a little of the grass and rubbish in front of her to reveal a small patch of dirt floor. Now she smoothed the dirt with the back of her hand and traced a drawing with her fingers. I had seen many drawings like it made by women and children in idle moments and recognized it as the stylized design of a pig's carcass. Ko II divided it up with straight lines, as was the custom. This portion, she said, was for Ko I, this for me, and that for herself. She apportioned the other sections among various absent relatives.

Ko I said nothing. She was plainly bored. I noticed on a second patch of dirt that was incompletely covered sure signs that they had tried this pastime before. She unrolled a handkerchief that contained her supply of tobacco and found that she did not have enough to make a cigar. There were no children to send for some, and her mother's deserted house was half a mile away. Ko II had no tobacco at all. I rolled cigarettes, but the fine and faintly sweet imported tobacco was a poor substitute for a coarse and strongly flavoured cigar and Ko I threw hers away after a couple of puffs. Ko II did not seem to have any ideas to relieve her age-mate's boredom, and she sat awkwardly with her legs stretched out in front of her, her fingers sifting the soft rubbish on the floor.

Suddenly, noticing Ko II's legs stretched out beside her, Ko I glanced across at her companion. Her interest sparked quickly and she swung both her own legs over one of the other girl's. Ko II grinned broadly and locked her age-mate's legs with her ankles.

'I am a man,' Ko II joked, as they played at carrying leg.

'And I am a girl,' Ko I answered, gaily but with obvious pride. 'You mustn't carry leg with all the girls— only with me!'

Both girls plainly enjoyed carrying leg with their male partners, but there were no men in Kondambi on that day. As they carried leg with each other they reminded me of girls at country socials in Australia who so love dancing that they dance with each other when there are not enough boys to go round. Later, however, I wondered about the tender attachment the women of the Minj Agamp form for their age-mates in the days of their youth. They are inseparable companions until marriage forces them to live in different communities; up to that time they walk about with their arms round each other, and most nights they sleep in one another's arms. This was the only time I ever saw girls carrying leg together, but Ko II's easy response to her age-mate's joking advances made it seem that it may have happened before. Special friendships among age-mates can be lifelong among the Agamp; occasionally I have seen them renewed by mature women who meet at a mourning feast after a death that has affected the clans of both their husbands, though they have not seen each other for many years.

* * * *

As months went by, the dancing in the Pig Ceremonial grew more and more spectacular and more and more visitors came from near and far to view the waving plumes. People came from all over the Wahgi Valley, and one day a young man from Chimbu arrived. The men of Kugika clan carried leg with girl visitors and the girls of Kugika clan carried leg with male visitors on the patch of grass where Two Stay and the Ngeniga girl had been sitting when Apron interrupted them. Here also the young man from Chimbu was the centre of a small drama.

Ko II was the first girl to notice him when he arrived in the middle of the morning as the first dance was beginning. He was good-looking in a conventional way, with tawny-gold skin and a broad, flat nose and, though his dress was undistinguished in this company of colourful plumes and glittering ornaments, a visitor from afar is an exotic conquest and it was a feather in Ko II's cap to ensnare him before any of the other girls had done so. A little boy delivered her message to him, and he went at once to the patch of grass, where they carried leg together for the rest of the morning.

There was a lull in the dancing about midday while the Kugika men refreshed themselves with sugarcane, cucumbers, and cooked snacks. Most of the married women were away gathering vegetables in their gardens for the evening meal, and the couples who had been petting on the patch of grass had dispersed. But everyone reassembled in the afternoon, and the scene of the morning was repeated. Plumes waved gaily as the dancers pounded their hand drums and lifted their voices in unison. The patch of grass was covered with flirtatious couples, but there was one significant difference. The men of Penkup subclan were only singing intermittently while they whispered to one another.

'Look at the man from Chimbu!' one of them hissed. 'Ko I's giving him love now.'

'But I saw Ko II with him this morning.'

'Yes, Ko II was carrying leg with him first.'

'But where's Ko II now?'

'I can't see her anywhere.'

'What will she say when she knows Ko I's got him?'

'Ko I is very bold to carry leg with the man from Chimbu when everyone knows Ko II had him this morning.'

'Will Ko II attack her?'

'Ko II will be jealous, of course, but they're very special friends and Ko I is the leader of their age-group.'

The whispered speculations continued, and the men of Penkup subclan stared so hard at Ko I and her partner that they were soon out of step. At last they stopped dancing altogether, though the Burikup and Koimamkup sang and danced on awhile longer. Some of the Penkup youths darted away eagerly to find Ko II and tell her that Ko I had taken her man. Ko I sat stolidly beside the young man from Chimbu, her legs clasped in his ankles, though she must have been well aware of what was happening.

Ko II received the news calmly. Ordinarily she would have attacked another girl who carried leg with a man she herself had summoned earlier the same day, for at least temporarily he was hers, but she did not want to fight with her age-mate, particularly with her special friend among age-mates as Ko I was. The question of her being Konumbuga, not Kugika, by birth did not suggest to anyone that she might have had less right to entertain visitors at Kondambi than the daughter of a Kugika man, for her long association with her maternal uncle's clan had led her to identify herself in many respects with her age-mates in her adopted clan.

All the Penkup watched as Ko II strolled along to the patch of grass where the couple sat. Without a word and with no emotion showing, she bent down and lifted Ko I's legs gently from those of the young man, then she walked away. She had made the gesture her adopted clansmen required her to make, but she had not offended her age-mate. In fact Ko I expressed amusement, but the young man from Chimbu looked uncomfortable, for the incident had shamed him before strangers.

The men of Burikup and Koimamkup subclans had also stopped dancing by this time, and they had seen Ko II's action. They were indignant with her for interfering, and several of them protested to the Penkup men. But the Penkup men, like Ko I, were amused. It was indiscreet of her, they said, to carry leg with the young man from Chimbu so soon after Ko II had done so, and Ko II had acted with tact and decision.

* * * *

The men of Kugika clan had built my house, at Big Insect's urging, only six feet away from a new house belonging to his second wife, Goodly, beside the ceremonial ground. In fact Goodly was so busy tending her pigs at Weeping Bamboo, three miles along the ridge, that she never moved to her new house but simply visited Kondambi daily when the dancing began. A man named Vomit became my neighbour instead. Vomit was a birth member of a different division of Penkup subclan, but he had attached himself to Big Insect, helping the *luluai* in a thousand small chores; in return, Goodly looked after his pigs. Vomit was a middle-aged bachelor, a man of the type the Minj Agamp called a 'knockabout man', a short and ugly fellow who could never hope to find a wife. He was a quiet neighbour. The girls had never bestowed their favours on him. Whenever the clan was holding a particularly important dance and many visitors were expected, the leaders of Penkup subclan told him not to bother decorating himself to participate in the dance because they wanted to impress the visitors as a body of well-built and handsome men. Nevertheless, Big Insect was glad to include Vomit's pigs, which Goodly had tended, among those he was responsible for distributing at the climax of the Pig Ceremonial in which the owner was forbidden to participate fully.

When the festival was more advanced I acquired more neighbours, this time a family. My house had been built at the boundary between Penkup and Koimamkup territory on land belonging to Forest Tree, a man of the third subclan, Burikup. Soon Forest Tree built two houses next to mine. One was ostensibly for himself and the other for his wife, Courting Ceremony, but actually they used Courting Ceremony's house for cooking their meals and Forest Tree's own house for sleeping. The houses built ostensibly for particular married women in the temporary ceremonial village were not 'women's houses' built to accommodate pigs but were the same kind of structures as the houses built for men. No especial taboos were associated with these houses, so they could conveniently house visitors when necessary. Forest Tree built his own house so close to mine that the wall was less than two feet from that of my bedroom and the grass thatch of the two roofs was touching. The temptation to eavesdrop on family discussions was irresistible.

Forest Tree was a perfect miniature of a man. Most of the Minj Agamp males grew to about five feet six inches tall, and one man in Kugika clan was nearly six feet in height, but Forest Tree was below five feet. Nevertheless his well-set head with its crop of curly hair and trim black beard, his broad shoulders and slim hips, and the rippling muscles of his arms and legs were beautifully proportioned. No one called him short— partly because the Minj Agamp Yu word for 'short' implies stockiness and ungainliness, and partly too because 'knockabout men' are supposed to be short in stature and they are always 'rubbish men'—dependent, like Vomit, upon a man of means to act as their sponsor. Forest Tree was himself a man of means. Though not of outstanding wealth like Big Insect's, he was an independent farmer and pig-keeper. He had inherited his brother's widow, Courting Ceremony, and was hoping to acquire a second wife within the next year or two. He had been a competent warrior and sorcerer; though he had not practised sorcery since his clan had been forced to live in an uneasy peace with others, the knowledge that he could do so enhanced his prestige. He still maintained a small war-sorcery house hidden in a grove of bamboos near his usual place of residence. He had shown great initiative in deciding to cultivate a long-abandoned burial ground near his home, arguing that the human remains had enriched the soil, and had transformed it into a≈productive garden. He was a man of moderate consequence.

One evening, Banana, Forest Tree's eight-year-old son, called to see me as he did nearly every day.

'I cannot stay and talk with you, White Woman-o,' he said. 'My father went home to fetch firewood, but he had been gone a long time and my mother has sent me to see what has happened to him. Come for a walk with me while I go and meet my father.'

I understood the boy's reluctance to go alone. Adults among the Minj Agamp never walked alone, for if they did they might be suspected of practising witchcraft or going to an adulterous assignation. Even a youngster might be accused of witchcraft, but a healthy lad like Banana was unlikely to be thinking of such things. Darkness was approaching, and he was more likely to be sensitive to the dangers from ghosts and bush demons lurking in the scrub. Anyway, he and I enjoyed each other's company. He picked up my notebook and carried it for me, as was his custom, although I doubted whether I would find anything to record during our evening walk to Forest Tree's home and back apart from a few more names for plants and insects I had little hope of ever identifying botanically.

We had gone no further than the ceremonial ground, now deserted by its dancers, when we saw the tiny figure of Forest Tree approaching from the direction of his home under a load of firewood. A group of his clansmen were sitting about idly gossiping, and he made his way towards them. They looked up as he swung his heavy load to the ground and began to address them.

'You all saw the fight young K- had yesterday with the Ngeniga girls,' he said. They all knew K-, another Konumbuga girl whose whole family lived with the Kugika. They had seen her fighting the day before against a girl she had found carrying leg with a man who interested her. I had also seen the fight develop into a flurry of brawling women. Out of the general hubbub one could distinguish screams of agony and abuse and the sharp crack of a stick landing on someone's head or shoulders. On the fringe of the crowd a hefty young girl was dragging a scrawny matron along the ground by her hair; the older women's thin dugs flapped against her ribs, and her string apron was immodestly askew.

'All the Ngeniga girls helped their age-mate, but not one of the Konumbuga girls helped K-,' Forest Tree grumbled. 'The girls of a clan ought to stand up for one another. But none of K-'s age-mates stood up for her, so all the Konumbuga women who are married to Kugika men fought by her side.'

'That is so,' one of the men replied. 'My wife and yours were among them. After seeing my wife hit a Ngeniga girl on the head with a stick, I'll be careful what I say to her in future.'

There was a mild ripple of amusement, for the speaker was known to have a hard time controlling his wife, but Forest Tree did not smile.

'It is not fitting that married women should fight,' he said with the air of a man who proclaims a well known truth; and indeed this was a set phrase some man or other always reiterated when women were brawling. 'The girls who attend courting ceremonies should have fought on K-'s behalf.'

Forest Tree's clansmen did not answer. Plainly they agreed with him but did not feel strongly enough to stir up trouble among the young girls. He shouldered his firewood and went on his way.

'Hurry, Banana!' I whispered. 'Your father will get home before you do.'

'But I can run fast, as you know,' the boy grinned. 'I'll put your book inside your house first. I knew there would be something for you to write.'

* * * *

The Minj Agamp's Pig Ceremonial is clearly divided into two phases. The first was called Pig Houses, a name signifying the period from the erection of a white post in a high part of the clan's territory where people from miles around could see it and know that the clan was preparing to kill its pigs until the ceremonial ground was cleared and a temporary village was built around it. The main work of this period was the construction of the long-houses, the Pig Firewood Houses which gave their name (shortened to Pig Houses) to this period and also to the site of the pig festival, whether it was being currently held there or not. The second phase was called Pig Songs, for the main work of this time was for clan members to gather daily and dance in formation while they sang and pounded their hand-drums. Pig Songs could not begin until the long-houses lining the ceremonial ground had been completed. Whenever one of these buildings was finished the builders notified their affinal and maternal relatives in nearby clans that the roof would be thatched on a certain day. They invited these relatives to participate. The visitors arrived, their womenfolk stooped under loads of kunai grass which they placed in an impressive pile before the newly completed long-house. Their≈hosts danced around the heap of grass while their wives brought food to present to the visitors. The men visiting from other clans had come to do the work of thatching, and when the preliminary festivities were over some of them climbed to the roof while others handed up bundles of grass for them to fasten. There were always many willing workers, and the thatching was done quickly and skilfully.

The ordinarily slothful girls of the thatchers' clans were always eager to help their mothers in gathering and carrying the kunai grass on such an occasion, for this provided an excuse for them to attend the festivities and they knew that they would be meeting the handsome young men of the host clan. The thatchers themselves, who were mostly young, were looking forward to being invited to carry leg with the girls of the place.

People of the neighbouring Ngeni-Muruka and Konumbuga clans had come to Kondambi to celebrate the completion of one of the long-houses for the Kugika Pig Ceremonial. The men were dressed for dancing: coloured plumes waved in their head-dresses, and pieces of pearlshell dangling from their waistbands clicked together as they strode proudly along the well-trodden paths. Their womenfolk were clad simply in drab and meagre string aprons that swished from side to side as they plodded along with their loads of grass.

The dancing and the thatching were over by the time the women of the Kugika began to arrive. Their bodies leaned forward and the loops of their net bags were stretched tight across their foreheads from the weight of the vegetable food they carried on their backs. The Kugika were treating their visitors royally, and even the young girls who were not generally expected to do women's work had been pressed into service to bring still more food from the gardens and the cooking groves. After some speech-making, bags of raw vegetables changed hands. The mood was one of feasting, but the Minj Agamp did not gorge themselves on these occasions. The important thing was the presentation, not the consumption, of food. Nevertheless, the women distributed light snacks for the visitors to eat with their hosts.

Two of the Penkup girls, Ko I and Or Nothing, leaned against the wall of the new long-house, resting after their unaccustomed exertions as they surveyed the visitors.

'I can't see Stony,' Ko I said. Her great brown eyes searched the groups of Konumbuga people sitting around the ceremonial ground but could not find the handsome youth she had been carrying leg with earlier in the day. 'I want to carry leg with him again.'

Ko I was unusually attached to Stony. She carried leg with him nearly every day, and she had even asked her father to let her marry him, but he had replied gently that he had other plans for her.

'There he is,' Or Nothing answered. 'He's already carrying leg with a Ngeniga girl.'

Ko I regarded the couple with blazing eyes, bur Or Nothing spoke again.

'They are going against the customs of our fathers and our grandfathers' she said wisely. 'This is Kugika territory. A Ngeniga girl cannot carry leg here unless it is with a Kugika man, and a Konumbuga man can only carry leg here with Kugika girls. Let us drive her away.'

Ko I was not concerned with the customs of her forefathers at this moment of discovering that she had a rival.

'Yes,' she agreed. 'I don't like other girls to carry leg with Stony. Let us drive her away.'

Together they went to the girl and pulled her roughly to her feet. Stony stood up and walked away as unobtrusively as he could while the two attacked her. Only one girl of Ngeniga clan had come, and she had no age-mates to help her, but she hit Or Nothing a nasty blow on the head and Or Nothing had no chance to retaliate before the Kugika men separated them. The Ngeniga girl fled, and Or Nothing resolved to get even with her later.

The next day the Konumbuga also celebrated the completion of a long-house by holding a similar feast at Konmil, and the Kugika girls went along to help their mothers in gathering and carrying the kunai and to watch their clansmen dance. Suddenly there was a disturbance at one end of the ceremonial ground. Or Nothing had seen the Ngeniga girl carrying leg again with Stony and had attacked her with her fists. This time Stony decided to help the girl, for he was on his own clan land now and she had every right to invite him to carry leg with her. He picked up a stick, which he held horizontally to ward off the blows. Stripping herself of her ornaments, which might have got broken in the fight, Or Nothing gave to one of the Kugika girls the goldlip shells, the bailer shell, and the trade rings she had been wearing and returned to the fray. Stony did not try to hit Or Nothing; he merely warded off the blows that were meant for the Ngeniga girl and pleaded with them both not to fight. Other men remonstrated, but the girls did not heed them. Or Nothing, joined now by other Kugika girls, was winning the battle and was chasing Stony and the Ngeniga girl across the ceremonial ground. Some of the girls armed themselves with sticks. Their own clansmen urged them on, but the Konumbuga men were alarmed lest a full-scale brawl should develop on their land. When Or Nothing overtook her opponent she attacked her again, but the Ngeniga girl hit back. The girls continued to struggle for a quarter of an hour before the Konumbuga men intervened and managed to separate them.

* * * *

Sometimes a girl would choose one particular man as her constant partner, and her brothers might then suggest that she should go and stay with his clan in order to spare him the labour of walking daily from his home to hers in answer to her invitation. She would stay for a couple of days, and then her brothers arrived to take her back. During this time she had been carrying leg several times in public with the man of her choice, but ordinarily she seems to have slept with one or two of the women of his clan. She and her lover had little time for privacy during her visit. He and his clan relatives bathed her with pigs' grease on the day her brothers were to arrive, and loaded her with costly decorations which she wore home. The plumes and ornaments were for her brothers, though they usually gave her for her personal use a pretty bird skin of little value; she kept the new garments (the fluffy strings, netted skull cap, and any cane bands one of her lover's clansmen might have plaited for her) and often a single goldlip shell. The rest of the bounty went into her brothers' stock of valuables, from which they unfailingly supplied her with decorations when she needed them. Sometimes she returned home willingly, proud that she had been able to contribute to the wealth of her brothers and their clan as a whole. But sometimes she was so attached to her lover that she wanted to stay with him and be accepted as his wife.

Good Bird was an important man among the Kugika Penkup. In middle age he was the oldest direct descendent, in the senior line, of the man who had founded his subdivision of the subclan. When the previous leader of the group had died Good Bird had been too young to succeed him and Raggiana, the oldest member of a more junior line, had taken his place. Now that he would have been old enough to succeed if the role had been vacant again, he helped Raggiana administer the affairs of his subdivision and of the whole subclan. Good Bird already had one wife, Creamy, who had borne him two sons, but he was ambitious to have more wives and sire more boys to add to the strength and glory of his clan. Creamy always objected when he wanted to get another wife, and she had driven away several new wives he had tried to keep.

Good Bird had been visiting Omngar clan in the northern part of the Wahgi Valley. On each of his three recent visits Waiting, a young girl of the clan, had invited him to carry leg. At last, at the suggestion of her brothers, Waiting accompanied him home to Kondambi and stayed there a couple of days. Creamy did not show any jealousy, as she knew that the girl's brothers would be taking her back as soon as Good Bird had bathed her with pigs' grease.

Good Bird waited impatiently for Waiting's brothers to arrive. She had told him the evening before that she did not want to go back with them but would prefer to stay with him and be his wife. She told him that her parents had said she could marry him if she wished. Her mother had told her that she was not formally betrothed and so would be able to marry any man she had carried leg with and wanted to marry. But Good Bird knew that Waiting's brothers would have the final say. Perhaps one of them might want to exchange her for a bride for himself. Good Bird knew that he could not provide a girl in exchange for Waiting, for other marriages were already planned for all the Kugika Penkup girls as well as for all the girls among Creamy's relatives. Nevertheless he hopefully lined up some plumes and ornaments ready to offer to Waiting's brothers as a betrothal payment.

It was a busy morning for the Kugika. The Konumbuga had brought a large marriage payment for a Kugika girl, who was decorated and handed over to them. The pole bearing the payment had been driven into the ground, and it still stood there when Waiting's brothers arrived. They eyed it admiringly, exchanged a few words softly, then went behind the long-house to meet Good Bird.

'Why haven't you bathed Waiting with pigs' grease?' one of them demanded while the other stood by in silence.

Raggiana, ceremonial leader and leading war sorcerer of Kugika clan and orator and government-appointed *tultul* (deputy headman) of Penkup subclan, indicated with a grand gesture the plumes and shells Good Bird had laid out on the ground for inspection. Waiting's brothers could have this payment, he said, if they permitted the girl to stay with Good Bird. If she had to go back, Good Bird would bathe her with pigs' grease and give them only a few plumes and shells.

Waiting's brothers eyed the payment greedily for a moment, then the one who was spokesman made a long and earnest speech to the Penkup, facing Raggiana as he orated. He said he understood that their father and mother had pronounced that Waiting could marry any man she liked, and he wanted to respect their wishes. But he had to insist on a generous payment for her—as large a payment, in fact, as the one he had seen on the ceremonial ground that morning. He indicated Good Bird's payment with a disparaging gesture, saying that it was obvious that Good Bird himself had provided the plumes and shells. He could not contemplate leaving Waiting, the brother went on, unless the big men—Raggiana and his brother, Big Insect, and perhaps others as well—also contributed toward the payment.

Good Bird replied that he was willing to give only this little pay[2] at present, though he could well afford more. The brothers, he said, could understand the unwillingness of the other big men to give plumes and shells at this stage. The girl might leave him after awhile and go to another man, and the payment would have been given for nothing.

---

2   Reay is probably adopting common Tok Pisin usage here, 'pay' for 'payment', here with reference to shells and other valuables, not only money.

The brother agreed that he appreciated this point, but stressed that he himself wanted some plumes. After all, his sister was a good-looking girl and the Kugika should be prepared to pay well for her. He preferred to hold out for a substantial payment.

The discussion had been amicable. Good Bird agreed to send the girl back, and he prepared to bathe her with pigs' grease. Waiting was not consulted; the men had settled her fate between them.

* * * *

The Kugika headman, Big Insect, was considerably younger than his brother, Raggiana, but he was also a mature and wealthy man. He had three wives, but he wanted more. This was partly because the Minj Agamp judged the importance of a man by the number of wives he had, and both he and Raggiana used to boast that their father had ten wives. (They could only remember six when I questioned them on details.) It was Big Insect's ambition to have ten wives also, in order that he might be known as more than a 'strong' man (his people's term for 'big' man). Occasionally a leader among the Minj Agamp achieved such wide renown that others said of him 'His name is up on top', and this was the reputation Big Insect coveted. A more pressing reason for his wanting more wives quickly was the barrenness of those he had already. Indoors, his senior wife, had borne him only one child, who had died young; the faithful Goodly had borne him one son and was to give birth to another soon after my departure; Wailing was a recent wife, but Big Insect suspected that it was by her own wish and the furtive skills of the older women that she was not yet a mother. He was a 'strong' (that is, eminent) man, headman of his clan and a leader among his people, but he had one son and the foetus in the belly of his second wife might turn out to be merely a daughter. He wanted ten sons, the greatest number that could be counted on two hands, to carry on his line.

Some men of Waga clan had invited Big Insect and a few other Kugika to visit them at Nondugl, and they had instructed the young girls of their group to be kind to their guests. A plump and personable girl asked Big Insect to carry leg with her and he did so, with the Waga and their other visitors watching. He and his companions stayed for several days, and Big Insect spent some part of every day carrying leg with this handsome creature. He learned that her name was Weeping, and he surmised from the generous curves of her body that she might bear a man many sons.

Weeping's father and mother and a man called Good Little, her father's elder brother's son, urged her to go with Big Insect to stay for a couple of days and be bathed with pigs' grease and decorated. Big Insect, they told her, was a wealthy man and would be generous in loading her with plumes and ornaments for her 'brother' and father. They themselves would accompany her as chaperones; they would take this opportunity to visit Mountain Tree, a man of Big Insect's subclan who had married Weeping's paternal aunt.

Walking across the valley to Kondambi, Big Insect fell into step with Good Little and began to discuss with him the possibility of marriage with Weeping. He knew that Good Little, as the girl's closest 'brother', had the most say in disposing of her. There had been no marriage between the Waga and the Kugika in recent years; the son of Weeping's aunt was twelve years old, and he suggested that they should give the Kugika more brides if they wanted to keep their friendship.

Back at Kondambi, Big Insect lost no time in lining up a betrothal payment for Good Little and Weeping's father to inspect. Women of his subclan brought food, and the men joked with one another in high spirits as they ate. Beside them, the sun touched with gold the rich plumes Big Insect was offering with the shell ornaments for his betrothal. The women had retired. Weeping and her mother were in a nearby house with their relative, Mountain Tree's Waga wife.

Good Little said that he and Weeping's parents wanted to give her to Big Insect. He was a great man and their friend, and they were happy to help him by giving him a bride. Also, of course, they hoped that the Kugika would be giving women to the Waga in exchange for her. He regretted that Original Woman, another Waga girl who had come to stay with the Kugika, was already betrothed elsewhere and so could not marry a Kugika man, for he would have liked their two clans to exchange many women.

Mountain Tree brought up the question of Weeping's own choice.

'I am married to a Waga woman,' he said, 'and I too would like our clans to exchange many women. But has anyone asked Weeping whether she is willing to marry Big Insect? Kondambi is not far from the Government Stations, and a girl who is taken to a man she does not like can go to the Court of Native Affairs and complain. The officers say we should not give girls to men they do not like, and if the case comes up some of us will go to jail.'

No one had asked Weeping whether she was willing to marry Big Insect. He himself admitted that he had not discussed the matter with her. But he assured Good Little that if Weeping were given to him Mountain Tree's young son, Now Spirit, would be entrusted with the duty of seeing that she did not run away. If she did not want to marry him, the Government officers would only discover that the Kugika were keeping her against her will if she succeeded in escaping and went to Minj.

Mountain Tree insisted that girls who were being held against their will were cunning in devising ways of escaping. Now Spirit was young and inexperienced, and he could not guarantee that the boy would succeed in preventing Weeping from going to Minj with her complaint. It would be wiser, he urged, to consult the girl herself and, if she were unwilling to marry Big Insect, try to persuade her. Weeping was brought on to the ceremonial ground, and Good Little addressed her.

'We want you to stay and marry Big Insect,' he said. 'Your aunt is here, so you will not be lonely. Are you agreeable?'

Weeping wasted no time in replying.

'No,' she cried clearly. 'I agreed to come to Kondambi with him and be bathed in pigs' grease and decorated and returned to my people. There was no question of marriage. I expect to stay here tonight, but tomorrow I want to go home.'

'Your aunt is a Waga women,' Good Little reminded her, 'and she is here.'

'There are Waga women closer to home,' Weeping insisted. 'They also are my aunts. I do not want to live at Kondambi, and I do not want to marry Big Insect.'

The men watched her stalk away in the direction of her aunt's house. Some of them commented that she was strong willed and knew what she wanted and what she did not want. Mountain Tree muttered that if they were to marry her to Big Insect they would all find themselves in jail.

The girls of Big Insect's subclan held a courting ceremony that night for the Waga men who had come with Weeping and Original Woman. The two girls watched the ceremony, but did not participate. Big Insect slept at Kondambi in the house he had built for Goodly, with the bearded Vomit as his only companion. He dreamed that he gave love to Weeping and then discovered that it was not Weeping at all but a bush demon masquerading in her form. This was a common nightmare among the Minj Agamp.[3] It was generally assumed to portend some evil, perhaps sterility in the dreamer's wives. Did the nightmare mean that marriage with Weeping would bring him no more sons?

The next morning Now Spirit, Mountain Tree's young son, greeted me as I was eating breakfast, and I asked him whether Weeping was going to marry Big Insect or be bathed in pigs' grease and sent home.

'She will stay and marry Big Insect,' he answered. 'I shall claim her and give her to him.'

I knew that Now Spirit could do this. Weeping's father was his mother's brother, and in Minj custom a man who wanted a wife for himself or a clansman asked his mother's brother to supply one. If this man had a daughter who was not bespoken he could not refuse to give her to his nephew. Now Spirit could not claim Weeping for himself, as she was his cousin, but he could claim her for a clansman. If he himself wanted a wife he could ask Weeping's father to find him a Waga girl who was not related.

'I shall tell her,' he continued, 'that I want her to stay with the Kugika so that she can bend my legs for burial when I die.'

The Minj Agamp were traditionally buried in a sitting position with their knees touching their chins. It was the duty of a dead man's maternal cousin to break his knees to make this possible.

'Then,' Now Spirit told me, 'if Weeping tries to get away and go home to Nondugl I shall restrain her.'

We walked together on to the ceremonial ground where Original Woman, who had slept with Two Stay's wife, Apron, was already bathed with grease and decorated for her return. Big Insect, seeing her, went to get a gourd of pigs' grease to wash Weeping.

'If the girls don't want to stay,' he said resignedly, 'they won't stay. So let us bathe Weeping with pigs' grease and send them back.'

Two Stay heard him, and a wicked smile lit his face.

---

3   Australian National University Archives: ANUA 440. 2013. Marie Reay collection (item list): 440:466: Myths and Legends, A Draft of a Paper by Reay entitled: Fiddling with the Future in False Creations: Standardised Dreams and Visions among the Kuma. Available at archivescollection.anu. edu.au/index.php/uipue (accessed 26 February 2014).

'Apron is good at capturing girls,' he said slyly. 'Some of the women and some of the men can grab Weeping for you.'

Big Insect turned to his senior wife, Indoors, with a mischievous gleam in his eye.

'When the girl comes to be bathed with grease, Indoors,' he said in a conspiratorial whisper, 'hold her and say "Stay with me".'

A man of Big Insect's subclan told him that he had been talking with Weeping's mother and brother.

'They said "We'll tell her that Big Insect has gone to Minj and that we're tired of waiting for him to come back and bathe her with grease. We'll say that she can come home later with some of the Kugika who want to visit us. We'll be pretending, and just leave her with you". That's what they said.'

A crowd had gathered in the yard where Big Insect still stood holding the gourd of pigs' grease. When Weeping herself appeared, he made a speech that was designed to reassure her.

'Original Woman has been washed with grease and has gone,' he said. 'I wanted to marry Weeping. Her father and her mother and her brothers told the interpreter Arrow at Minj that they wanted to give her to us, and Arrow said it would be all right.' Big Insect was referring to an interpreter who enjoyed the confidence of both the Minj Agamp themselves and the Government officers, and whom he and his clansmen were accustomed to consulting in order to predict official reactions to various courses of action. Arrow and other interpreters acted informally as legal advisers to the Minj Agamp.

'So we have been thinking a lot,' Big Insect continued. 'But let us hurry and wash Weeping and decorate her and send her back with her father. She doesn't want to stay with us; she has said so. She has no need to be frightened of us. We don't kill girls and eat them as we eat pigs; we're not like the barbarians of Goroka, who we all know are cannibals. The girl may go when we have decorated her. But let us hurry' he joked 'in case she runs away first!'

The men and women stood ready to hold the girl and make her stay. One of the women addressed me in an excited whisper, 'Have you heard that we're going to capture Weeping?'

A girl of Big Insect's subclan brought a pandanus mat for Weeping to sit on while being decorated. Goodly screamed at her, 'Spread it neatly, or the girl won't be comfortable. When you're washed with grease, you want everything nice.'

The pigs' grease was rubbed into Weeping's skin until she gleamed. Goodly fastened two furry new aprons over the old one the girl was wearing. Mountain Tree handed over some goldlip shells to hang about his niece's throat. Others came forward with plumes, a headband sewn with *tambu* shells, some earrings of fur from the tree-kangaroo, and other decorations. These splendid gifts were really meant, as everyone knew, for Weeping's father and brothers; she would keep little for herself. As the dressing proceeded, the crowd began to disperse. Indoors had departed to tend a wayward pig. Nobody grasped Weeping's arm and said 'Stay with me.' The people who remained hung about quietly; I am certain they would have captured the girl if Big Insect had told them to do so, but he gave no such order. He looked thoughtfully after the party of Waga as they walked homeward with the girl who was nearly his bride.

3

A Girl is Marked

Black-bearded As If was an ageing hypochondriac who had neglected his gardens since his younger brother, Proud, had died some months ago. Proud had been a young man of fire and promise; so long as he had lived As If derived a certain prestige and respect from being his older brother and no one realized how fully the older man depended upon his initiative and labour. After Proud's death the true character of As If gradually revealed itself. He had married, many years earlier, a woman of Ngeni-Muruka clan who had given him two daughters and then died. Snailshell, the older girl, was twelve and she was about to participate in her first courting ceremony. Grass Woman was several years younger. The two girls lived with their father. When Proud died, As If lamented loudly and announced in tones of despair that he had nothing to live for because he had lost his wife and now his only remaining brother had died and left him bereft. He did not actually try to commit suicide, for when the other men of Penkup subclan saw how stricken he was they guarded him constantly in case he should hang himself from a tree and end his life through grief. The guard was relaxed as soon as it was clear that As If was reconciled to his brother's death. He continued, however, to complain, whenever an occasion arose, that he was a lonely man with no wife and no brother. The other Penkup men were glad to see him inherit Proud's widow, for they sympathized with him in his loss and loneliness. When As If sought their help in building a new house at Kondambi for the Pig Ceremonial, they gave their labour willingly and the house was soon completed.

The wife As If had inherited from his brother was a Konumbuga woman by birth, so it was natural for him to assure the young people of his subclan that they could use his house for a courting ceremony at which they proposed to entertain young people belonging to that clan. But the rain that had begun at four o'clock that afternoon was heavier than ever in the evening and the Konumbuga did not arrive. Some of the youths and girls who lived nearby had come to the house early, as soon as they had finished their evening meal. They were so eager to hold the courting ceremony that they waited for some hours before accepting the fact that the Konumbuga were not coming.

Ko II had come with the Penkup girls to await the guests. Being Konumbuga by birth and Kugika by long residence, she was in an ambiguous position. She treated the Kugika girls, especially those of Penkup subclan, as age-mates, but she was unequivocally a Konumbuga girl in courting ceremonies and in her private love life. A Kugika boy could give love to her, and indeed everyone expected that she would eventually marry a Kugika man. She could find partners in courting ceremonies and in carrying leg with Kugika, not Konumbuga, boys. This afternoon she had been carrying leg with Good, a handsome and well-built young man of Kugika clan who was the acknowledged leader of the young men of Penkup subclan. Now they slept in each other's arms in the inner room of the house.

In the outer room two young men, Head and Konangil, sang courting songs with three young girls of their own clan, Kugika. One of the girls was Or Nothing, an age-mate of Ko II and, like her, well versed in the actions and songs of the courting ceremonies. The other two were As If's elder daughter, Snailshell, and her age-mate. This first courting ceremony was to mark the beginning of a new life for them, but there was no ritual to signify their transformation from girl children into nubile adolescents: they would simply begin to take part in the courting ceremonies and public petting parties that were the business of marriageable girls. They were learning the songs and the movements of the courting ceremony from Or Nothing and the two youths.

There was a lapse in the singing just after I arrived, and Konangil began to joke with the girls.

'Do you want to get married, Or Nothing?' he asked. 'Or do you want to go to courting ceremonies all your life? You want to get married, don't you?'

Or Nothing hung her head and did not answer.

'Or Nothing has been attending courting ceremonies for a year now,' Konangil said, turning to me. I knew that it had been longer, but I did not shame him by correcting his statement. 'In another year she will be married, and a year after that she will have a child.'

Or Nothing simpered and started another song. As they all sang softly, she demonstrated to Snailshell and the other girl the movements they would soon have to perform, swaying their bodies and turning their heads first towards their partners and then, provocatively, away from them—in flickering firelight, looking as sinuous and devious as snakes slipping almost unseen through the bushes.

* * * *

A crowd of Penkup had gathered at Mountain Tree's house to hear a complaint that Blood had to make. Mountain Tree was not directly concerned, but he was head of the subdivision to which Blood belonged and so had a right to be present and represent him when necessary.

Blood, a little man with perpetual lines of anxiety on his face, gave a lengthy harangue. He began on a note of self-pity, stressing (as he often did) his misfortune in having no sons but only daughters, who were therefore his particular concern. Now his eldest daughter, Ko I, was causing him to worry. She and her age-mate, Or Nothing, were continually carrying leg and he was continually cross with them. This judgment surprised me until I discovered that he was cross because they carried leg unvaryingly with the same man, without distributing their favours among many. Their latest offence was that they had dared to tell him that they wanted to marry Stony and Strong Stone, although they were both betrothed to other men. They were trying to upset the arrangements the men of Penkup had made for them, simply on account of the foolish whims that were common in young girls. A girl, as everyone knew, was like the branch of a casuarina tree: the wind blew this way, and it would follow; the wind blew the other way, and it would go that way instead. Ko I and Or Nothing were trying to decide their own future, deluded that they were responsible persons.

Blood's wife, Flying, and a man of his subdivision, Struck Arrow, added their comments. Blood had been cross with Ko I the day before, and she had run away and slept with one of his clansmen's wives. Early this morning she had run away into the bush but Struck Arrow had found her and brought her back.

Raggiana delivered a speech with an air of wisdom and authority. He said that it was unthinkable that the girls could marry men who had not been chosen for them. The brother of Or Nothing, Tail,[1] had promised to give her to a Konumbuga man who lived some distance up the Minj River in exchange for the other man's sister, and this promise had to be honoured if Tail were to get a wife. Kobia, the brother of Go Insect, had betrothed Ko I and established his claim by giving Blood a pig. Kobia lived in adjacent Konumbuga territory, but Go Insect lived with the rest of this family inside Kugika territory and acted as a go-between in arranging many marriages between the two clans. All had agreed, Raggiana said, that Ko I would be bathed in pigs' grease after the Pig Ceremonial was over and would be given to Go Insect for his brother.

Struck Arrow reiterated that Ko I wanted to marry Stony and Or Nothing wanted to marry Strong Stone. He thought it would be better to give the girls to their affianced husbands straight away, without waiting for the end of the Pig Ceremonial. They had had enough freedom, and should not be encouraged to think that it could last forever. It was time they both submitted to the discipline of marriage.[2]

Several of the men contributed to the discussion. One said that as the Konumbuga men had betrothed Or Nothing and killed a pig and given it to the Kugika, she should not carry leg with other men. This was the only time I ever heard this view expressed; everyone else had told me, both spontaneously and in answer to my queries, that betrothal was no impediment to a girl's participation in courting ceremonies, public petting, and private love life: the only difference was that she now actively avoided carrying leg with the betrothed himself—not because the avoidance was

---

1 Tail and a man named Head were age-mates who began life with the same given name. The new names to distinguish them sprang from their eating these particular parts of a possum they shared as children (see Strathern, Andrew, 1977, 'Melpa food-names as an expression of ideas on identity and substance', *Journal of the Polynesian Society*, 86: 503–511).

2 'Freedom' and 'discipline' are not literal translations of what Struck Arrow said. He used circumlocutions contrasting what it was fitting for the two girls to do now and what it was fitting for them to submit to later.

prescribed by the men but because she herself felt that she had a lifetime of marriage in which to be intimate with him and only a limited time, before her marriage, to be intimate with other men. No one, however, corrected the man who had uttered this unconventional opinion and I am inclined to think the others took the statement as referring to a girl's habit of carrying leg with one particular man instead of distributing her favours among many.

Raggiana strolled through the crowd, talking quietly.

'I have something to say to you,' he said to Mountain Tree, Blood and Struck Arrow. He retired to Mountain Tree's cooking grove, behind a screen of trees.

Big Insect was giving an address on the differences between marriage now and before the white man came. Before, he said, if a man wanted to marry he would simply capture the girl without bothering to betroth her first. (Perhaps this did happen in fact, but there was certainly a clear rule requiring formal betrothal.) Now it was the custom to give a betrothal payment. Now girls married men with whom they had carried leg instead of the men their fathers had chosen for them.

Mountain Tree, Blood, and Struck Arrow followed Raggiana into the cooking grove. Raggiana nodded to Blood, and the worried-looking little man began to speak.

'Ko I told me that she had a perfect right to carry leg with Stony,' he said. 'Kobia had promised to give me a betrothal payment as soon as he came back from his trading expedition. He has been back for some time now, and he hasn't given me the payment yet. That is what Ko I has been thinking about.'

Ko I, I thought, is growing into an astute woman. I had no doubt that her unwillingness to marry Kobia was based simply on her overwhelming preference for Stony. But she knew that the only arguments that were likely to impress her father and his clansmen were those that touched their own interests in her marriage: the acquisition of material gain, and the cementing of friendly alliances. She was the oldest of the girls who were still going to courting ceremonies. For years now she had supported her age-mates in fights against rivals from other clans; for years she had helped her clan brothers by entertaining their honoured guests and by refusing to entertain any who had insulted or fallen out with them; for years she had identified herself proudly as a girl of the Kugika, the clan that had declined in numbers but, small though it had been in recent years, had vanquished its worst enemies. It is likely that she identified herself so closely with her clansmen that Kobia's failure to provide the betrothal payment had genuinely offended her, though his giving it would have been against her own present interests. But I could not help admiring her astuteness in appealing to her clansmen's greed for wealth. Blood's report that Ko I was concerned with securing a betrothal payment for them so impressed Raggiana that he announced, 'Ko I must be called, so that she can speak for herself.'

Struck Arrow called out for Ko I to come and dismissed a crowd of small boys who accompanied her through curiosity. Ko I's mother, Flying, stayed with her. The older woman's demeanour suggested that she knew she had not been invited to be present at the discussion but was determined to stay until she was told to leave.

'Kobia hasn't given your father the payment,' Raggiana said to Ko I, 'so you are not inclined to marry him and want to go to another man. Is that correct?'

'Yes,' said Ko I sullenly.

'If Go Insect and Kobia give the payment,' Flying interposed, 'Ko I will behave herself and she will wait and marry Kobia.'

Mountain Tree silenced her with a gesture, and said: 'We men are dealing with this.'

Big Insect had finished his speech about the changing marriage and betrothal customs of his people, and he strode into the cooking grove in time to hear what Flying had said.

'If they give the payment,' he repeated, 'Ko I will behave herself and marry Kobia. You may remember,' he continued, 'that True House marked Go Insect's mother for another man, just as Go Insect marked Ko I for Kobia; but then he married her himself. The other man killed one of us. Bloodshed, strife between friends: that is what will happen if Ko I marries someone besides Kobia.'

There was an uncomfortable silence while the men remembered the incident and its aftermath. Go Insect's mother was a Kugika woman; his father, True House, was a Konumbuga man but not the man to whom she had been betrothed. The Kugika had condoned the marriage, since True House was willing to live with them and give them substantial help in addition to enabling a beloved daughter to stay close to her people after her marriage. But the disappointed fiancé had tried to claim his bride; a brawl developed, and a Kugika man was killed. Generally a man's clansmen would avenge his death by killing, as soon as possible, someone from the clan of the murderer. But Kugika and Konumbuga clans were 'as brothers'. There had been so much intermarriage between them that there was scarcely a member of the small Kugika clan who did not have close relatives among the Konumbuga. This death had never been avenged: the debt of blood could never be repaid without damaging the Kugika's valued friendship with their powerful neighbours.

Blood addressed his daughter loudly, so that all the assembled company could hear: 'Shall we wash you with grease now and give you to Kobia, or shall we wait until the Pig Ceremonial is over?'

No one expected Ko I to answer, and the men agreed that it might be better to give her to Kobia quickly. But Ko I herself spoke.

'I am thinking of the payment,' she said, to attract their attention. 'I shall wait until the Pig Ceremonial is over. If Kobia gives the payment I'll behave myself and not carry leg with the other man. But I would rather marry Stony.'

Big Insect and Struck Arrow reminded her that if she married someone else Kobia would resent it and there would be bloodshed and killing.

'Before,' Ko I told them, 'Stony told Blood and Struck Arrow that he wanted to marry me. He promised to give them plenty of pay when he came back from the coast at the end of his term as a labourer. But Blood and Struck Arrow refused. They said they wanted to give me to Kobia. Now that Kobia's payment hasn't appeared, I like to carry leg with Stony. At the time of the Pig Ceremonial there is plenty of pay about, and yet Kobia hasn't given you the payment he promised.'

'To mark a girl isn't enough without paying,' Mountain Tree said dubiously. 'When Go Insect comes, we'll tell him we want plenty of pay quickly.'

'Ko I can't just go and marry as she likes,' Big Insect stated. 'We shall wash her with grease and give her to the man we choose. Ko I is silly, carrying leg and getting fond of a man who is not her betrothed.'

'When we kill the pigs at the end of the ceremonial,' Raggiana said, 'we'll wash Ko I with grease and give her to Kobia. When Go Insect comes, we'll tell him we want a large betrothal payment now.'

Big Insect made an impatient gesture.

'Let us wash Ko I with grease and give her to Go Insect when he comes,' he suggested. 'Don't wait for the pig-killing.'

'Yes,' Blood agreed, 'let us wash her with grease and give her to Go Insect when he comes. This morning I was very sad. All my brothers are dead, and my daughter is carrying leg with the wrong man. I don't want to wait for the pig-killing. Let's get it over.'

'When Go Insect comes,' Big Insect resumed, 'we'll tell him to take Ko I. We'll put her inside her mother's house and wash her with grease … When the Konumbuga killed one of our men because of Go Insect's mother, they did not give us enough compensation. They know about it, and they will have to give us plenty of pay when they marry this Kugika girl.'

There was much discussion of the arguments already mentioned. Finally Big Insect agreed that as Raggiana wanted to wait for the pig-killing they should do so. Raggiana looked pleased, for he had not expected his brother to support him. I wondered cynically whether Big Insect was ceding a point in order to win Raggiana's support on some other issue affecting the subclan. But I knew he was fond of Ko I and he may have had the sentimental motive of wishing to delay her departure from Kondambi.

The men in the cooking grove turned expectantly when the young Konumbuga man, Go Insect, arrived. Tall and graceful, he wore a grubby red *lap-lap* fastened with a leather belt, instead of the long net apron, dark with pigs' grease, which was the uniform of the others. Go Insect had worked as a labourer at the coast, and more recently he had been a cargo-boy on the Government Station. He listened carefully while the Kugika told him of the discussion they had had.

'Go now,' Raggiana told him, 'and get the pay. Ko I will stay with us until the Pig Ceremonial is over.'

Ko I began to stroll away, but Big Insect called her back.

'Don't go,' he instructed her. 'We have to deal with Or Nothing now.'

The men began to discuss Or Nothing. They summoned her to their presence and told her that she must not carry leg with Strong Stone while she was betrothed to another man. At the pig-killing, they assured her, they would wash her with pigs' grease and give her to the Konumbuga.

* * * *

Two months later, the dancing in the Pig Ceremonial was at its height, and scrambling on top of one of the long-houses for a better view one looked down upon a sea of gaudy plumes. The Penkup men stopped dancing when they saw that Ko I was carrying leg with Stony, the young man she had wanted to marry. They told her to stop. Ko I said sulkily that she wanted to marry Stony. She walked away. Go Insect, whose role in betrothing her to Kobia gave him a special interest in these events, had helped the Penkup men to separate her from her lover and he watched her to see where she was going. He realized that she had gone in the direction of the Minj River, the stream that flowed swiftly through the deep gully dividing Kondambi from the Government Station. Sensing what was in her mind, he ran after her and dragged her back. Ko I protested that life had no meaning for her if she could not marry Stony and that, as Go Insect had guessed, she wanted to throw herself into the river.

In the evening, Tail found his sister Or Nothing carrying leg with Strong Stone in one of the Penkup long-houses. He ran forward with an angry cry and struck her. Strong Stone ran away and went home to Konmil. Tail continued to hit Or Nothing about the head.

Dog walked on to the ceremonial ground and saw them struggling. He was a handsome young man, strong and well-built, and Tail, who was a few years younger, looked a mere boy beside him. Dog had a special interest in Or Nothing. Although he belonged to the Koimamkup subclan, he was her half-brother: their mother had been wife to their fathers in turn. Now he attacked Tail for hitting her. He made it clear that he intervened because of his blood relationship with the girl, not because he agreed with her view. He tore Tail's waistband and bark corset off him, while Or Nothing sat crying on the ground.

Several Penkup men arrived and separated the two young men. Head and Tail tried to drag Or Nothing away and take her to her home, but the girl sat stolidly on the ground. One of the men succeeded in grasping her arms in a strong grip and, handing one arm to another man, was able to pull her away. Tail found a slim switch of bamboo and threatened to beat Or Nothing with it if she did not go quietly. He struck her with it whenever she tried to break away from her captors on the journey home.

* * * *

Another month passed. Then Tail told me that he had broken off his betrothal and taken back the payment he had made. The Konumbuga girl up the river had wanted to marry him and he had promised to give Or Nothing to her brother in exchange. But now he was cross because his betrothed had been carrying leg constantly with another man, who had kept her for a few days then bathed her with grease and sent her home. Tail did not want to marry her now. Later, he said, if he were to find a girl he wanted to marry he would give Or Nothing to her brother. If Or Nothing herself wanted to marry someone, it would have to be a man who could provide a sister to marry Tail.

* * * *

Snailshell had been attending courting ceremonies for about two months now. She was a slim, awkward girl, with none of the dimpled roundness of Ko I and Or Nothing, and her characteristic expression was a vacant stare. She helped to swell the numbers at the courting ceremonies, but no one had composed a song about her yet. One of the favourite songs at the courting ceremonies of the time was one which told of an old man coming from the east, seeing Or Nothing, and deciding to stay.

As If's other daughter, Grass Woman, was looking forward to attending courting ceremonies in a year or two. It was a shock to the two girls when their father told them that he had arranged for them both to be betrothed to the Konumbuga.

'I am only a little child!' Snailshell protested. 'I have not been attending courting ceremonies long. I can't marry Konumbuga Vomit. He is an old man, and I won't marry him.'

As If did not argue with her. There could be no argument. Snailshell would have to marry Vomit, for As If could repay his debt to the Konumbuga man in no other way. He was a poor man, and all his brothers had died. He himself had recently been ill, and the men of Penkup subclan (aggrieved with him for being lazy and begging from them) neglected him. Vomit, his Konumbuga friend, had faithfully nursed him through his illness, even carrying his excreta out of the house. He had no way of reimbursing Vomit for his kindness, other than promising him his daughter in marriage. In fact he had a double debt to Vomit, for his father had been wounded in warfare and Vomit's father had nursed him in the same way. When Vomit suggested that Grass Woman would be a fitting bride for his brother, As If found himself concurring.

'You are giving too many girls to the Konumbuga!' Snailshell cried. 'They have only given you one.' This was the wife As If had inherited from his dead brother. 'My mother belonged to a different clan, and her ghost will come and make you sick.'

'Stop that talk!' As If growled, rubbing his beard.

* * * *

Seven months had passed since the meeting in Mountain Tree's cooking grove. The dancing in the Pig Ceremonial had become more spectacular, but the Kugika had not yet killed their pigs. One morning there was a stir on the ceremonial ground. Konangil appeared panting at my door and told me to come quickly.

'Today we are giving Ko I and Snailshell and Or Nothing to the Konumbuga,' he said. 'Yesterday Ko I went to Stony, and some of the Kugika pulled her back. All the girls have been playing up. Ko I bosses the other girls, so when we give her we are going to give them all.'

There was a great gathering of Penkup people in Mountain Tree's long-house. Big Insect addressed the crowd at length, saying that the Kugika were giving Ko I and Snailshell to the Konumbuga Pipikanim and Or Nothing to the Konumbuga Gaimakanim. He told Blood and Tail to get some feathers to decorate the girls.

Ko I and Or Nothing were crying. Snailshell sat near them, looking bewildered but apparently unmoved. Ko I and Or Nothing laughed faintly when Big Insect made an obscene pun on the word for 'drum'. He was referring to a northern custom Or Nothing had adopted: a girl's direct approach to a man when he was dancing, and snatching his drum as a signal that she wanted to carry leg with him.

The men guarded the girls closely. Ko I tried to enter a yard beside the long-house, but Konumbuga Vomit, Snailshell's betrothed, blocked her way. She waited until Vomit's attention was diverted and entered the yard, but some of the other Konumbuga men pulled her back.

Tail grumbled that Ko I had given Stony her decorations, including a goldlip shell of his own. Stony had run away when the Penkup arrived to take Ko I back yesterday, and Tail knew that his goldlip shell would never be returned to him.

'Ko I has been attending courting ceremonies for a long time,' one man ventured, 'so it would be better to give her to the man of her choice. Snailshell is a different matter. She is rather simple-minded, so she can go to the man who has marked her.'

No one heeded this interesting opinion, for the man who had voiced it belonged to Koimamkup subclan. This was a Penkup matter; it was none of his concern.

Tail had brought some ornaments with which he intended to decorate Or Nothing, and he fetched a gourd of pigs' grease with which to bathe her.

'No, no!' she cried. 'I don't want to marry the Gaimakanim.'

Tail held Or Nothing's arms and called to the Konumbuga Gaimakanim men while she squirmed in his grasp.

'Take her now,' he commanded them. 'I'll bring her back tomorrow and grease her and decorate her. She is too determined now.'

The Konumbuga Gaimakanim took her from her brother and dragged her from Kondambi screaming.

Ko I and Snailshell were prisoners in the little yard of Blood's house. Go Insect and Struck Arrow held Ko I, and As If and Konumbuga Vomit held Snailshell. Guards stood at all the gates. Both girls struggled when the men tried to fasten new waistbands on them, and Ko I trampled hers on the ground. At last the men managed to fasten the waistbands, new bunches of cords, and some goldlip shells. The girls were crying with grief and frustrated rage. Snailshell was biting and kicking her tormentors, while Ko I strained away from the men and sat down violently in an effort to wrench herself free. At last their struggles ceased, and the wives of Struck Arrow and As If rubbed pigs' grease on to their skin.

of visitors—the legitimate exercise of an adolescent girl's power over men. But looking after her little sisters could have had another meaning for Big Insect besides the obvious one. As the oldest of the Penkup's nubile girls, she had 'looked after' or led her 'sisters' or subclan age-mates and seen that they acted in their clansmen's interest too.

Big Insect burst into tears, and his shoulders heaved with great sobs as he handed Ko I to Go Insect. Or Nothing came quickly down the aisle. Big Insect, who was still holding one of Ko I's hands in one of his, took Or Nothing's hand in the other.

'Or Nothing has not been with us as long as Ko I has,' he said, 'but it has been a long time. We do not like losing her. Look after Or Nothing well. If she is not happy she will come back to us. Look after her well. Her own mother is dead and Tail's mother is crying because she is going.'

Big Insect gave Go Insect both the girls at once, and Go Insect took them to where the Konumbuga were waiting.

The ceremonial ground is a public place, and many of the Koimamkup people had gathered to watch the proceedings. They huddled together while the Konumbuga men passed with the three brides, and they discussed the day's events with interest.

'We do not follow the customs of the Penkup,' they said self-righteously. 'Our girls can wait until they want to marry. They can certainly wait until we kill the pigs, and if they want to stay longer they may do so. We certainly shan't grab them and fasten them like fowls when we want to give them to another clan.'

* * * *

The next afternoon, Or Nothing ran away and hid in the bush on her way back to Kugika territory. Some Konumbuga men found her and took her to one of their wives' houses, but she ran away again in another direction. Eventually, she was discovered and taken to her husband, a long way up the Minj River. Tail told me he did not think she would run away again.

Another day passed. Late at night, some young men returned from a courting ceremony at Konmil and brought the news that Ko I and Snailshell had escaped. They thought the girls had gone north of the Wahgi, where Snailshell had a lover, but soon the two girls arrived at Kondambi. The Kugika Penkup gave them back to the Konumbuga.

More than a week later, Snailshell ran away and sought refuge with her mother's brother, a man of the neighbouring Ngeni-Muruka clan. He brought her to Kondambi to interview As If.

'Snailshell is only very young,' he said, 'and you have given her to the Konumbuga already. She does not belong to Ko I's age-set; she is much younger. You want to get the Konumbuga's payment, but you haven't given us our payment yet as compensation for the death of Snailshell's mother. Have your old enemies the Kondiga routed the Kugika and burnt all your houses, that you are so anxious to give little girls to the Konumbuga?'

As If objected that he had pressing obligations towards the Konumbuga, and told his brother-in-law how Vomit's father had nursed his father and Vomit had later nursed him.

'You see,' he said, 'I am obliged to give Snailshell to the Konumbuga. I cannot do anything else.'

'Let us go to Minj,' Snailshell suggested, 'and settle this at the Court of Native Affairs. I don't want to marry.'

The Ngeniga man left and Snailshell stayed with As If. Good Bird and Struck Arrow came on to the ceremonial ground and, hearing that Snailshell had come back, they went to As If's house. Snailshell and As If were inside.

'Snailshell!' Struck Arrow shouted. 'You must go back to the Konumbuga at once!'

'I don't want to go back,' Snailshell replied. 'The Konumbuga have a lot of girls who are really big, with breasts that hang down, whereas the Kugika give the Konumbuga little girls with breasts that have scarcely begun to develop.'

'Come outside!' Good Bird commanded.

'No!' Snailshell replied.

Struck Arrow lounged against the fence and let Good Bird do the talking. The two men had been visiting another clan, and they wore the long black plumes of the Princess Stephanie Bird of Paradise on their heads. They did not want to risk breaking their plumes by crawling through the low doorway into the house.

'Go back to the Konumbuga at once,' Good Bird commanded 'before we have to go in and grab you.'

'No,' Snailshell objected, 'I shall stay here.'

'If you stay here,' As If's voice rumbled from inside the dwelling, 'whose house are you going to sleep in? Certainly not mine.'

Good Bird looked around for some Konumbuga women who were married to Kugika men, and saw Indoors (the headman's senior wife) in company with Good's wife, Talking Woman. He called them over and sent them into the house. As If tried to push Snailshell through the doorway while the two women pulled her by the arms. He slapped her hard. The shock of the blow released Snailshell from the women's grip. She seized a length of firewood from the shelf above the fire and hit her father. Indoors and Talking Woman helped As If to wrest the stick from the girl's hand. She seized another stick and hit As If again before Indoors took it from her. Talking Woman and As If pulled Snailshell through the doorway, urged on by Good Bird's cries. 'You are a couple of strong women. You are not weaklings, and she is only little. Hurry up!' Snailshell clung to the fence, but Good Bird and Struck Arrow pulled her away. She went without resistance on to the ceremonial ground, but suddenly darted inside one of the Penkup long-houses.

The Konumbuga man who had been guarding Snailshell on Vomit's behalf had arrived at Kondambi, hearing that she had gone there. Seeing her escape from the two Kugika men, he shook his head sadly and said, 'She doesn't like me. I can't do anything with her.'

Big Insect's second wife, Goodly, who was also Konumbuga by birth, was inside the long-house tending her fire when Snailshell dashed in. Goodly grabbed the girl's arm as As If arrived. Together, they struggled with Snailshell.

'Your father has a sore leg,' Goodly reproached Snailshell. 'He is sick and will die soon. Aren't you sorry for him?'

'I am only a little child,' Snailshell objected, 'not a big girl.'

Eventually, Goodly and Indoors led her away to Konmil. Good Bird called to the Konumbuga man who was following them, telling him not to let Ko I and Snailshell get together and talk in case they planned to escape again.

The excitement subsided on the ceremonial ground. Then news came that Or Nothing had run away from her husband and was staying with her mother's brother, halfway between her husband's home and Kondambi.

A fortnight after Big Insect had given Ko I to the Konumbuga, the Pipikanim brought her to Kondambi. Kobia and his clansmen were now ready to give the marriage payment.

The Penkup bathed Ko I in pigs' grease and decorated her splendidly. They also decorated Go Insect's mother, Bluebell, who had been a Kugika woman, and her daughter.

The Konumbuga had brought three cooked pigs. Go Insect handed pork-fat around to the Penkup, and everyone feasted. Then Big Insect handed the women to Go Insect, who led them over to the Konumbuga as he had previously led Ko I with Snailshell and Or Nothing. The Konumbuga women embraced Ko I and Bluebell and [space in original] and made them sit with them and eat some more pork.

The Penkup were pleased with the marriage payment the Konumbuga had brought. Plumes waved and ornaments dangled from a heart-shaped bamboo frame attached to a pole which the men stood in the ground. It was a very satisfactory payment. The Penkup let it stand there for several hours before pulling it down and dismantling it to distribute the valuables, to remind them what good friends the Konumbuga were.

* * * *

Or Nothing came back to Kondambi a week later. Her mother's brother, himself a Konumbuga man, had been angry with the Kugika for giving her to his clan so soon. He made them promise that she could attend courting ceremonies again and be considered unmarried.

'Snailshell will be angry when she hears about this,' Tail predicted. 'Or Nothing attended courting ceremonies for a long time before Snailshell began.'

* * * *

Two Konumbuga girls had come to stay with Kugika men and carry leg with them. Both the men belonged to the Penkup subclan, so all the women of this group contributed fruit and vegetables to present to the girls. Big Insect and the other men arranged the food in three generous piles. Ko I, who had come to visit her parents and was watching the piling of the food with interest, knew that one of the heaps of food was for her.

'Ko I was a girl we hated to lose,' Big Insect said at the end of his speech about the Konumbuga girls. 'But fortunately she has married a Konumbuga man and is living nearby, so we still see her and she can come to visit us. Look, she is with us today. This food is for you, Ko I.'

* * * *

But Ko I was not yet reconciled to her uncongenial marriage. A month later she and Snailshell ran away again. Big Insect, Raggiana, and Mountain Tree went northward across the Wahgi River to find them, and the girls came sullenly back to Kondambi. Raggiana announced that the Penkup should beat the girls before giving them back to the Konumbuga. Go Insect and Vomit, who had arrived to take the girls back, agreed that they should be punished.

A man of Ko I's subdivision, Together Little, cut two bamboo switches and gave one to As If. As If hit Snailshell four times on the buttocks. Snailshell did not resist, but she put her hand out, with the palm facing As If, to urge him to stop. He did not hit her further. Snailshell stood quietly with tears coursing down her cheeks. Together Little hit Ko I, who was sitting on the ground. She screamed, but he continued. When he had hit her a dozen times, she put up her hand as Snailshell had done and he desisted. But when he was passing behind her to take his place beside Mountain Tree and the other men he hit her a few more times.

The men had a lively discussion, trying to decide what the girls had intended to do. Their natural suspicions were that Ko I and Snailshell had intended going to their lovers, but, though Snailshell had a lover on the other side of the Wahgi, it was well known that Ko I's lover was Stony, who lived nearby. Finally, the men agreed that the girls were probably speaking the truth when they said that they wanted to stay unmarried until their breasts dropped.

Or Nothing's father delivered a long tirade against the three girls the Penkup had given to the Konumbuga. Or Nothing had heard that her new husband was taking another wife, and she had run away to a Tengalap man. Tail looked on without saying anything. It was true that Or Nothing had not been seen that day, but rumours were prevalent. Goodly rebuked Snailshell severely, stressing the facts that Snailshell's mother was dead and that Vomit had cared for As If.

Big Insect delivered an oration, rebuking the two girls and expressing his disappointment with Ko I. He said that they must stay in their own houses and must not visit Kondambi again.

'But they may need to get food from their gardens,' Go Insect's mother objected.

'Very well,' Big Insect agreed, 'they may come to Kondambi for that purpose alone, so long as they go back promptly.'

Vomit took Together Little's switch and threatened to hit Ko I if she did not hurry up and go back with them. Ko I, who was sobbing convulsively, took no notice. Snailshell cried in sympathy. Big Insect was plainly sorry for Ko I, but he could do nothing.

Raggiana ridiculed the two girls.

'Did you smell your menstrual blood and find it good?' he cried. 'Is that why you want to walk about?'

Snailshell protested that they had not gone to any other men: they simply wanted to stay unmarried until their breasts fell.

'We walked about nothing,' she said, meaning that they had walked about with no ulterior motive.

Go Insect, who was sitting at Snailshell's feet, laughed and flicked her bunch of cords with his hand.

'Did you really walk about nothing,' he asked, meaning with no clothes on, 'or did you wear your cords?'

The men and the women exchanged other ribald jokes and puns within hearing of the two girls.

Later in the day, Blood and his wife, Flying, came back from visiting relatives and learned what had happened. They were angry with Together Little for beating their daughter, Ko I, and they tried to find him. He was not at Kondambi, so they went to Mountain Tree.

'You are the big man of Kumnga subdivision,' Blood said to him. 'You needn't have let that happen.'

Mountain Tree listened to the protestations of Blood and Flying, and then he told them that he had gone across the Wahgi River to find the girls and had brought them back. He had thought that they had run away to their lovers, but they merely objected to being married.

'But I am Ko I's father,' Blood protested. 'Only a girl's father may hit her.'

'Ko I deserved it,' Mountain Tree said. 'I think you will find that all the Penkup agree.'

* * * *

Tail was looking dispirited, and I asked him what was wrong.

'It's Or Nothing,' he said.

A man of Waga clan had taken Or Nothing to carry leg in Waga territory. She had stayed there for a couple of days, and then had said, 'I don't want to go back to Kondambi. I shall stay here and marry you.'

Or Nothing might have expected some trouble about her own clansmen's attitude to such a marriage, but nothing had prepared her for her lover's own reaction. I myself have never heard of any other man among the Agamp who spoke to a marriageable girl as this man did according to Tail's account.

'I don't want to marry you,' he told her simply.

Or Nothing was infuriated.

'You have deceived me!' she cried. 'All right, I shall go to another man and look after his pigs, and you can watch me.'

Or Nothing went to Mountain Tree's brother-in-law, Herb, one of the men who had approached Tail about marrying her.

'Now I am annoyed too,' Tail told me. 'Or Nothing has married Herb, and I wanted to exchange her for a bride for myself.'

He said that he was so annoyed that he would not go to see her, even to bring her back.

As we talked, we saw two young women coming from the direction of Konmil, bent beneath the weight of their bulging net bags. They came nearer, and we could see that they were Ko I and Snailshell. They paused to speak to us in subdued voices. They were taking a load of green vegetables to Bluebell, Ko I told us.

4

A Rubbish Man Takes a Wife

The Government road passed through the territories of many clans. Talk Eastward and his two companions were going home from the Government Station, and they had just crossed the bridge over the Minj River into their own Kugika territory when they saw two figures climbing the steep hill in front of them. Talk Eastward recognized them as Pain and her brother. He had heard that the white man she was living with had sent her home, and he assumed that the brother had gone to Minj to take her back to Tangilka territory.

Pain was a handsome girl by local standards. As he told me later, a man could be proud of having a wife like that. He himself had one wife, but Eaten was an old woman in his eyes. He had appealed to Two Stay, his elder brother, to help him collect a marriage payment, but Two Stay had said that he could spare no valuables for that purpose. Two Stay was *tultul* of Burikup subclan and the head of Baimankanim subdivision; surely he could spare some plumes and shells for his brother's marriage payment? But Two Stay had said that Burikup was not a wealthy subclan like Penkup and Koimamkup. Talk Eastward would have to wait. Talk Eastward had waited. His beard had grown, and still he could not get a young wife. Perhaps, Two Stay told him, a girl would carry leg with him and insist on marrying, or a married woman would run away to him. Talk Eastward knew that Two Stay was joking. No girl ever asked him to carry leg. He could not help being ugly and awkward. He would have to get a nice young wife somehow.

Walking along the road, Talk Eastward remembered that two Burikup men, including a brother of his, had been killed in warfare. They had been helping the Tangilka in a fight against the Dambilika, so the Tangilka should have paid compensation for their deaths. They had never paid. He told this to his companions and outlined a scheme in which he needed their help. He would capture Pain to settle the old score with the Tangilka.

The three men captured the girl. She struggled violently, and the beads she had been wearing around her neck broke and fell to the ground. Talk Eastward told her brother that he was taking her to be his wife, and explained to him the debt the Tangilka owed the Kugika. The brother replied that he did not mind his sister marrying a Kugika man, so long as she did not marry a man of Penkup subclan. The Tangilka had given the Penkup Big Insect's youngest wife, [space in original] and the Penkup had not yet given them a woman in exchange.

Talk Eastward and his companions dragged the unwilling girl to Kondambi and took her as far as Two Stay's house on the track to Gwaip. By the time they arrived, Pain was bruised and cut about from being dragged unwillingly over the pointed palings of pig-fences. A crowd assembled in Two Stay's house to discuss Talk Eastward's acquisition of a bride. They were mostly Burikup people, but Big Insect came when he heard that Talk Eastward had captured a girl of [space in original, presumably Kugika] clan.

'The Pingya are coming tomorrow to pay me compensation for my brother's death,' he told Talk Eastward, naming a clan that lived north of the Wahgi. 'As you know, he was killed when he was staying with them a long time ago. I shall give you part of the death compensation as a contribution towards your marriage payment.'

A native policeman arrived. He had been walking along the Government road and had found Pain's beads, stained with blood. He was directed to Two Stay's house. He satisfied himself that Pain was not seriously injured. Big Insect said that it was local custom to capture girls in this manner. The policeman looked dubious, but he was not a local native so he changed the subject, asking where Pain was going to sleep, for it was now nearly dark.

'Here with me, of course,' Talk Eastward told him. 'She is my wife now.'

Pain objected loudly. She said that she wanted to sleep with her 'sister'.

'No!' cried Big Insect. 'The Tangilka will hear of it, and they will think that I have slept with the girl.'

The policeman, who could not countenance Talk Eastward's marriage until he had consulted either the Government officer or at least one of the local interpreters at the Government Station, said that Pain should sleep with [space in original]. The two women occupied the little sleeping cubicle of [space in original] house, and Talk Eastward kept watch in the ante-room. He had to get up once during the night to stop Pain from escaping. Big Insect expected Pain's clansmen to arrive the next day bringing the death compensation for Talk Eastward's brother, so that they could retrieve her. They did not arrive, so Talk Eastward took the girl to his house at Gwaip.

Three days later, I came to my house and found the step in the doorway broken, my table upset, and papers scattered on the floor. I learned that Pain, trying to escape from Talk Eastward, had sought sanctuary in my house. Two Stay and some other Burikup men had forcibly removed her. They had called for her to come out, but she had refused, so they had rushed in, seized her, and dragged her out. They had carried her back to Gwaip. I went to visit her. She was sitting in Talk Eastward's garden, under the watchful eyes of Two Stay's wife, Apron. We talked in Neo-Melanesian, which Pain spoke fluently, so that Apron could not understand us.

Pain told me she had decided to let Talk Eastward think she was resigned to marrying him. Then, when he relaxed his guard, she would run away to Whitewood, a Native Medical Assistant. When she was with the European, Pain had discovered that she was pregnant and had taken Whitewood as her lover to counteract this. For pregnancy, in Minj Agamp belief, resulted only from many acts of intercourse with one man, and a girl who was promiscuous was in no danger of having children.

Pain reasoned that it would be useless for her to return to her parents, for Big Insect had already met her father and the Tangilka *luluai*, and they had both agreed that it would be all right for a Kugika man to marry her. Her father had even told Big Insect to advise Talk Eastward to tie a rope around the girl's waist and fasten her inside his house as if she were a pig, in order to prevent her from escaping. She had tried several times to escape. Each night Talk Eastward fastened the door of his house and tried to rape her. Each night she beat him off with sticks she pulled from the fire. Soon, she said, he would grow tired of pestering her.

When Big Insect had met the Tangilka, they had decided that Talk Eastward need not give them a marriage payment until Pain bore a child. If she succeeded in running away before this was possible, the Tangilka undertook to pay Talk Eastward the compensation owing to him for his brother's death. This explained her father's anxiety that Talk Eastward should guard her carefully, for he would rather receive a payment than give one.

Whitewood was transferred to a medical post about four days' walk from Kugika territory, and Pain revised her plans when she heard this. She would run away to her parents. Perhaps they would agree to give her to a Kambilika[1] man, she preferred him to Talk Eastward.

Pain pretended to be resigned to her marriage, and Talk Eastward soon relaxed his guard. She fled to the Tangilka. The Kugika were amused when they heard that she was again attending courting ceremonies, for they regarded her as a married woman. Her pregnancy was now becoming noticeable, but it was never publicly discussed. Her father advised the Kambilika to come and get her before she ran away to another man. The Kambilika captured her, and her parents put up a token show of resistance then let her go.

The Kugika were quick to remember that the Kambilika, against whom they had fought in the past, were potential enemies. They felt that they were unquestionably right in regarding Pain as Talk Eastward's wife and quite justified in kidnapping a Tangilka girl when her clan had failed to pay compensation for the death of Talk Eastward's brother. They appealed to the Court of Native Affairs at Minj, and they were told to inform Pain, the Kambilika man, and her father that they must attend the court the next day.

The Kugika armed themselves with spears and bows and arrows. They were prepared to fight if the Kambilika offered resistance. They marched along the Government road to the beginning of Kambilika territory. They yodelled from a safe distance, commanding the others to send Pain

---

1   Pers. comm. from John Burton of 17 August 2013 on the form of these group names. Kambilika is correct.

and her husband and father. The Kambilika refused, alleging that the Kugika would again capture Pain on the way to Minj. They demanded a police escort. The Kugika returned to Minj and reported that the Kambilika had refused to attend the court unless a policeman were sent to escort them.

Finally, the case was heard. The court ruled that Pain should stay with the Kambilika. Further, the Kugika could not exact compensation for the death of Talk Eastward's brother because the war with the Kambilika had occurred a long time ago, before the Government had come to Minj. The Kugika returned to their homes, muttering that the Kambilika and Tangilka still owed them a bride in exchange for the 'Kugika woman', Pain.

* * * *

When You Heard's father, a Konumbuga man, died her stepmother married his brother, who became the girl's guardian. He arranged for You Heard's betrothal about a year after she had begun to attend courting ceremonies. He made the arrangements with Good Bird whose marriage to Creamy had initiated an exchange of women between Penkup subclan of Kugika clan and this particular subclan of Konumbuga clan. You Heard was to marry Original Man.

Original Man was shy, for, although he was handsome enough by European standards, he was not attractive to Highlands women. He had given up attending courting ceremonies when he had found that none of the girls was willing to press her nose against his. They never summoned him to carry leg. A Berebuga man by descent, Original Man had lived with the Kugika all his life. Both his parents had been killed by Berebuga witchcraft, and his mother's brother, [space in original] had reared Original Man as his own child and as a fully incorporated member of Kumngakanim sub-subclan.

The girl You Heard used frequently to stay at Minj with an older sister, the wife of a policeman. She carried leg with a coastal native employed as a servant there. When members of the Kugika clan went to Minj on Government work, they heard that she had gone to live with this man and wanted to marry him. They complained to the Court of Native Affairs, and You Heard was ordered to return to her parents until the Pig Ceremonial was over.

You Heard's parents had gone to Minj for the court case, and on their way home they discussed the possibility of her running away to another man before they could give her to Original Man. Perhaps she would run away to the coastal native again. No one believed her when she protested that she had merely been staying with her sister and that her relations with the coastal native had been confined to carrying leg. Her parents sent a message to Good Bird and [space in original] to come and capture her and marry her to Original Man. Good Bird and some of the Kumngakanim men captured You Heard. Her parents pretended to resist the Kugika, and two of the men were injured slightly. There was no pretence in Your Heard's resistance. She struggled and screamed, pummelled her captors, bit them, and tore their hair. They dragged her to Kondambi and deposited her outside Mountain Tree's house, closely guarded. You Heard's mother followed. She laughed with the two wounded men, apologizing for having to hit them so hard to convince her daughter that she was sorry for her, and promising them that they would have a generous helping of pork from the first pig You Heard reared for Original Man.

You Heard slept that night in Mountain Tree's house with Long, an older Konumbuga woman, guarding her. She made several abortive attempts to escape.

The next day Good Bird and the other men took You Heard back to her parents, who were to bathe her in pigs' fat and decorate her before giving her finally to Original Man. Creamy and Long carried a pig the Kugika had cooked to present to the girl's parents.

You Heard told her family that she did not want to marry yet. She wanted to take part in the Pig Ceremonial, which the Konumbuga were celebrating at the same time as the Kugika. They did not head her, and they beat her whenever she tried to run away. She tried to prevent members of her family from eating the pork the Kugika had brought, knowing that the *kiaps*[2] used the eating of pork as an index of the validity of marriage. Her brother became so angry that he attacked her viciously, inflicting several cuts and bruises. Her step-sister reproved him, 'Don't hit her like that! You are too strong. You'll kill her, and then we shan't get any marriage payment. Let me hit her instead.' She beat the girl until You

---

2 Patrol officer.

Heard lost consciousness and fell to the ground. When she recovered, she made a few more futile attempts to escape, and finally allowed her brother to imprison her in her mother's house.

In the morning Good Bird dragged her back, protesting, to Original Man. She had successfully prevented her parents from bathing her with pigs' grease and decking her with ornaments.

More than three weeks passed. During this time, Original Man shut her in the house at night and consummated the marriage by rape. He cut her hair and forcibly removed her woven waistband and armbands and the beads she wore, for a man does not want other men to find his bride attractive. She tried many times to run away, but the Kugika brought her back. Once she managed to reach her parents, but they sent a message to Original Man and he took her back immediately.

One night the guard was relaxed and she was alone with Original Man. She waited until he was asleep, then crept outside and went to her sister at Minj.

The Kugika could not hope to capture You Heard at Minj in the presence of Europeans and police, and she stayed with her sister for nearly two months. The case of Pain was heard at the Court of Native Affairs, and an officer warned the Kugika that if they captured any more girls by force they would all go to jail. The Kugika wanted to continue their Pig Ceremonial and kill their pigs. You Heard's sister and her policeman brother-in-law persuaded her parents to let her stay at home. She returned to her family, and the Kugika were amused to hear that she had resumed courting ceremonies as though she had never been married at all. The policeman threatened to report his parents-in-law if they gave You Heard to Original Man before the end of the Pig Ceremonial.

Original Man was deeply distressed.

'You Heard will go to another man,' he told me. 'I cannot bear to think of her going to another man. If she does, I shall kill her with my hatchet. If I don't kill her, I'll hang myself.'

We have already met two of You Heard's sisters—the vicious step-sister who lived with her husband near her parents' home, and the kindly policeman's wife at Minj.[3] You Heard had a third sister, who had recently married a Ngeniga man. Three months after the Court of Native Affairs had reviewed You Heard's case, she went to stay with this third sister. Ngeniga territory adjoins that of the Kugika, who soon learned where You Heard was staying. Early in the morning [space in original], Together Small, and two other men lay in wait for her. When she came out of her sister's house, they took her by surprise and captured her. She struggled with them, but when she injured her wrist she gave in and walked quietly back to Kondambi with them. [space in original] took her to his cooking grove.

I asked [space in original] why they had not waited for the pig-killing. He answered that the officer at the Court of Native Affairs had told the Kugika to wait for three months and then capture You Heard.

'It is a lie!' You Heard hissed.

I told [space in original] that the Kugika had told me the officer had forbidden them to capture You Heard and had advised them that she should not marry until the pig-killing was over. Then [space in original] told me why they had captured her.

You Heard's parents had given the Kugika a pig at the time of Original Man's 'marriage'. This was a pig the Ngeniga had given them as part of the marriage payment for Your Heard's sister. The girl's parents could not themselves eat this pig, because of their part in warfare with the Ngeniga a long time ago, so they had handed it over to the Kugika. They had told them that it would be a convenient time to marry You Heard, because of this circumstances. The Kugika gave You Heard's parents a pig in return, and they had eaten this. You Heard was staying with the Ngeniga when they objected that her parents had never given them a pig in exchange for the one they had given them. They decided to keep You Heard with them and marry her to a Ngeniga man, to compensate for the pig that had not been returned. You Heard's parents and brothers told the Kugika to capture the girl and later give them a pig to present to the Ngeniga.

---

3   This may reflect an earlier version.

You Heard was chatting to me when Original Man arrived and went into [space in original] house.

'He is a rubbish man,' she said, an expression of distaste clouding her noble features when she saw him. 'I don't like him. He is no friend of mine, and certainly not my lover. Why did they all have to capture me? Why? I want to run away, but where can I go?'

You Heard did in fact run away, this time to the coastal native with whom she had previously carried leg. Original Man and You Heard's brother reported them to the Government officer, and You Heard was again the subject of a dispute at the Court of Native Affairs. The Kugika told me about it afterwards. The officer had asked You Heard's brother whether he would be agreeable to the coastal native giving him a marriage payment to return to Original Man.

'Definitively not.' The brother of You Heard was adamant. 'His family live at the coast, and I can't visit them.'

Original Man supported him, saying, 'I don't want the marriage payment back. I want to marry her myself.'

'Shut up!' said the officer. 'It is plain that You Heard doesn't like you.'

You Heard was told to go home and stay there until she found a local native she wanted to marry. In fact, she was told, she could stay at home until she died, if she wanted to stay single.

5

Lothario Gains a Bride[1]

The two youths Head and Tail were age-mates belonging to Dambakanim subdivision of Penkup subclan. They had the same bestowed name, but they were such close associates that the use of the original name for both of them would have been confusing. They had gained the distinguishing nicknames in their childhood, when Head had eaten the head of a possum and Tail had eaten its tail. Now they were handsome young men who spent much time attending courting ceremonies and carrying leg with girls. Neither was married yet, though Tail had tried several times to obtain a bride for himself in exchange for his sister, Or Nothing.

Head had lived all his life with Kugika clan, but he was not Kugika by descent. His father had belonged to Mindjinga, a clan that had died out. This man and his brother had married Kugika Dambakanim women and had settled with their wives' relatives. Head grew up as a member of Kugika clan. His father had died, but his father's brother, Sicklebill, behaved as a member of Kugika clan, Penkup subclan, and Dambakanim subdivision.

As the Pig Ceremonial progressed, several girls came to stay with Head— to carry leg, be washed with pigs' grease and be returned to their brothers with plumes and shells. One evening, Song arrived. She had carried leg with Head, and now she said that she wanted to stay with him as his wife. She begged him not to bathe her with pigs' grease and return her to her brothers. Song belonged to Ngeniga clan, and Head knew she was

---

1   Appendix B contains some of Reay's fieldnotes relating to Chapter 5.

betrothed to a man of Bambilngya, a clan in the extreme north of the Wahgi Valley. He was uneasy, for he knew that her relatives would object to her going to the Kugika.

Three days passed, then Vain Tears, Song's step-father, visited the Kugika clutching his bow and a bundle of arrows. He demanded to know why the Penkup had not bathed his daughter with grease and returned her to the Ngeniga. If the Penkup did not give her back to him, he said, he would shoot an arrow into her side. The Penkup replied that Song did not want to go back.

'The Bambilngya marked Song when she was a child of about four years,' Vain Tears told them, 'though they did not give the betrothal payment till recently. I was on a long trading expedition when a European came to Pugamil to take Song to live with him. He gave her brothers ten goldlip shells and some shovels, which they accepted, and she went with him. When I returned, I took the pay back to the European and demanded Song's return. I wanted Bird of Paradise plumes, which I knew I could get from the Bambilngya. Soon afterwards, the Bambilngya gave me the betrothal payment, which included two Raggiana plumes. I showed Song the pay, and she didn't say anything.'

'That's not true,' one of Head's age-mates stated. 'Song saw the payment and said that she did not want to marry the Bambilngya man. She wanted to marry Head, so she ran away to him when her father received the pay from the Bambilngya.'

'I shall come to Kondambi again tomorrow,' Vain Tears said. 'Big Insect and Raggiana will decide what is to be done. If they are not willing to send Song back to us, I shall complain to the Court of Native Affairs.'

He came back the next day, still clutching his bow and arrows. A crowd gathered on the ceremonial ground to hear what was happening.

'I want to speak to Song,' Vain Tears said, 'and then I shall go.'

'You can't speak to Song,' Big Insect replied firmly. 'She herself has chosen to come to this man, and you can do nothing about it.'

A Ngeniga man who had come with Vain Tears complained that another Ngeniga girl had run away to the Kugika a long time ago and she was still married to the Kugika. He said that they had taken the case to the Court of Native Affairs and had also fought with hatchets. If Song were to stay with the Kugika, the same thing would happen.

Big Insect wanted Song to stay, but Raggiana advised Head to bathe her with pigs' grease and give her back to the Ngeniga.

'You will get her in the end,' he said wisely. 'She will run away after they give her to the Bambilngya, and she will come back to you.'

Defecating In-Law, a Burikup man who had a Ngeniga wife and associated closely with the Ngeniga, had come along to support Vain Tears. Now he began to cry loudly.

'When the Ngeniga gave us pay for a woman recently,' he wailed, 'they gave my little son a small Princess Stephanie plume and that is all. He didn't want a little black plume; he wanted a big red one. I'm sorry for my little son, and I don't feel very kindly towards the Ngeniga.'

'Song's brother wants to exchange her for a bride for himself,' a Koimamkup man said, grinning. 'If another girl goes to him, he can have her.'

Defecating In-Law repeated his lament about the small plume the Ngeniga had given his little son.

'The Ngeniga and the Kugika do not fight,' a Ngeniga man intervened. 'Later, when we give you the marriage payment for the last woman you gave us, you will realize that we are not enemies. Now you seem to be deaf. This afternoon you will recover from your deafness and hear what I am saying. Then you can bring the girl and let her go back with her father.'

'When the Ngeniga came here to Kondambi to dance with the Kugika,' another Ngeniga man said, 'Song wanted to sleep here, but we wouldn't let her. We wanted her to come with us the next day to Konmil, where we were to dance with the Konumbuga. You think, Song. If you want to stay with Tobacco Woman, your 'sister' who is married to a Kugika man, say so. If you don't want to stay, come with your father. The Kugika cannot force you to stay.'

'The Bambilngya brought pay for me and made me think,' Song replied. 'My mother's people aren't Bambilngya. If they were my mother's people, I could stay with them. I have a 'sister' here with the Kugika, so I want to stay here.'

'The white man brought ten goldlip shells and ten shovels,' Vain Tears reiterated. 'He said he wanted to buy Song. I said I didn't want this pay. I wanted Bird of Paradise plumes, so I told him to take the pay back. Then the Bambilngya gave me Bird of Paradise plumes for the girl. Don't let's stay here talking. Come back now.'

'Don't get angry,' Defecating In-Law interposed. 'Let's settle the matter and go.'

'We have not many men,' Vain Tears said. 'Only two men and myself have come. Our throats are sore from talking.'

'The girl comes,' Big Insect said laughingly, 'and you have talked yourselves hoarse. We haven't, because we haven't anything to say to you'.

'If you want to stay,' Defecating In-Law said to Song, 'just think. Later, when the Kugika want to give a marriage payment for you, the Ngeniga won't take it'. (The only circumstance when a payment was declined was when war was impending.) 'That will make you think. Think well. Later, you may want to go back to your father, or you may want to stay. Think, and tell us now what you want to do.'

'You're a crazy girl to have come to the Kugika,' one of the Ngeniga men said. 'I stay in my own house.'

'The girl herself wanted to come,' Big Insect pointed out, 'so she may stay'.

Sicklebill, Head's father's brother, spoke.

'Yesterday,' he said, 'when Vain Tears came for Song, I didn't tell her to stay inside the house. I didn't imprison her. Her father wanted to take her back, but she herself hid inside one of the houses. We asked her whether she wanted to go back with her father, and she said she didn't. She said she wanted to stay here. Now we have work to do. You have heard what we have to say.'

'If you want to give us a marriage payment later for Song,' said Vain Tears, 'we shan't take it'.

'The girl herself says she doesn't want to go,' Struck Arrow pointed out impatiently. 'We're not going to capture her and give her back to you. It is a matter for the girl herself to decide.'

One of the Ngeniga men, who was Song's subclan brother, complained, 'Yesterday I stood talking until my legs went to sleep. If you have a young girl you can give me in exchange for Song, you may have Song. If you haven't a young girl to give me in exchange, I'll take Song back. It's getting late if anyone wants to work.'

'That's true enough,' Big Insect said resignedly, for indeed the sun was high.

'You know the practice of the trade stores,' Song's brother continued. 'You don't get the goods until you have given the pay. We'll follow the same practice, and wait until you have paid.'

'Think well,' Defecating In-Law warned Song. 'If you think your parents ought to eat the pork the Bambilngya have given them, come back. And if you think Head may divorce you later, you'd better come back.'

'The Ngeniga talk a lot,' Sicklebill said sneeringly. 'If we give you a marriage payment, you'll take it,'

'It is a matter for the girl's parents,' Defecating In-Law stated heavily. 'It is no good for the boy and girl themselves to decide.'

Tultul Unavailing of Koimamkup subclan arrived, carrying a length of bamboo.

'Look!' he said, aghast. 'There is a dispute going on, and the Government officer has ordered us to bring a load of bamboo to Minj. It is getting late.'

'That is the work we've been referring to,' Big Insect said. 'Let us settle this matter quickly.'

Defecating In-Law walked across to where Song was sitting on the ground.

'If you want to go,' he said, 'get up and go now. If not—well, you have heard what I have said.'

Song left the group and walked slowly northward in the direction of Gibbis, where Head lived.

'Song's brother wants to exchange her for another girl,' Defecating In-Law stated.

'We've talked a lot,' Vain Tears said. 'We want to exchange Song for another girl. If a Kugika girl comes to us, we'll exchange.'

'We have no girls to spare,' one of the Kugika replied. 'If we had, we would give you one.'

Big Insect ended the discussion by pointing out that Song had gone away in the direction of Head's house and by commanding the Kugika to get about their work of taking bamboo to Minj.

A few days later, Vain Tears and his two companions came again. Vain Tears held his bow and arrows, and the girl's brother and the other man carried spears. They arrived at nine o'clock in the morning.

'Vain Tears is constantly coming here,' one of the Kugika grumbled. 'We wait around and don't get any work done. Let us wash Song with pigs' fat and send her back, so that we may get on with our work.'

'We have to get our decorations ready for tomorrow's dance,' Tultul Unavailing agreed. 'Why not simply wash her with grease and let her go? We have work to do. Wash her with grease quickly. If you don't want to, then talk it over quickly so that we can get back to work.'

'We intend to talk agreeably,' Vain Tears said gently. 'We don't want to quarrel with the Kugika. If we don't talk amicably, a fight may arise like that of the Konumbuga. If you keep the girl here, you will all go to jail, just like the Konumbuga.'

Vain Tears referred to a fight that had taken place when a girl who was betrothed went to stay with a Konumbuga man and refused to let him bathe her with pigs' grease and return her to her parents. Forty victims of the fight were still in the Native Hospital at Minj, and about a hundred and twenty men were in jail.

The men of Penkup subclan huddled together at their end of the ceremonial ground and discussed the case quickly before advancing to meet Vain Tears.

'Song's mother saw her come,' the leader of the girl's subclan brothers was saying. 'Vain Tears came to get her, and she said that she wanted to stay. Vain Tears did not turn his back on her.'

'This dispute must die down,' Big Insect stated. 'If it doesn't, and if you capture the girl, later there will be a court case at Minj. Song's brother did not suggest to me that he should exchange her for another girl. We didn't capture Song. She came because she wanted to. If a girl comes to the Kugika, it is a matter of her own choice whether she stays or gets bathed with grease. Bring Song.'

Song came shyly. Big Insect told her not to sit at the back of the crowd, and she sat in the second row from the front.

'The Ngeniga and the Kugika cannot have big disputes,' the leader of her brothers said. 'Song has come, and you have kept her a prisoner. My legs are going to sleep from standing up so long talking. The first time you Kugika saw Song, you thought she was a nice girl and you wanted to marry her. Later you will not think so, and you will want to send her away. It is better for her to come now. Her mother told her to go, and she came. Now her mother has come and we shall hear what she and Song have to say. We'll talk about payments later.'

'If she marries and later leaves for another man,' Defecating In-Law said, 'it will be because the payment given for her was not enough. So send her back'.

'She is young and good-looking,' said Big Insect, 'and we should like to marry her. Later she will be slightly older and she will still be here. We want her to stay here.'

'We have much work to do, and cannot talk all day,' Defecating In-Law complained. 'Let us hear what the girl has to say.'

'A man brought red Bird of Paradise plumes,' Vain Tears stated, 'and Song's mother said, 'This man's place is a long way away. We cannot see the smoke from their fires'. Song heard her say this, and I think her mother sent her to the Kugika. She has slept with Head for two nights, not a long time. I think her mother sent her here to stay a couple of nights.'

'That conversation took place,' Song agreed, 'but it was forgotten. I myself decided to come.'

'I have already told you to bathe Song with pigs' grease,' Vain Tears complained to the Kugika. 'You're taking a long time.'

'Song's mother sent her,' Big Insect stated. 'The place you wanted to send her is too far. She told us this herself. What do you think the Government officer would say about this?'

'Vain Tears and Song's brother wanted Bird of Paradise plumes,' said the Ngeniga man who had accompanied them. 'My own wife is a Kugika woman, but they didn't give me any of the Bird of Paradise plumes.'

'Song used to sleep at Konmil with the Konumbuga,' the girl's mother said irrelevantly. 'I told her to come back.'

'A long time ago,' the Ngeniga man resumed, 'I said that if Song were to go to the Kugika we should gather some food together and give her to them. I didn't see her go.'

'You have kept her a prisoner,' Vain Tears told the Kugika.

'We're not making her stay,' Big Insect rejoined.

Vain Tears and Song's brother suddenly tried to seize her, but the girl shrank back amongst the Kugika.

'When a Kugika girl comes to our place,' her brother grumbled, 'we don't keep her a prisoner. We let her go back.'

The Burikup orator, You Ate, noted my presence and he interrupted to make a pronouncement on the customs of the white people. I wondered where he had gathered his information.

'When a white man marries a white woman,' he said with an air of wisdom, 'he only gives a marriage payment if the woman tells him to. Now a white woman is here watching us, and she has seen you trying to seize Song.'

'Song has talked to me,' Big Insect said, 'and I have listened.'

'I told you before what to do,' Defecating In-Law said impatiently. 'You ought to have washed her with grease the first time she came and married her next time.'

'When her father tried to seize her just now,' Good Bird stated, 'she held Mountain Tree's leg and she hung on to Witchcraft So, and we told them not to hold her. You saw it happen.'

That was indeed what had happened. The Penkup had allowed Song to shrink against them and cling to them, but they had not held her.

'I talked to the girl myself,' Defecating In-Law said. 'I told her that if she married Head he would send her away.'

'One old man,' said Raggiana obliquely, not looking at Vain Tears, 'stood up and talked about eating pork. He said nothing about marriage payments. We are not cross with him.'

Big Insect spoke to Song: 'Your father came to get you. Do you want to stay or go back? Have we kept you here against your will?'

'I want to stay,' Song declared.

Defecating In-Law said that Head had been silent all this time.

'What do you want me to say?' Head asked him. 'If you want to wash her with grease, that is all right. If you want her to stay, that is all right.'

'At first,' Big Insect said, 'we wanted to wash her with grease, and we prepared some valuables to give her brothers. But Song said that she wanted to stay. That is all right; she can stay.'

'Head is an attractive young man,' You Ate said without malice. 'The Konumbuga girl House Tongue wants to marry him, but she can't because she is already betrothed to another man. Another Konumbuga girl has carried leg with Head, and if she comes to him later we'll keep her.'

'We're not talking about later,' Vain Tears objected. 'I want to take Song back now. The Kugika have to dance at Konmil tomorrow, and you will all have to be in good breath. We can't stay here talking all the time, but we shall stay until you give us the girl.'

Konangil and Tail, both age-mates of Head, were whispering together. They agreed that if the Ngeniga tried again to seize Song they would hold her and help her to escape.

'We want to go,' Vain Tears resumed. 'We shall go as soon as Song is ready to come with us.'

'We have talked enough,' said Tail's father. 'The girl is adamant in wanting to stay. It is a matter for her.'

'The first time Song visited the Kugika,' Vain Tears remembered, 'she came to a courting ceremony. Later, she came with the dancers for the Pig Ceremonial. Then she came with us when we brought plumes and shells for your Pig Ceremonial. Then she came again. Now her fathers want to take her back. Her own father wanted to seize her, but she resisted and held on to the Kugika man.'

'The *luluai* has asked the boy and the girl what they want to do,' one of the Ngeniga men said. 'That is not enough. I want to see the two girls together. If Tobacco Woman and Song come and sit down together, that will be all right.'

'If Tobacco Woman and Song come at once and say that they want to stay,' Vain Tears echoed, 'that will be all right. But Tobacco Woman hasn't come.'

'When a man asks a woman something,' Defecating In-Law stated wisely, 'she does not tell him what she thinks. She only tells women what she thinks.'

Song and Head drifted away from the crowd and began to walk towards Gibbis.

'You can see for yourselves,' Sicklebill said, 'that the girl herself wants to stay.'

'Why had Head taken Song away?' Vain Tears demanded, but nobody heeded him.

'I'm going home,' said Defecating In-Law. 'I can't be bothered talking any more.'

'Now that you've heard it all,' Big Insect said to the Ngeniga men, 'you can go back. The girl held the men's legs when you tried to take her back. You saw her. There is no point in talking further. We have work to do.'

'Don't go!' Vain Tears commanded. 'Stay here!'

Big Insect laughed, shrugged, and walked a little distance away.

'What do you think?' one of the Ngeniga men said to Raggiana. 'Is the dispute over?'

'No,' Raggiana answered, 'it is not over'.

'It is all right for you and us to go when the dispute is over,' Vain Tears said. 'But it is not over yet, and all the Kugika are going.'

'We have plenty of work,' said Raggiana, 'but we cannot go while Vain Tears is still here'.

'Say something clearly and quickly,' Big Insect commanded, 'and I shall hear it and go. I myself have a few words to speak, and then I shall go. Song came to us, and she and Head said that they wanted to marry. We told the girl to go back, but she didn't want to.'

'Her mother and Vain Tears sent her to the Kugika,' ventured one of the Ngeniga men, 'but her brother thinks otherwise'.

'We have heard all this before,' Defecating In-Law protested. 'The *luluai* spoke truly about Song.'

'If she wants to come,' Song's brother said, 'let her come quickly. You have heard her say that she wants to stay.'

'Tomorrow,' Big Insect reminded the Kugika, 'we have a big dance at Konmil. Now we have finished talking about Song.'

Raggiana shouldered his hatchet and departed while Big Insect was talking. Then Big Insect himself left. The crowd of Penkup people dispersed when their own leaders had gone. Two young men stayed to gossip with some of the Koimamkup.

'Before,' a Ngeniga man said to Vain Tears, 'the Kugika and Kondiga fought. The Ngeniga are not going to fight the Kugika. If the girl wants to stay here, let us go without her.'

'We're not talking about fighting,' one of the Koimamkup men protested. 'If we don't settle this matter, we shan't be able to dance well tomorrow.'

'It is true,' said Sicklebill, who had not gone far, 'that if we have disputes on the dancing ground we shall not be able to dance well. Let us go somewhere else. We have talked about Song, and Song has gone back to Gibbis with Head. What is this talk about the Kondiga? We have no quarrel with the Ngeniga. It was the girl's idea to stay here.'

Vain Tears visited the Kugika again the next morning, but they were busy preparing for the big dance at Konmil and refused to discuss the matter further. He asked them to give Song back to him. When they refused, he promised that if they were to give her to him he would bathe her with pigs' grease and give her back to them. The Penkup laughed. 'You would be more likely to bathe her with pigs' grease and give her to the Bambilngya,' they said.

A couple of days later, Vain Tears came again and seized Song. The Penkup did not resist him, but let him drag her back to Pugamil. 'Never mind,' they told one another. 'Later she will run away and come to Head again.'

* * * *

Several months passed, and the Kugika recognized that Head had lost Song. He continued to carry leg with other girls. House Tongue, the Konumbuga girl who had previously expressed her intention of marrying him, stayed with him for a few days and was bathed in pigs' grease and returned to her parents with a payment of plumes, shells, two hatchets, and a dog. She told Head that she would come again and stay to be his wife.

Ginger, the full brother of House Tongue, had arranged to give her to the Djegga of the northern Wahgi in exchange for a bride for himself. Ginger already had one wife, Witchcraft Flower, who was a mature woman, but he wanted a young wife. Head knew that Ginger would object strongly if House Tongue wanted to marry him.

House Tongue arrived one evening to stay with Head, and the men of Penkup subclan met on the ceremonial ground the next morning to discuss what they were going to do. Opinions varied as to whether they should allow the Konumbuga to take her back. Head had already lost Song, and all were in favour of House Tongue staying and marrying him, but there was little agreement on what resistance, if any, they should offer the Konumbuga when Ginger and his friends came to take her away. A Pingya man who was visiting the Penkup had a lot to say. The Kugika, he said, should help the Konumbuga to take House Tongue back in order that Ginger might obtain another girl in exchange for her. Tail, who was still hoping to obtain a bride in exchange for his sister, Or Nothing, echoed this opinion. Big Insect was against giving House Tongue back. He listened attentively while Dog, the young Koimamkup man, who was related to the Konumbuga, outlined a scheme for keeping her. Dog suggested that they should allow the Konumbuga to take House Tongue as far as the clump of strong bamboo that grew on the ceremonial ground. Then, having allayed the Konumbuga's suspicions, they could rescue House Tongue from her captors and take her back to Gibbis.

They could do this with little violence, he said, if they managed to surprise the Konumbuga. They did not want to fight their 'brothers-in-law', the Konumbuga. Big Insect approved of Dog's suggestion.

Sicklebill and Head did not take an active part in the discussions, but their views were well known. They wanted House Tongue to remain, but they were not willing to do anything to ensure this against the wishes of the strong Penkup group. Raggiana and Good Bird said that they would not resist the Konumbuga's attempts to take House Tongue, as they did not wish the Konumbuga to get the impression that the Kugika were determined to keep her. At the same time, they said, it was plain that Head had lost Song because he did not guard her closely and prevent the Ngeniga from finding her.

The Konumbuga arrived the next morning to settle the fate of House Tongue.

'We have come to take House Tongue back,' announced Stony, her half-brother.

House Tongue, who had slept with You Ate's Konumbuga wife, You Did, at Kondambi, strolled on to the ceremonial ground.

'Are you cross,' her mother asked her, 'that you have run away from us?'

'No,' House Tongue answered, 'I am not cross. I want to get married, that is all. I am tired of staying at Pagnga, and have come here.'

Witchcraft Flower, the wife of Ginger, looked at the girl and said scathingly, 'Your stomach is fat and your nose is so close to your eyes that you look as if you only have eyes. We have looked after you well, and you have grown big. So think well. Do you want to be with your mother's brothers and your father's sister, that you come here?'

'My mother's brothers and my father's sister may die,' said House Tongue 'but I shall stay here'.

Stony said, 'We have brought back your dog, the hatchets, and the shells the Kugika gave us when you stayed with Head last time. The Kugika can take these things back, and you can come back with us.'

'Did your mother tell you to come?' asked Witchcraft Flower.

'This woman and I,' said House Tongue, indicating her mother with a deprecating gesture, 'do not hold hands and sleep together. I myself came because I wanted to.'

'Well,' said Witchcraft Flower, 'You can marry Head if he gives his sister to Ginger to marry. I need someone to help me with the pigs.'

Silence greeted this remark, for everyone knew that Head had no sister. The mother of House Tongue grew impatient.

'We came here early in the morning,' she complained. 'Now the sun has come up strongly, so come with us and let us go.'

'House Tongue only sleeps in men's houses,' Witchcraft Flower said nastily. 'She never sleeps in women's houses.'

'You Kugika haven't bathed House Tongue in pigs' grease,' Stony said accusingly. 'I am waiting for you to do so.'

'I don't want to be washed with grease,' House Tongue protested. 'I want to be married.'

Stony looked enquiringly at the Kugika. They were mostly sitting around munching groundnuts, relic of a recent exchange between clans.

'We have nothing to say,' a Koimamkup man told Stony. 'If you have anything to say to House Tongue, she can answer you. We are only waiting.'

'Did you come here to eat groundnuts?' Stony cried angrily at House Tongue.

'If the Kugika are eating groundnuts,' his half-sister replied, munching placidly, 'I can eat with them.'

Stony crossed to where the Penkup were standing and sitting. He carried two hatchets, and House Tongue's 10-year-old brother carried the little dog Head had given them. They put these on the ground. Stony stretched forward and grasped House Tongue by the arm. He pulled her to her feet, and dragged her towards the strong bamboo. House Tongue struggled with him, but the Kugika did not help her. House Tongue's mother, Stony's mother, and Ginger's wife came forward. The girl's mother held up a bush knife and struck her on the head. Fortunately the blade turned and the blow glanced off. The mother helped Stony to pull the girl along. When they drew level with the strong bamboo, Dog and another Kugika man grasped House Tongue and wrested her from the grip of Stony and his companions. House Tongue went to You Ate's house and was greeted by You Did, who sympathized with her for the blows she had suffered.

'I made you a nice new bunch of cords,' Ginger's wife, Witchcraft Flower, called after the girl, 'and I want them back'.

'Not now,' Stony said, 'You can see about it tomorrow. Tomorrow Dog and this other man can bring House Tongue back to us. If they don't, we'll complain to the Court of Native Affairs.'

6

The Amazonian Mood

A man of the Minj Agamp was always hospitable towards his brother-in-law. You Ate's wife, You Did, was a Konumbuga woman, and he frequently entertained her relatives. Their daughter, South River, had married a Konumbuga man, Westerly, and had gone to live at Konmil. But Konmil is not far from Kondambi, and when You Ate and You Did moved to the temporary village on the edge of the ceremonial ground for the duration of the Pig Ceremonial, South River visited them so often that it was hard to say whether she was living with her husband at Konmil or with her parents at Kondambi. Westerly asked her grumblingly to spend more time attending to his pigs and gardens and preparing his food. But soon his sister Small Cold returned and took over these tasks. Small Cold was a big, strong girl who had been married to a coastal native stationed as a policeman at Minj. Her husband had been sent back to Goroka, so she had gone home to her brother at Konmil. She drifted into the habit of preparing Westerly's meals.

You Ate had given Westerly some land near Kondambi, in the hope that his son-in-law might settle there and help him in his work. The gardens were bearing, and Small Cold often came to Kondambi to gather food. There she saw Good, a young Kugika man with whom she had carried leg before her marriage. She watched him dancing, and told You Did that she wanted to marry him. You Did was delighted at the prospect of having yet another Konumbuga ally among the women of the Kugika. Whenever Small Cold visited Kondambi, she would go to You Did's house and talk to You Did and South River. She spent more and more time at Kondambi.

Early one morning, Westerly sent Small Cold to Kondambi to get some sweet potatoes for him to eat while making geru boards. These were small boards, about six inches square, which the Agamp decorated with colourful geometric patterns and wore for certain dances of the Pig Ceremonial. They were known by the name of the great spirit concerned with pigs. Westerly worked all day at carving his boards. Small Cold had not yet brought him the sweet potatoes by 4.30, and he was hungry. He stormed down to Kondambi and found her gossiping in a leisurely way with You Did and South River.

'Starve me, would you?' he screamed, beating Small Cold several times over the head.

South River helped Small Cold and shouted insults at her husband. You Ate helped South River, and You Did urged them on. A great crowd gathered.

Westerly was afraid to hit South River, as a man had recently been detained in jail for beating his wife and Westerly wanted to participate in the Pig Ceremonial. He kept shouting that he was only angry with Small Cold, his sister.

South River mocked him and tugged his hair, dragging the skull-cap and trade-rings from his head. Then, holding him by the hair of his head, she threw him to the ground. Westerly was a slight man, and South River was strongly built. She let him scramble to his hands and knees, and then she thrashed him on the buttocks with a stout stick. Twice Westerly collapsed, sobbing, and pretended to be seriously hurt. South River continued to mock him.

The crowd of Kugika who had gathered on the ceremonial ground to watch the fight found it an hilarious diversion. They gave a triumphant cry when South River threw her husband to the ground, and they urged Small Cold to help her. Young Dog, whose wife was a sister of Small Cold and Westerly, came forward to help his brother-in-law, and Two Stay, *tultul* of Burikup subclan, tried to separate the women from Westerly in the interests of good order. Two Stay's wife, Apron, rushed at Westerly with a stick, but her husband restrained her.

When Westerly collapsed, crying, South River heard him sob out that he was only cross with Small Cold, not with South River.

'Small Cold is not your wife!' she cried. 'I am your wife. If you want someone to dig sweet potatoes for you, why don't you ask your wife? That is my work, not Small Cold's.'

'Yes, why did you hit me?' Small Cold asked him. 'Am I your wife? Haven't you got a wife? You're afraid of your wife, so you ask your sister to dig sweet potatoes for you. Am I your wife?' she continued mockingly.

'You harlot!' Westerly screamed, rushing at Small Cold. 'You don't heed anything I say.'

'Why should I heed you?' Small Cold mocked him. 'Am I your wife?'

South River intercepted him in his rush at Small Cold, pummelling him with her fists and then hitting him with a stick she grabbed from You Did.

Dog helped Westerly, overcome with pain and fear, along the track from You Ate's house to the ceremonial ground. The women followed. As You Did was passing the new fence around her house, she tested a paling she knew to be loose, moving it and putting it back. She did not look back at South River as she did this, but it was plain that she meant her daughter to see that one of the palings was loose. South River, following her, pulled out the paling and swiftly attacked Westerly with it. Westerly drew his hatchet from his belt and waved it at his wife, but she was not intimidated. She knew that he did not want to go to jail at this stage of the Pig Ceremonial. Westerly raised his hatchet in earnest, but Dog and Two Stay held his hand and rushed in front of South River.

'Whose hatchet are you holding, anyway?' mocked South River, trying to snatch it from him. 'I think it is *my* hatchet.'

Westerly knew that he was beaten, and he began to walk from Kondambi in the direction of Konmil.

'Wait until you are at Konmil tomorrow,' he warned his wife. 'I shall kill you with this hatchet then.'

South River danced around playfully and continued to mock him until he left.

He returned 10 minutes later to retrieve his skull-cap and trade-rings. South River began to mock him again, and another fight seemed to be threatening. Then You Did brought the skull-cap and two rows of trade-rings from You Ate's house and gave them to Westerly.

Westerly objected that he had been wearing three rows of trade-rings, not two. He noticed that Konangil was wearing a *negints* bird's wing in his hair, and recognized it as one he himself had been wearing when he came to Kondambi. Konangil had snatched it during the fight. Westerly alleged that Konangil had probably stolen the trade-rings also. He lunged at the young man, but Konangil dodged swiftly and ran away laughing.

* * * *

In 1963 the Burikup men gave a party for Westerly. He was now a man of substance. He worked at Minj as cook at the native jail and was a prominent member of the native community on the Station. He drank beer regularly at the Minj Club and was indistinguishable in his dressing from the important Konumbuga councillors with whom he associated. The Burikup were obliged to give a party for him as an expression of their gratitude for his helping some of them when they had been in jail. The Burikup men jailed had included two distinguished war magicians who, by virtue of their special position in the Kugika community, were unable to eat food cooked on the same fire as other people. Westerly, being You Ate's son-in-law and therefore a relative by marriage to all the Burikup, went to the trouble of cooking individual meals for the two sorcerers in order to prevent them from breaking the taboo or starving.

Flowers were strewn to mark the path to the party house at Gwaip. The house itself, an open pavilion roofed with kunai grass, was furnished with a long trestle table and lined with benches. Cigarettes, sticks of trade tobacco, and rolls of newspaper hung from the roof and the table was crowded with food. Plates of cooked pork jostled with thick sandwiches. The Burikup women were crouched over fires outside, making tea to serve in pannikins. They panicked when Banana told them that many more Konumbuga were coming that they had expected: Westerly had invited the president of the Council and several other important men who could be expected to eat a lot and drink more tea than the Burikup could provide. There proved to be plenty, however, when the guests walked in single file along the path of flowers and entered the party house.

You Did was wearing the dress she had obtained from the missionaries, as she always did when she was to be in the presence of people from other clans. Her daughter, South River, was helping her. This woman was almost unrecognizable as the harridan of eight years before who had beaten up her husband. Her fuzzy hair was cropped close to her head, signifying that she had accepted the teachings of the missionaries, and she always wore a dress. She was trying to persuade her mother to become a Christian too, and You Did was confused and distressed: she had admitted to a missionary that she had killed another woman in a brawl a long time ago, and had been admonished severely, as she told me, for being a murderer condemned her to go straight to a big fire after death unless she was first baptized and received everlasting life. You Did did not want to live forever, as she would be lonely after all her pagan friends and relatives died, but she was terrified of being burnt. South River did not seem to share or sympathize with these anxieties.

The same year, when the Kugika had been dancing towards Minj in readiness for the food presentation, I had seen South River guarding a reluctant bride. The two seemed to be standing quietly side by side as they watched the dancing, the prim wife with cropped hair and old-fashioned, ill-fitting dress, and the new bride with gleaming skin and fluffy new strings and shiny ornaments. Only from behind could one see how a large kerchief belonging to South River bound their wrists together to prevent the girl from escaping.

Love had been the wife of Stone Flower, a Koimamkup man, for several years. She tended his pigs and gardens well, and she cooked his food regularly. She had borne him a son, a little boy of three who still sucked at her breast. Stone Flower had no complaints, but he was a moderately wealthy man and wanted a younger wife. Both his brothers, Tree and Girl Wealth, had married Konumbuga women, and now he negotiated to marry a Konumbuga girl himself. Love had belonged to Kambilika clan, an old enemy of the Konumbuga. She had at first been hostile to Staying and Daisy, the wives of Tree and Girl Wealth, but she was the sole representative of her clan and gradually she had learned to live at peace with these women.

Making, the girl Stone Flower had betrothed, was beautiful by Minj standards. She was plump, with a round face and swollen breasts. She had gone to a Ngeniga man, Grieving, wanting to marry him. Grieving had formerly been a household servant at Minj, and he gave her handkerchiefs and scent. Making's parents complained to a patrol officer who was conducting a census in the area. He elicited the information that Grieving already had another wife, a Konumbuga woman who had also been betrothed to the Kugika. He ruled that the second wife, Making, should go to the man her parents had chosen for her. Her parents notified the Kugika and bathed her with pig's grease.

Girl Wealth and another Koimamkup man went up to the mountain above Konmil to fetch Making. Apron and North Clan, two Konumbuga women of Making's subclan who had married Kugika men, accompanied them, with Apron's little son astride her shoulders. The Konumbuga bathed the two women and the little boy with grease and decorated them nearly as splendidly as they had decorated Making. Making walked sullenly back to Kondambi with them, plumes waving and a new bush knife clutched in her hand. Her brother, Strong Bamboo brought a live pig and a cooked one.

A crowd gathered in the cooking grove while Strong Bamboo explained to Stone Flower that he must guard her carefully in case she ran away to Grieving. Stone Flower, who knew that Love resented his acquiring a new wife, said that Making would sleep for three nights with North Clan, who belonged to her subclan. Then she would sleep with Daisy and Staying until Love had learned to accept her. Strong Bamboo stayed with Stone Flower for three days, then he and North Clan bathed Making again with pigs' grease and gave her to the Koimamkup. The next morning, Stone Flower told Love to go with Daisy to find a pig that had strayed. Love flared at him.

'You send me to look for a pig so that you can walk about with this new wife of yours and sleep with her,' she accused him. Then she flounced away to get vegetables from her gardens.

A couple of days passed then Love had a prolonged quarrel with Stone Flower.

'I have been married to you a long time and everyone knows me,' she declaimed. 'Everyone knows me and listens to what I have to say. I am just like a boss-boy[1] or a Government officer!'

Stone Flower and the assembled company laughed loudly, but Love continued.

---

1 Mihalic (1971:75) spells *bosboi*: a native overseer, work foreman in a village, leader of a line or team (see Mihalic, F. 1971. *The Jacaranda Dictionary and Grammar of Melanesian Pidgin*. Milton, Qld: The Jacaranda Press).

'I have been with you a long time,' she asserted. 'If you want to walk about with this new Konumbuga woman, you can walk about somewhere else, not at Kondambi. My clan fought the Konumbuga, so I don't like cooking food for the Konumbuga. All these years I have been married to you, I have cooked food for the Konumbuga. Now you have got yourself a Konumbuga woman, and I don't like it.'

'You don't like the Konumbuga?' Stone Flower mocked her. 'What were you doing, then, when you came with us the other day and mourned for the Konumbuga man who died? Practising illicit magic?'

'For years,' Love protested, 'I have been your only wife and I haven't quarrelled with you. I have stayed with you and borne a child. You can't give any of my pigs to the Konumbuga when you kill them. If you do, my son Tree will see. He is a big child now.'

Everyone laughed, for it was well known that little Tree II was only three. The laughter became ribald and uproarious when Stone Flower taunted Love, 'You're cross with me. If you get cross with me, I'll sleep with the Konumbuga woman, not with you.'

'All the other women told me to hit you and be angry with you,' Love told him, looking confused. 'They told me not to let you acquire a new wife when I have cooked for you so long. Why do you want a new wife, anyway? Aren't I enough? You think to yourself: "Love can cook my food, and I shall sleep with the new wife". But for a long time I have been your only wife. Now either the Konumbuga woman or myself will have to go. I'm not going to stay with you while you have this other woman.'

'Before,' Stone Flower said to the crowd, remembering, 'I had two other wives, [space in original] and another girl whose name I can't remember. I myself sent them away. I myself got rid of them. Now Love says that she will leave me. She does not wait for me to send her away.'

'I didn't see these other wives,' Love said, meaning that they were before her time, 'or I would have sent them away. Why don't you hit me, if you're so angry? Daisy objected to Girl Wealth getting another wife, and he shot her through the leg with a spear.'

'Yes,' Stone Flower answered, 'and Girl Wealth went to jail. If this were any other time, I would do the same. I am not afraid of going to jail. But now I want to celebrate the Pig Ceremonial, and I don't want to go to jail. So I am not going to hit you. If you are still cross with me after we've killed the pigs, I'll hit you as much as you like. The Konumbuga woman will still be here.'

'You're a wicked man,' Love grumbled, her anger rising. 'I'd like to kill you … I'll kill the Konumbuga woman … I'll leave you … I'm going to kill a pig.'

'You're not going to kill one of my pigs,' Stone Flower objected in some alarm.

'It is my pig,' Love told him. 'I'll kill it if I want to.'

Apron began to support Stone Flower on behalf of her clanswoman, Making. Earlier that morning, Stone Flower and Love had argued about the ownership of a Bird of Paradise plume the Ngeniga had given them. The Ngeniga had named Love as the recipient, meaning her to give it to her husband. Daisy had supported Stone Flower.

'The Konumbuga women always help one another,' Love grumbled. 'That is why Daisy won her fight over Girl Wealth's second wife. Girl Wealth will never get another wife, from now until he is an old man. But everyone heeds what I have to say. I am just like a boss-boy. The Government officers know me, and they will give me a brass badge to wear on my head.'

Stone Flower and Love quarrelled again the next day, and Stone Flower punched his wife in both eyes. Love went outside early the next morning, with both her eyes painfully swollen, and hit Making. She chased the girl on to the ceremonial ground. Staying, emerging from her house, was angry because none of the Konumbuga women had come to Making's assistance. She herself went away to get a stout stick. North Clan, Daisy, and Apron helped Staying to belabour Love. Love, hopelessly outnumbered, was trying to defend herself. You Did and Red Paint came to her rescue. They were Konumbuga women by birth, but there were already four Konumbuga women helping Making so they themselves decided to help the Kambilika woman who was alone. They tried to prevent Staying and her clanswomen from hitting Love. Staying had already given Love a scalp wound, and blood was flowing freely. A couple of the men tried vainly to separate the women.

'I'm going to report you to the Court of Native Affairs,' Love shouted, seeing Stone Flower approach, 'for hitting me yesterday and causing this blood to flow'.

'I didn't cause the blood to flow,' Stone Flower protested, knowing that he could go to jail. 'One of the women hit you this morning.'

Girl Wealth was standing with his arms folded in a determined way and a smug expression on his face. He had recently been released from jail, and was not going to be drawn into women's fights.

Sugar and Tree intervened. Tree grasped Staying's arm as she was hitting Love, and she slewed round and tried to hit him with the pole she was using. North Clan pulled Sugar's hair, and Apron helped her to chase him.

Staying and Love, charging each other with poles, cried 'Go hence! Go hence!' as they approached. This was a battle-cry the men used in warfare. Staying cried out that You Did and Red Paint, who were defending Love, were traitors to their clan. At last Staying looked at Love, cowering and bleeding, and announced that the Kambilika women had had enough. The women went to their houses.

Tail passed me on his way to the Penkup houses.

'Did you know,' he asked in his gossipy fashion, 'that Stone Flower sent away his other two wives because Love fought them? There is no doubt that Making will have to go.'

Making's parents heard about the fight that had taken place, and they came to stay with the Koimamkup and help their daughter. Love hit Making again, and Stone Flower was so angry that he pulled some of the thatching grass off his wife's house. One of the Koimamkup women told me that there would be a big fight that night. Making's parents and all the Koimamkup would help Making, and Love would call out for all the Penkup and Burikup to help her. Before the white men came, the woman continued, the new wife's whole clan and the old wife's whole clan would come to help them and there would be a great fight between the women. Now that fighting was banned, only the parents came to help the new wife. No member of Love's clan had come to help her. But the fight did not eventuate. Making's parents stayed for a few days and then went home.

One day Love resumed her quarrel with Stone Flower, telling him that she wanted him to send the girl home.

'I have had six wives,' Stone Flower said in an exasperated tone, 'and you sent away all the others.'

'I was with you,' said Love, 'when the casuarinas were planted at Kondambi. See how big they are now!'

'Never mind,' Stone Flower replied, 'you can go. I want Making to stay, and in a little while I want to get another wife. I can't get more wives while you're here, because you fight them and send them away. I have had six wives, and you have sent the other five away.'

'I only sent four of them away,' Love objected. 'You yourself sent away two wives. Were there five or six of them? The first was a young girl of Ngeniga clan, who left before you slept with her. The second was a Konumbuga girl. The third was a Ngeniga who is married to another man now. The fourth was a very young girl; she left when she was still a young woman. I was the fifth. You sent the sixth away yourself.'

'With the name Love,' Stone Flower said jokingly, 'which means "man" in Neo-Melanesian, you think you are a man and can send away wives as you wish'.

'"Love" is a name of the Agamp' his wife replied. 'My parents were in love before they married, and they named me after giving love or carrying leg. They didn't know the Neo-Melanesian language. My name means "love" or "carrying leg".'

'Well, you can't carry leg now,' Stone Flower continued. 'You're an old woman. Go back to your relatives, and I'll take our son, Tree II.'

'Tree II is my child,' Love objected. 'I can't go away. I'll have to stay.'

'He is my child too,' said Stone Flower, 'and I mean to keep him. You can go. I don't want to lose Making, and I want to get other wives soon.'

Their argument continued for an hour, Stone Flower commanding his wife to gather up her belongings and go back to her relatives and Love remonstrating that she had been married to Stone Flower a long time and did not want to go. She began to plead with him to let her stay, because she did not want to leave her child. But Stone Flower was adamant. Finally, he gave her a beating and she left Kondambi. She returned the next day to feed little Tree II, and went back to her relatives that night. Several days later, she stayed at Kondambi instead of returning to her relatives. She did not fight with Making. When I left Kondambi it was not clear whether Love was going to resign herself to being one of two co-wives instead of being Stone Flower's only wife, or whether she was going to obey her husband's command to leave her small son with him. The new bride, Making, seemed firmly entrenched. But when I came back to Kondambi in 1963 Love was again Stone Flower's only wife. She remembered Making, who was now married to another man, as one of the girls she had driven away. Stone Flower was under the impression that Making had run away to another man in preference to staying with him, and he shrugged indifferently when asked whether Love had caused her to go.

* * * *

Ko II, the young Konumbuga girl who lived with the Kugika, had been with her mother's brother, Shield, of Penkup Damba subdivision, ever since her own father had died. Her brother remained with the Konumbuga. He told Shield that he wanted to exchange Ko II for a bride for himself, but the uncle replied coldly that Ko II could choose a husband when she had carried leg and found a man she liked. He assured her brother that he would give him the marriage payment when that happened, so that he could use it to obtain a bride for himself.

Ko II had been carrying leg with Good, a young man of Baiman subdivision in Penkup subclan. She went to stay with him and told him that she wanted to marry him. Good was agreeable, but Shield objected. He said that he did not want Ko II to marry yet. When Good pressed him to give a reason, he said that Good belonged to Ko II's mother's subclan and was too closely related. She should, he said, marry a man of Burikup or Koimamkup subclan. Good would be marrying his 'own' cousin, not a classificatory one. Good rejected this reason, saying that Penkup was a large subclan and he belonged to Baiman, not to Damba, subdivision. The subdivisions were as large as the subclans in some groups, he said. Shield was insistent. He had a way of being insistent. A squat little man with a rugged, determined look, he was known as Bozip Shield because the earliest Government officers had appointed him a *bosboi*. He still wore the white bone ring of office on his forehead, although there was no longer any place for a *bosboi* in a system of *luluais* and *tultuls*. Big Insect helped

Good to bathe Ko II with pigs' grease and give her back to Shield with three red Bird of Paradise plumes, two yellow Bird of Paradise plumes, one Princess Stephanie plume, and some other valuables.

Ko II went to stay with Good again a couple of months later. Good had built three houses at Kondambi, one for each of his two wives and one for his mother, Guardian. Big Insect had built houses for Indoors and Goodly nearby, but his wives continued to live at Weeping Bamboo. Big Insect's male visitors used the house he had built for Indoors, and he let the young people hold courting ceremonies in Goodly's house. Good slept with Ko II in this house and the little man who had been sleeping there while Goodly looked after his pigs good-naturedly retired to a communal men's house.

Good's mother, Guardian, was a wizened little woman with a round face and an [word unclear] sense of humour. She did not concern herself with the young people's doings. Her friend and age-mate, Outsider, had found some edible fungi and the two women were cooking them for a private feast. The fungi were of a kind that the Minj people believed responsible for producing a kind of madness when eaten at a particular time. Men became aggressive and ran amuck; women became light-headed and insisted on dancing. Both Guardian and Outsider had experienced the 'effects' of eating the fungus in season. They had made their menfolk decorate them splendidly, and had danced on the ceremonial ground holding spears and hatchets. It had been an exhilarating experience. But the time of the 'mushroom madness' was over now and the fungus should not have had any of these strange effects. Good was therefore alarmed when he heard that Guardian and Outsider had gone mad through eating fungi.

When women were experiencing the collective hysteria associated with mushrooms, they used to boast of real and imaginary love affairs. I knew that Guardian, who must have been nearly fifty, had had an extended affair with Raggiana, *tultul* and orator of Penkup subclan. Raggiana had told me that he was the father of Good, not simply in a classificatory sense, and I had asked Guardian whether this was true. 'How can I tell?' she had said, dissolving into giggles. 'I slept with my husband, and I slept with Raggiana. I don't know who his father was.'

Guardian was now a widow. But when the two old ladies had finished their meal and staggered hand in hand on to the ceremonial ground, she declared publicly that she was married to Raggiana. Further, she asserted laughingly, Bozip Shield had raped her. She demanded, in a mood of great hilarity, that the people should call the *luluai*, Big Insect, so that he could hold a court about it.

The crowd, which had quickly gathered, recognized that she was hysterical. People laughed at her, and no one bothered to call Big Insect.

'Where is Raggiana? Where is Shield?' she cried. She called out for Raggiana to come. Some of the men tried to address her, but she threw stones at them.

Raggiana appeared at last, hearing his name. Guardian chased him and threw stones at him. He retired, laughing, to a distance.

Bozip Shield came on to the ceremonial ground, looking very puzzled. His generous lower lip dropped when he was addressed by Guardian, blinking her eyes at him flirtatiously, 'Oh Shield! Naughty, naughty Shield!'

The *bozip* did not immediately grasp that the widow was hysterical. He stood bravely before her and denied her charge. He seemed afraid lest people should believe that he had raped her, but the crowd rocked with laughter. Outsider alternately helped and fought with Guardian. At one stage Guardian hurled a stick as though it had been a spear.

In the evening, Outsider cooked some bean leaves in Guardian's house and they ate together. They both seemed in good spirits and light-headed. Guardian continued to talk about the men she would marry and the men who had captured her. Outsider said sullenly that she did not want to marry.

More than a month passed, then Bozip Shield told Big Insect that he wanted to marry Guardian, as she was still a widow. Guardian protested that she was an old woman and did not want to marry anyone. In that case, Shield asserted, Good would have to give him a compensation payment for the death of Ko II's mother, who was accidentally killed a long time ago in a fight with Guardian.

The case was discussed the next evening in Big Insect's cooking grove at Weeping Bamboo. Big Insect had the most to say. He stressed that the Penkup, particularly the Baiman subdivision, women were mostly childless and there were few male children to carry on the line. Guardian had two male children, Good and the little boy Man Bamboo. So, having done her duty, she could please herself whether she married again or not. If she wanted to marry again, she could please herself whom she married.

Shield protested that he had plenty of work and only two wives to help him.

Big Insect replied that Shield should be the last person to claim Guardian because he had no children, even with two wives. Big Insect asked whether it was true that Shield had stated that he would take Ko II back if Guardian would not marry him. Shield replied that it was not true that he had said this, but that he would indeed take Ko II back. The Baiman subdivision should make reparation for the death of Ko II's mother.

'Guardian's husband has been dead a long time,' Big Insect stated. 'Long ago we told her she ought to go to another man. We suggested Raggiana, but she said she would get into strife with his other wives. We suggested [space in original] and she would not go to him. We suggested the Konumbuga or the Baiman, but she would not go to them. Has she changed her mind? Let us hear what Guardian herself has to say.'

'My husband has been dead a long time,' said Guardian. 'When he was alive, I used to hit him if he did no work. Now he is dead and I have no man of my own. I am an old woman. I don't want to go to Bozip Shield, but I shall go to him if he is prepared for the consequences. If I marry him and he does not work hard, I shall strike him as I used to strike Good's father. Tomorrow morning, let Bozip Shield do some work—make a fence, or build a house. We can talk more about this in the afternoon. If he has worked well, I'll marry him.'

Guardian walked back to Kondambi. The *bozip* did not undertake any special project to demonstrate to her that he was a good worker. But later, after I had left New Guinea, he renewed his efforts to get the widow to marry him. Guardian was evidently persuaded, but Shield's own wife, who had ignored his attempts to win the widow when they seemed to be fruitless, now tackled Guardian and broke her finger in a brawl. Guardian decided that she would be better off as an unattached widow, and by 1964 she had not acquired another husband.

7

Meri Tultul[1]

One thing I have always felt to be wrong about this book is that it makes no mention of one quite extraordinary Kuma woman, a woman at Kudjip who was a *tultul* when I was in New Guinea. I had no idea of writing a book about women when I went to New Guinea, or I would certainly have obtained her life history. As it was, I met her briefly on two occasions. I did want to find out how a woman could become a *tultul*, but in those days there was a very bad road to Kudjip and only one vehicle at Minj which was always in administrative use whenever I wanted to go west. Consequently I walked to Kudjip and also rode there on the back of a motorbike, but never had any appreciable time there. When I was certain my trip later this year would come off I resolved to get this woman's life history and include it in the book. Now I learn that she has died. I am informed that the Nazarene mission at Kudjip has collected a lot of information about her; I only hope it is the kind I want, the kind that may explain how she could become a government official.

* * * *

---

1 This is the only material relating to the subject Marie intended to cover in this chapter.

8

Wandering Wives

Love Woman was a morose character in her early twenties, quite plain by both Australian and Agamp standards, and with a rare smile that seemed shame-faced and tinged with bitterness. When I first met her, she was staying with her mother, Dance, and her stepfather, Forest Tree, who was her father's brother. Every morning Forest Tree asked her when she was going back to her husband, but Love Woman said nothing and went to help her mother in the gardens. Some of the other Kugika women told me that Dance's daughter was a wandering woman, 'a real harlot'. Gradually I learned her history.

When Love Woman had been attending courting ceremonies for a couple of years, Forest Tree had arranged for her betrothal to a Konumbuga man, Ginger. But Love Woman liked Go Insect, who belonged to the same subclan as Ginger did, and she went to stay with him, asking him to let her remain as his wife. When Go Insect learned that Love Woman was betrothed to Ginger, he told Forest Tree to take her back. Forest Tree bathed her with pigs' grease and gave her to Ginger. Love Woman had some misgivings, because she knew that Ginger already had a wife, but she was not a rebellious girl and when the marriage ceremony was over she walked to Konumbuga territory with her new husband and his clansmen. Ginger's senior wife, Witch-Flower,[1] did not receive the new bride kindly, but picked a quarrel with her whenever an opportunity arose. Eventually, Witch-Flower beat Love Woman with a stick and drove her from the locality where Ginger had built his houses. Love Woman went to Go Insect.

---

1   Referred to as Witchcraft Flower (see Chapter 5).

Ginger said generously that, as it was clear that Love Woman liked Go Insect, he himself would relinquish his claim to her and let her marry her lover. But Go Insect refused, saying that he did not want a married woman. 'When you were a young girl,' he said to Love Woman, 'I let you stay when you came to me. But now you are a married woman, and you cannot stay with me.' He gave her back to Ginger. But Ginger said he wanted a bride who did not go to other men, and he sent her back to Forest Tree. Forest Tree assumed that she had run away, and he made her go back to Ginger. This time, Witch-Flower beat Love Woman and drove her away again. Love Woman went home to her family.

Ginger visited Forest Tree and insisted on taking back the payment he had given. If he himself had sent the girl away, he told him, there would be no question of reimbursement, but it had been his senior wife who had driven her away. Forest Tree grudgingly collected the items Ginger wanted and gave them to the younger man. He was both distressed by the loss of the marriage payment and angry with Love Woman for occasioning this loss. He arranged a further marriage for her and gave her to Oak.

Oak was a member of Aiikup, a clan settled on the northern side of the Wahgi. The journey to visit her family would be longer than it had been when she was with the Konumbuga. She said goodbye to Dance, who embraced her with tears in her eyes, to Banana, her young half-brother, and to her little half-sister, Ma'am, whom she had often minded when Dance was gardening. She had heard that Oak, like Ginger, already had a wife, and she hoped that this senior wife would not resent her as Ginger's had done. Forest Tree was now well disposed towards her, because Oak had given him a handsome marriage payment to replace the plumes and shells Ginger had claimed back. Forest Tree needed the ornaments badly, for his clan was going to celebrate its Pig Ceremonial. Also, Oak had a widowed sister whom Forest Tree himself hoped to marry later.

Love Woman found that Oak's senior wife had her widowed mother living with her and that this woman supported her daughter in arguments. She lived with them as quietly as she could, although she knew that they resented her presence. It soon became obvious that Love Woman was pregnant, and the two women began to attack her with little or no provocation. One day they beat her with sticks, and she ran away to Go Insect. Go Insect knew that her husband would be angry with him if he let her stay, and he told Forest Tree that Love Woman had come to him. Forest Tree sent her back to her husband. The baby was born prematurely and died.

Oak was goaled for neglecting to work on the Government road, and while he was away Love Woman went to visit her parents. She told her mother how unhappy Oak's senior wife was making her, and Dance counselled patience. The senior wife attacked her on her return, thinking that she had gone to visit Oak in the jail at Minj.

'You can't go and see my husband without asking me to go with you!' she cried, beating Love Woman with a stick.

Oak returned, and the two women complained to him that Love Woman could not cook and was not looking after his pigs properly. He decided to give her to a clansman.

'I am not a moron or a wanderer!' Love Woman cried. 'I will not be passed from one husband to another. I'll go back to my parents.'

Forest Tree, Dance, and their children were now living next door to me at Kondambi for the duration of the Pig Ceremonial. The dancing was at its height, and Forest Tree was wearing his finest plumes and shells nearly every day. He was angry with Love Woman for leaving her husband, because he was reluctant to return the marriage payment. He urged her to go back to Oak, and when she refused he beat her viciously. Dance supported her daughter, saying that she should not go back to a man who wanted to divorce her.

Some months passed, and Love Woman remained with her parents. Oak wanted to know whether she would be returning to him and Forest Tree said that certainly she would be returning when she had seen some of the dancing. Forest Tree had a conversation with a man of Ngeniga clan, a neighbour of both the Kugika and the Konumbuga.

'My daughter, Love Woman, wants to marry you,' he lied. 'She has left her husband and has asked me to give her to you.'

The Ngeniga man was flattered and raised the required marriage payment, enabling Forest Tree to return the plumes and shells to Oak. The Ngeniga man came to take Love Woman to his home, and found her reluctant to go with him. Angrily, he turned to her stepfather.

'Forest Tree!' he cried, 'You did not listen to Love Woman. She doesn't want to marry me. You want the pay for yourself and have no other motive for arranging this marriage. Give me back the pay, and let Love Woman wait until she finds a man she wants to marry. If you want your daughter to marry a man you have chosen, ask her first. If she says no, forget it. You did not ask her this time. You were greedy for the pay.'

Three weeks passed. Forest Tree had not returned the marriage payment, so the Ngeniga man came and retrieved it. Oak still had the other marriage payment, which Forest Tree had returned to him, and had not yet used it to acquire another wife. Now that Forest Tree had failed to marry Love Woman to the Ngeniga man, he urged her to return to Oak. He invited Oak to visit him and try to persuade Love Woman to return.

Oak invented the story that a patrol officer taking a census of Aiikup clan had asked about Love Woman and, hearing that she had returned to her parents, had threatened to send her to jail if she did not go back to her husband. Love Woman did not believe the story. Than Oak brought a load of firewood to the house where she was living and told her that he intended to stay there as her husband and take her back to the Aiikup. Love Woman objected, and fled to seek support from her parents. Dance was sympathetic, but Forest Tree responded by beating her and, thoroughly enraged at her stubbornness, tried to strangle her. Love Woman escaped and complained to the *luluai* of Forest Tree's treatment of her. Big Insect held a meeting on the ceremonial ground.

A few tall casuarina trees were still scattered about the ground, but most had been cleared for dancing and the earth was levelled by the stamping of hundreds of feet. Only one patch of grass remained where young lovers could sit and 'carry leg' while a big dance was in progress. A crowd of about fifty men and women gathered to listen to the dispute.

You Ate, the head of Forest Tree's subdivision and the orator of his subclan, was present. He berated Forest Tree.

'You're hungry for the marriage payment,' he said with discernment, 'but you should listen to Love Woman. If she does not want to go back to Oak, you should not make her go. I don't want my daughter to throw herself into the river or hang herself with a rope.'

When Love Woman heard You Ate supporting her against her stepfather, she said that she would like to stay with You Ate's family. The meeting agreed that she could do this, provided that when she eventually remarried Forest Tree should receive the marriage payment, since he had cared for her for such a long time. Love Woman went to stay with You Ate's family, and Oak returned to his clan.

You Ate was a genial, easy-going man dominated by his wife, You Did. They had three young children. Dance called to see Love Woman each day on the way to her gardens and found her contented. The general interest in the case the *luluai*'s meeting had aroused died down. I heard from several people that Love Woman intended to return to Oak, and traced the story to Forest Tree. He had discussed the marriage again with Oak, who had agreed to come with his clansmen to take Love Woman back by force. Weeks passed without this happening.

One day, Love Woman had brought me some vegetables and had stayed to chat with me and her half-brother, Banana, when the *luluai* arrived. He greeted me briefly, and then asked Love Woman why she was staying so long with her own clan, as it was time she found a husband. Love Woman replied that she intended to go back to her original husband, Ginger, when the Pig Ceremonial had finished. The *luluai* was obviously surprised at this, but he made no comment. You Ate's wife, You Did, was a Konumbuga woman by origin, from Ginger's subclan, and had probably influenced Love Woman's decision.

At last Oak came again, this time with several of his clansmen. Forest Tree helped them to capture Love Woman, and they dragged her back to Aiikup territory. I did not hear of her for two weeks, and I thought that her wanderings were over. Then young Banana told me that Love Woman and Oak's senior wife were in the jail at Minj, having been arrested for fighting each other. When Love Woman was released she came to Kondambi to tell Forest Tree and Dance what had happened. Oak had wanted to give her to another man, and she had refused again. Angered, he had told his senior wife and this woman's mother to attack her. Forest Tree was angry with Oak when he heard this, and advised Love Woman to stay at home with her parents.

Love Woman was still with her parents when I left Kondambi in 1955. Soon she would go to another man, perhaps to Ginger. She continued to be friendly with You Ate and You Did, who had given her support when she had needed it. Members of other subclans, who did not know her well, had noticed and commented on her periodic return to her parents, and they knew that she had had at least two husbands. 'Wandering woman!' they would whisper disgustedly when her name was mentioned.

I do not know the full story of Love Woman's further adventures, but by 1963 she was back with the Aiikup and had worked out an adjustment to uncongenial circumstances which were made tolerable by a private plan, a hope which may have been no more substantial than a dream. When I saw her she looked much more than ten years older than she had been when I knew her first. She worked fanatically hard in her husband's gardens to produce vegetables to take home to her mother, and carrying loads of sweet potatoes and greens across the valley enabled her to see Dance and Banana and her little sister more often than many women married into neighbouring clans managed to visit their families. These journeys enabled her to avoid becoming closely identified with her husband's clan, so she appeared to get into few fights with the other women of the Aiikup. She was plainly hoping that she and Forest Tree might finally persuade her husband to settle with the Kugika and save her making the long and frequent journeys, but I came across no evidence that he might be persuaded.

* * * *

The people of Kugika clan regarded Red Earth too, as a wandering woman. I did not know Red Earth: she was married to a Kondika[2] man, one of the traditional enemies of the Kugika, who glimpsed the Kondika when they visited the Government Station but had no social relations with them. Someone had seen Red Earth at Minj and had come back with the news that 'the wandering woman of the Kondika' was going to have a baby. The men of Penkup subclan had a special interest in Red Earth, so I asked some of them for the story.

Red Earth was a girl of Konumbuga clan. She had been attending courting ceremonies for at least a year when her father arranged for her betrothal to Good, the son of Eastern Mother and protégé of Big Insect. She continued to attend courting ceremonies. The Roman Catholic Mission had established a small station in Kugika territory, and two native catechists from Chimbu were stationed there. Red Earth was attracted by one of

2   Reay alternately spelt this group name as Kondiga and Kondika.

these men and went to live with him. Good did not mind her having casual affairs, but he objected to her going to live with one particular man. He and some other members of his subclan captured her and took her to his house. She tried to escape, but Good guarded her carefully. At last, evidently after about a month, he judged that she would no longer try to escape and he set off for the Jimmi River on a trading expedition.

Good was a handsome young man by Minj standards. His eyes sparkled above a flat nose and generous lips, and his face was round. He was tall and well-built, and his light skin had a golden glow when he rubbed it with pigs' fat or pandanus oil. He was popular with the youths of his subclan, who looked up to him as their leader, and the older men expected him to be the next head of Raggiana's group. He was the kind of man over whom girls fought jealously, and his success with women brought him great prestige.

Good already had one wife, Talking Woman, a gentle creature who belonged to Red Earth's own clan, Konumbuga. Her parents had lived with Kugika clan, the clan of her mother, so she had grown up with Good. The Kugika had given her father land on the understanding that his daughter would marry a Kugika. When Talking Woman attended courting ceremonies, she and Good were constant partners and everyone knew they slept together. Talking Woman's father said to Good, 'You two are continually sleeping together. You may as well get married. Don't bother about the marriage payment yet.' Good handed over the marriage payment two years later as a gesture of sympathy when Talking Woman's father died. The payment was a generous one, for Talking Woman had exhibited all the domestic virtues. She worked hard in the gardens he allotted her, and cooked his meals both willingly and well; she tended his pigs carefully, and was never involved in disputes with other women; she helped him spontaneously in any work he was doing.

Talking Woman never displayed jealousy towards other women, and she accepted Red Earth (already a 'sister' and age-mate) quietly. Red Earth's only complaint was that she did not want to be Good's wife. As soon as he had departed on his trading expedition, she went back to her parents.

When Good returned home, he found that Red Earth was living in Minj as the mistress of a white man. He complained to the Court of Native Affairs, and she was returned to him.

Good was no longer interested in keeping Red Earth as his wife, though he had taken her to court to establish his right to dispose of her. Another Konumbuga girl was already betrothed to him, and, being a wealthy and attractive man, he could easily obtain more wives. He decided to give Red Earth to his father's father's brother's son, Good Bird.

Good Bird was more than ten years older than Good. He was neither outstandingly wealthy nor handsome. He had one wife, Creamy, by whom he had two little boys. Creamy was one of those rare people among the Agamp with extremely pale skins. She was a spirited woman, who did not want to share her husband's attentions. She made it plain that Red Earth was unwelcome, beating the younger girl and forcing her to run away again. Red Earth went back to her parents. They were annoyed with her for running away, and they notified Good Bird that she was with them. Good Bird and his relatives captured her and brought her back.

Creamy could not be induced to accept her as a co-wife, so Good Bird decided to give Red Earth to As If, a member of his subdivision whose only wife had died and who had not yet inherited a further wife. Red Earth protested that As If was an old man, and pleaded not to be given to him. He was indeed older than Good Bird, but Good Bird would not listen to her protests and she was taken to As If's house. Soon she ran away again. She did not go home to her parents, for she knew that they would simply return her to the Kugika and perpetuate the match with As If. This time, she ran away to a man of Kondika clan with whom she had attended courting ceremonies before going to live with the catechist such a short time ago.

Good Bird and As If could not go to snatch her back from the territory of their traditional enemies, so they complained again to the Court of Native Affairs. The court ruled that Red Earth should not have been given to three different men in succession, and she was permitted to stay with the Kondika.

Red Earth was still married to the Kondika man when I heard her story from Good, Good Bird, and other men of their subclan. Good Bird was excited by the news that she was pregnant, and wondered audibly whether the child she was bearing was his. (The Minj people did not know how much time elapsed between conception and parturition.) Now that she was going to bear a child, Good Bird regretted having given her to As If, for now she was able to produce children who would be reared as members of Kondika, the traditional enemies of Good Bird's own clan. It seemed that Red Earth had revenged herself on a man she disliked by using his seed for the increase of his enemies.

* * * *

Ko III was Konumbuga by birth. Her parents gave her to a Berebuga man as soon as she began to attend courting ceremonies, but she ran away to another man. She led the life of a 'wandering woman' who went from man to man and from place to place without settling down to tend pigs and work in gardens. Then she went to Fig, a man of Baiman clan who lived near Kerowil, and seemed content to stay with him.

Fig's mother gave Ko III two piglets to care for. The young wife could give them to her parents, she said, when they had grown. Ko III tied the two piglets to a casuarina tree. Later she found them fighting, and one broke its back and died. Ko III was frightened.

'You must have given me a pig that was sick,' she lied to her mother-in-law. 'See, it has died.'

Fig's mother butchered the little pig before cooking it, and she found that its spine was broken.

'You must have hit the pig across the back and broken its spine,' she accused Ko III.

Ko III told her what had happened, but the older woman would not believe her, since she had lied to her once before.

'You were hungry for pork' she said finally 'and somehow the pig was killed. You'd better eat some of it.'

Ko III left the other piglet fastened to the casuarina and forgot about it. The little animal died from neglect.

Ko III did not work. Fig's mother dug out his sweet potatoes and cooked his meals. Fig himself prepared his new gardens and planted all the foods his wife should have planted. He asked her to smooth the earth in the near garden, but she replied, 'I don't know how. I am only a little girl.' This was her standard response whenever he asked her to help him, though she was now a married woman.

Ko III did not greet visitors with a happy shout as the other women did. Instead, she would say quietly and stiffly, 'So you have come.' She did not give her sisters-in-law and brothers-in-law food when they visited her. Instead, she would say to them, 'I have just put the spinach on to cook. It will be a long time, so you'd better go.'

Fig's mother, puzzled at this behaviour, asked the girl why she was lazy and why she slept so much during the daytime. Was she thinking of a child? she asked, but her daughter-in-law made no reply. Soon it became obvious that Ko III was pregnant. Fig and his family thought that she would act more normally after the child was born. But when Ko III was walking about again after bearing a daughter, she still did not help her husband, she still did not tend his pigs, and she still neglected his gardens. Eventually Fig said, 'You are not a normal woman; you are another kind. Go back to your parents, and they can give you to a different man. You may take the child with you—it is only a girl.'

Ko III neglected her baby daughter, and it died soon after she returned to her parents. She stayed with her mother for a few months. Then she went to Kondambi to watch the Konumbuga dance with the Kugika, and she saw Dog. Her mother was talking to some Konumbuga women who were married to the Kugika.

'I think that Ko III wants to stay and marry Dog,' she told them. 'But she won't stay long. She is not a normal woman. She has the makings of a wanderer.'

'We'll look after her,' You Did and Hat assured her. 'Dog's sister, who was married to the Konumbuga, died and the Konumbuga didn't give the Kugika any death compensation. If Ko III marries Dog, this will balance things nicely.'

Dog was a handsome and popular young man. He swaggered a little when he found that Ko III intended to stay with him. She stayed for a week, then she ran away, to be captured and dragged back by the Koimamkup, Dog's subclan. She ran away several times.

Spinning Top, my servant, was sceptical.

'Why doesn't she run away during the night, when it is dark and everyone is asleep?' he asked rhetorically. 'She always runs away during daylight, so of course she gets brought back.'

The Koimamkup assumed, without asking Ko III, that she wanted to go to another man. That was the behaviour expected of a wanderer. They held an informal meeting to decide her fate. Most of the Koimamkup men made ribald comments and said they would like to have her. Dog decided to give her to You Ate. You Ate was Burikup, and the men of Koimamkup subclan objected that he should have given her to a Koimamkup man, but Dog was adamant. After all, he said, You Ate's wife, You Did, had made the girl stay. You Did was disconcerted; she had wanted Ko III to stay with the Kugika, but she had not wanted to gain a co-wife.

There was a heavy downpour of rain in the afternoon. Then the air cleared, and heavy beads of rain dangled from the edges of the long-houses. I heard You Did's voice raised angrily and went to see what was happening.

'What were you and Ko III doing in the house at Mangi during the rain?' she demanded of her husband. 'You were giving love, I know.'

'We were sheltering from the rain,' You Ate answered. 'Ko III is a wandering woman. There is no need for you to be jealous of her. You helped to get me this woman, so why are you cross? She doesn't stay long in one place. Dog and I are always looking for her and bringing her back. She was running away again, but when it rained she came into the house. She doesn't like me, and is determined to run away.'

'Yes, I saw her running away,' a Koimamkup woman asserted. 'I got wet watching her.'

'When the Konumbuga gave me Shell,' You Ate said, referring to a bride he had had about a year before, 'you all talked and she ran away. Now you do the same.'

'Ko III and I went to get some sweet potatoes,' You Did said. 'I gave her some sweet potatoes to give to the pigs. I knew that she wanted to run away, and I told her to go straight along the path and not to linger in the houses.'

You Ate began to walk back towards his house.

'Ko III doesn't want to stay,' he said resignedly. 'All right, she can go if you bring Shell and give her to me. If Ko III doesn't want to marry me, no matter. Go and get Shell and give her to me.'

'You Did won't go and get Shell for you,' Raggiana laughed, coming up to the group. 'You Did sent Shell away. Ko III, when you were at Konmil, did you yourself go to Dog, or did he capture you?'

'You Did went and captured her' You Ate told him.

'Dog's sister died, and the Konumbuga didn't give any death compensation, so we said we would take Ko III,' Hat explained. 'She said she wanted to marry Dog.'

'We can't sleep at night,' You Ate complained, 'in case she runs away. We are always getting up and building the fire. You Did said I was giving love to Ko III, so I was angry.'

'You were both in that house during the rain,' You Did explained, 'so of course I thought you were giving love. The Konumbuga can't take Ko III back, because you all say that she is a Kugika wife now and has to marry a Kugika man.'

Hat and the other Koimamkup women were discussing Ko III's escape and subsequent recapture. She had gone out in the rain, telling You Did's little boy that she would be back. One of the Koimamkup women had seen her crossing the ceremonial ground and had told her to go inside one of the houses, but she had ignored the advice and fled towards Mangi. The Koimamkup woman had called out to You Ate and Dog, and they had followed Ko III. They had found her at Mangi, and they had taken her inside a house there to shelter from the rain.

'We brought her back,' You Ate explained, 'because I want to keep her here until she decides which man among the Kugika she wants to marry.'

'Come here,' Raggiana said gently to Ko III, 'and tell me whom you want to marry. You Ate can't marry you. Tell me whom you want to go to, and you can marry him.'

Ko III was silent, her gaze stubbornly glued to the ground. Raggiana and Shield, a Koimamkup man, took her aside and spoke to her quietly.

'Do you want to stay with You Ate?' they asked her.

'No,' Ko III answered reluctantly. 'The wife he has already hits me.'

'Would you like to come with me and marry a Penkup man—say, Original?' Raggiana suggested, naming his own eldest son.

There was no reply. Shield began to speak, but Raggiana interrupted him, 'Wait for her to say. If she would like to go to the Penkup, I'll take her to my subclan.'

'First she went to the Berebuga,' Shield said warningly. 'I told them she wouldn't stay, and in fact she did run away. She went to the Baiman man, Fig. She came back. Then she went to Dog. At first it seemed that she wanted to stay, but then she began to run away. Now she doesn't want to go to another Kugika. She will run away soon to another clan. That is the way of wandering women. Ask her again, and if she wants to go to the Penkup she can do so.'

Shield left as Two Stay arrived.

'I'll go by this little path behind the long-houses,' Ko III said, 'to avoid the crowd on the ceremonial ground.'

Raggiana showed her the way to Penkup territory, but Two Stay, the *tultul* of Burikup subclan, blocked their path.

'This morning you said you wanted to go to [space in original],' he told Ko III, naming a Burikup youth. 'Now you talk differently. You can't sneak away like that. If you want to go to the Penkup, go through the ceremonial ground.'

'I don't want to go to the ceremonial group,' Ko III protested. 'There are too many people.'

'You ran away to Tunambauolg and were brought back, and then you ran away to Mangi and were brought back,' Raggiana said. 'It is better to go through the ceremonial ground and let everyone know what you're doing.'

'First she says one thing,' Two Stay grumbled, 'and then she says another. She won't stay permanently with any man.'

'If she doesn't,' Raggiana observed, 'everyone will call her a wandering woman.'

Ko III burst into tears.

'You Did hits me,' she wailed. 'I don't want to stay with You Ate.'

'Come,' said Raggiana, leading the way to the entrance of the ceremonial ground.

'Come, hurry up!' Two Stay urged Ko III. 'I can't understand you. In the morning you say one thing, and in the afternoon you say something different.'

'Wait until Shield comes back,' Raggiana suggested, 'and hear what the Koimamkup have to say'.

'This girl will run away,' Two Stay said, 'if we give her to another man'.

Wood Stone, who was the father of [space in original] had joined the group.

'You Ate told me that she would stay with him until she was given to another man,' he said now. 'I want to take her for [space in original] has been sleeping with other men's wives, and I am continually paying out plumes and shells as compensation for his adultery. It would be cheaper for me if I could take this woman and give my son a wife of his own.'

'We asked her once,' Raggiana said, turning back, 'what she wanted to do. We asked her, "Do you want to stay with You Ate". She said, "No, I shall go to the Penkup."'

Raggiana took Ko III into his long-house, and some of the others followed.

'You didn't consult You Ate when you brought Ko III here,' said Sinning, the Koimamkup woman who had seen Ko III running away in the rain. 'He will be angry, because he is a Burikup man.'

'Shield asked her whether she wanted to stay with You Ate,' Raggiana replied. 'She answered that she wanted to go with me. I thought You Ate had given her to me, as he did not object when I brought her here.'

'He will be angry,' Sinning insisted, 'because we didn't bring Shell when you took Ko III'. She turned upon the girl. 'Your father was a real man, not a wild pig, so why do you run away? I got wet watching this girl run away. Dog said, Ko III doesn't come into the house and cook my food, so she can marry You Ate. But she didn't like You Ate and she ran away. I got wet watching her. You Ate followed her to Mangi to bring her back, and You Did thought he was giving love to Ko III and got angry with him.'

'She told Shield she wanted to come to the Penkup,' Raggiana repeated. 'I didn't tell her to come to the Penkup.'

'Let's talk on the ceremonial ground,' Sinning suggested, 'not in a Penkup long-house. If she says the same then, the Penkup can have her.'

Ko III protested almost inaudibly that she did not want to go out among the people.

'Her father looked after me,' Sinning explained to Raggiana, 'so I have to watch her interests. Come with me, Ko III.'

Wood Stone entered Raggiana's long-house.

'Hat brought her to give to the orator [space in original] and the orator gave her to Dog when she said that was the man she wanted to marry,' he said. '[space in original] and Dog were both Koimamkup. Then Dog gave her to the Burikup. If she doesn't like You Ate, there are other Burikup men.'

Good Bird, who was secondary leader to both Raggiana and Big Insect, bent and peered under the roof of the long-house without entering.

'Bring Ko III to the ceremonial ground,' he advised Raggiana. 'This is a matter that affects all three subclans.'

'Come,' said Wood Stone, taking Ko III's hand. 'If you like a particular man, you can marry him. If not, we'll marry you to someone who has no wife.'

'If she had been given to Penkup,' Good Bird said bitterly, 'there are plenty of men she could marry, for there are plenty of men who have no wives.'

'If later she leaves the man and comes to the Penkup,' Raggiana said, aware of Ko III's habit of running away, 'we can't give her back to the Koimamkup or Burikup. You Ate said he didn't want her, and put his finger to his nose to show that he was speaking the truth. If she comes to Penkup, we can't give her back.'

'What is there to say?' Tultul Spear of Koimamkup subclan asked the assembled company. 'She doesn't like one man, so he gives her to another. She doesn't like the new man, so he gives her to someone else. She won't stay with You Ate, that is clear. If she knows a man she wants to marry, she can go to him—so long as he is a Kugika.'

Some of the men left to investigate a complaint about a pig. Among them were Tultul Two Stay and Wood Stone.

'If Two Stay and Wood Stone come to get the woman Ko III,' Raggiana said, 'I can't give her to them. If she comes to the Penkup, we'll keep her.'

'I wanted to marry her myself,' one of the Penkup men grinned, 'but the Burikup said I couldn't.'

'If she says today that she wants to marry some man, she can,' Spear pronounced. 'If not, she can wait. If she says tomorrow that she wants to marry someone, she can. If not, she can wait. There is no hurry.'

Later that afternoon, when Raggiana was busy elsewhere, Two Stay and Wood Stone went to his long-house and dragged Ko III away to You Ate's house. They were determined that the Penkup should not marry her.

A couple of days later, Konangil told me that Ko III had run away to him. He said he was pleased that she had done so but was afraid that he would not have enough valuables to give her family if she should become pregnant to him. Konangil said in a bored voice that Ko III was not a very good-looking woman and he did not like her particularly, but she had insisted on going to him. Knowing that he was a good actor, I did not know whether to believe him or not.

A little later, I saw Tail and asked him where Ko III was.

'Haven't you heard?' he asked me. 'Together Small captured Ko III from the Burikup and gave her to Konangil. She didn't like Konangil, so she has run away again and Together Small is very angry.'

It took me some time to learn the true story. When Raggiana learned that Two Stay and Wood Stone had taken Ko III back, he had a long discussion with Two Stay (as one *tultul* to another), who agreed to let him have Ko III for Konangil. Raggiana gave her to Konangil. Konangil had heard the other men's ribald joking and knew that they all considered Ko III to be a wandering woman. He watched her as she cooked some food for him. Like all Minj men, he had wanted his first wife to be a young girl untried in marriage, a girl whose skin gleamed with pigs' grease when her family decorated her and presented her to him. A woman who had previously been married, like Ko III, would have been satisfactory enough as a second or third wife, but his prestige would suffer if this were the only kind of wife he could find. Anyway, everyone knew that Ko III was a wanderer who would not work in the garden and look after pigs but would think only of men. His wife in name only, she would really be a concubine. Raggiana had even suggested jokingly that he might share her with another man. Konangil threw the food in her face, crying impatiently, 'You harlot! Why did Raggiana give you to me?' Ko III fled.

Mountain Tree's wife, Woman of Waga Clan, saw Ko III running away, and she told Together Small and Original Man, two members of her husband's subdivision, to go after her and bring her back. Woman of Waga Clan told Raggiana that Original Man wanted a wife, and he said that the Kumngakanim subdivision could have her for Original Man. Original Man took her to his house in the evening and tried to give love to her. Ko III scratched him and made his ear bleed. She managed to run away again. Together Small, Original Man, and Sleeping brought her back and guarded her during the night. Ko III ran away again the next day and took refuge inside my fence. Raggiana and Big Insect told Sleeping to capture her and take her back. Sleeping hesitated, because he did not want to break my fence. He knew that I had been angry with Two Stay for damaging the step when he had dragged the girl You Heard from my house.

Ko III told me that she now wanted to go back to her Baiman husband. She said that she would not have left him if Dog had not persuaded her to come to Kondambi. There had been nothing but trouble ever since. She told me tearfully that because she had left her husband all the Kugika thought that they could do as they liked with her.

'Of course we can do as we like with you,' one of the men interrupted her, 'because you're a wandering woman.'

Wood Stone suddenly swept through the crowd, grasped Ko III, and dragged her off to Gwaip to give her to [space in original]. The Penkup men were startled and did not resist him. Raggiana and Mountain Tree, who had been away at Minj, came and learned that the Burikup had taken Ko III.

'I don't want the Penkup to lose her to another group, even to Burikup,' Raggiana said. 'Married women who leave their husbands are unfortunately rare, and how else can we get wives?'

'True,' Mountain Tree agreed. 'Young girls are always given to young men who still carry leg. The older men who don't carry leg have no hope of finding new wives unless they take women who have run away from their husbands.'

'Who wants to hear what you two say?' Big Insect said jeeringly. 'No one wants to listen to you.'

Raggiana commanded the Burikup to bring Ko III to the ceremonial ground in order that everyone might discuss her fate. There was no response. He yodelled to Two Stay to bring her, but Two Stay did not appear. Then he sent Original and Konangil to Gwaip to interview Wood Stone. They reported that he was determined to keep Ko III for [space in original].

Ko III stayed with the wild young man, [space in original] as his wife. She was still with him when I left Kondambi two months later.

9

A Woman of the Kugika

Raggiana had married his first wife, Vine, when he had been warring in the north of the valley. He had brought her home as the widow of one of the vanquished, and with her was her small daughter, Cass, whom Raggiana learned to treat as his own. Cass was about nine years old when Original, son of both Raggiana and Vine, was born.

Raggiana acquired other wives including Spinach, who bore him three daughters, and Bluebell, the mother of his second son. Vine and Spinach joined forces to send away another wife he had obtained, and Spinach and Bluebell chased away yet another. When I knew Raggiana, he had four wives—Vine, Spinach, Bluebell (who died early in my stay), and Woman of Damba Clan. It was a long time before I realized that Woman of Damba Clan was married to him. I had learned that he had adopted her many years before. She was Original's age, and acted in every way as a kind of older sister to Raggiana's younger children by Spinach and Bluebell. But Raggiana had adopted her with the intention of making her the mother of his sons as soon as she was old enough. When her breasts began to develop, he took her quietly and without ceremony to sleep with him in a house where he sometimes entertained visitors from other clans. She did not go to courting ceremonies, as other girls of her age did, for her father-husband expected her to leap straight from childhood to womanhood. Her co-wives were already her 'mothers'; they did not resent her presence and try to drive her away. When she rebelled and Raggiana beat her with blazing wood from the fire, she ran to Vine and Spinach, assured of comfort and treatment for her wounds.

Cass had attended courting ceremonies when she was Woman of Damba Clan's age. She belonged by birth to a clan that was not that of her stepfather, so it was understood that she could marry a Kugika man. She could not, of course, marry Raggiana himself, because her mother had already done so. Raggiana would have to give her to a man of a different subclan if he wished to profit from her marriage, for he could not demand marriage payments from a member of his own subclan. Cass's age-mates were all Kugika girls by birth, and she associated with men of all the friendly clans as they did, but, unlike her age-mates, she was able to have love affairs with 'brothers' who were not too closely related—that is to say, with youths of Kugika clan who belonged to the only other large subclan, Koimamkup. She attended courting ceremonies and led the untrammelled life of an unmarried girl for an unusually long period.

Kugika clan held its long-spaced Pig Ceremonial at this time. Raggiana shifted his various households to Kondambi, where they all lived for the first time as a family unit. But soon afterwards the Kugika warriors, fired by the spirit of unity and the hatred of traditional enemies the ceremonial used to evoke, marched on their old enemies the Kondika and engaged them in a series of battles, from which there was little respite for several years.

The Kondika were formidable opponents who had once driven the Kugika from their territory in a defeat which was so decisive that the Kugika had given extra women to the Ngeniga in exchange for some land at the Wozna River. They had managed to build up enough strength, while living there, to go back to their old territory and risk further clashes with the Kondika. They cautiously maintained their rights to the new territory by hunting there for wild game and by using some of the land for desultory gardening, in case they should need it again as a retreat from their traditional enemies.

Kondika warriors crept into Kugika territory one night and set fire to a house where nearly all the men of Penkup subclan were sleeping. Some of the Kugika took their sons, who were to succeed them as warriors, to stay at the Wozna River. They did this partly because it allowed them to raid the Kondika from several different directions, and partly because they felt it was safer. The most distinguished warriors among the Minj people were by some standards, the least courageous, and certainly Raggiana—who had a long record of victorious fighting and a reputation for innumerable killings both by spear and by sorcery—was one of the first to move.

He took with him Vine and their little son, Original, and also Spinach—at that time a new wife by whom he hoped to have many sons. Bluebell had been with him for some years and seemed to be barren; her son was not to be born for several years yet. She was given the hazardous duty of taking loads of food to the Wozna River until Vine's gardens produced enough to serve the reduced household. Cass, too, was not worth protecting; Raggiana left her living at Kondambi with Bluebell and helping the older woman in her gardens.

The war with the Kondika ended with the Kugika returning in triumph to their own territory. They had often been defeated in the days when their clan had been strong and flourishing, but now they earned a unique reputation for having a strength in warfare that was unimpaired by their being greatly reduced in numbers. They resumed the ordinary business of life, tending their pigs and gardens without interruption, travelling far for trade, taking up the severed strands of the exchanges they had been conducting in pigs, women, and the plumes and shells they called 'pig-wealth'.

Kugika and Konumbuga clans were 'as brothers', because there had been much intermarriage which the members of both were eager to continue. Two of Big Insect's wives were Konumbuga women of Taukanim subclan, and Raggiana gave Cass to the Konumbuga Taukanim in exchange for one of them. The Taukanim gave yet another woman to the Kugika— again, to Penkup subclan. But Cass's husband died before she had become reconciled to being married to him, and some of the Taukanim wives who had relatives among the Kondika resented her presence among them. She pleaded with her stepfather to take her back instead of leaving her to be appropriated by another Taukanim man. Bird, a young Kugika of Koimamkup subclan, offered a generous payment for her. Cass returned to the Kugika, and her stepfather's subclan gave the Konumbuga Taukanim another girl, Smoking, to take her place.

Cass's rebellion was not over when her first husband died, and she did not go willingly to Bird. Raggiana advised the young man to tie her up with a strong rope, of the kind that is used for tethering pigs, until she had learned to accept her new situation. He pointed out to Cass the advantages she had over other girls who had to leave home to live with their husbands at marriage. Her new husband was a Kugika man who belonged to the same community as Raggiana himself, and Original, so she would be able to see them constantly. Their presence would ensure that Bird could not ill-treat her.

Cass bore two children to Bird. One day she showed me, at one side of her unused cooking grove, an old house which had once been inhabited but was now beyond repair. The grass thatching was grey and matted, and tall weeds had grown up through the roof.

'My children,' Cass told me. 'We put them in there.'

We trampled down the undergrowth to approach the doorway. It was fastened with cross-bars which had the driftwood appearance of wood that is long exposed to the weather. A small snake rustled in the undergrowth. Cass tore away some of the cobwebs and removed the cross-bars. We could see, just inside, the dim shapes of two bundles wrapped in mouldy bark cloth and *lap-lap* material, lying side by side.

'They just fell sick and died,' Cass told me flatly. Then she began to relate with a sudden surge of anger, something Bird had done. I had witnessed many quarrels between them. Trouble between Bird and Cass was not simply a domestic concern of a man and his wife, but a substantial threat to the traditional friendly relations between the two largest subclans of Kugika clan. Their quarrels were nearly everyone's concern, and their brawling was a signal for people to drop what they were doing to watch for the outcome. They had publicly voiced many grievances against each other, but these were often incidental to their deepest resentments.

I knew of the custom of depositing valuables with the dead. A person was ordinarily buried in a shallow grave, but an important man was laid inside a little house or mausoleum where his relatives might visit and watch him decay. They would decorate the body as for a great dance, with the richest plumes arranged about his head, goldlip shell at his throat, and green snailshell at his waist. These ornaments were removed from a man of no importance when he was lowered into the grave. But if the dead man were someone of renown, the decorations were offered with other valuables as a tribute to his greatness and a guarantee that the relatives who provided them had not hoped to benefit from his death. I had seen tubes of costly powdered paint emptied over a corpse, and valuable shells smashed into fragments to be strewn over it in an extravagant gesture.

Parents might demonstrate their grief at the loss of a well-loved child by treating the body in some respects as if it were that of a person of eminence. The dead child had this importance only for two people, the mother and the father. Parties of men visited the charnel house of a great man to see for themselves that the flesh had fallen away from the bones, then together gathered the bones and together disposed of the valuables. There were no clear rules a mother and father could follow if they decided to treat a dead child as a person of importance. The usual solution was to bury the child in an ordinary grave and, if they wanted to demonstrate that he had been especially important to them, they might build a little house on top of the grave. But Cass and Bird wanted to keep their children with them, even in death. They placed the bodies in Bird's house and fastened the entrance. Evidently neither parent felt any real obligation to watch the progress of decay and decide the fate of the children's bones. Each went to the house occasionally, removed the cross-bars blocking the doorway, looked upon the two bundles, and thought about the children.

On one such visit, Cass told me, she discovered that Bird had removed the valuables they had deposited there. The horror she expressed, crouching beside the torn cobwebs, made Bird's action sound like an unnatural crime, an act of violence against her babies. This was a different kind of grievance from the complaints I had heard so far. 'Look at my sweet potatoes! The pigs have been digging up the vines and making great craters in my garden, and Bird does nothing about it … This is my house. As you can see, it needs repairing!'

Bird had another wife, who had also borne him two children. Like the two who had died, they were a boy and a girl. Their mother had called the little girl Cass after her co-wife. But Cass had always resented Bird taking a second wife and, to prevent her from making it intolerable for the other woman to remain, Bird had built the two women's houses a mile away from each other. This woman told me her real name, but everyone knew her as 'Ugly Mouth'. The nickname referred to a grotesque facial disfigurement she had received a long time before in a fire. An unsightly scar drew her lips toward one eye in a lop-sided grimace. Cass was an attractive woman by Minj standards, and she resented being neglected in favour of a creature who was plainly hideous. She was jealous of Ugly Mouth, too, when her own children died and Bird could still stroll about holding his young son or little Cass by the hand.

Cass appealed to Raggiana and Original to help her when she quarrelled with her husband, but they remembered the valuables he had given them for themselves and the Taukanim, and were anxious to placate him. Bird had given them a further payment when Cass's children were born. They returned most of it later when the children died. But they had presented the couple at various times with pigs to rear, and they were expecting Bird to give them some of the offspring of these animals. Their account with him could not be settled in any simple fashion if they were to take Cass back and give her to another man.

Bird struck Cass for picking up a bundle of pandanus fruit he had put on the ground. She complained to her stepfather that Bird was ill-treating her, and showed her bloodied head and shoulders as proof. Raggiana refused to upbraid Bird, so she thought of asking her brother, Stone Herb, who lived on the other side of the Wahgi River, to come and help her.

Cass had already visited Stone Herb, at Raggiana's suggestion, taking a present of food as a gesture of friendship. This was Raggiana's implicit reminder to Stone Herb's clansmen that the Kugika would give them pork after the pig-killing in exchange for the loan of some ornaments to wear in the dances. As a further gesture of friendship, Cass had woven a net apron for Stone Herb and had sent a message that she would bring it to him on a further visit. Stone Herb had sent word for her to come on a certain day, and she had visited him without consulting her husband. Bird had beaten her when she returned, and then had said, 'You can't go over there again. If you go to see your brothers, they will give you to another man, but you are married to me and I won't stand for it.' Stone Herb received a message that Bird had threatened to kill him, and he came to Kondambi prepared to defend his sister against a husband who had beaten her without cause. A crowd gathered, as usual, on the ceremonial ground to hear and take part in the discussion.

'I just have to talk,' Bird complained, 'and Cass is tearful and angry … You're not a young girl who attends courting ceremonies—I married you! But if I say anything, you cry.'

'I married you, yes,' Cass agreed. 'Well, I'll marry another man.'

'The day after tomorrow,' Big Insect said, 'we'll give Bird a collection of valuables, and Cass can come back to us.'

This was Big Insect's tactful way of reminding the people of Penkup subclan that if Cass were to leave Bird and marry another man the payment he had given them would have to be reimbursed. At a time when they needed all their plumes and shells to wear in the dance.

Stone Herb asserted that the marriage was not valid, because he and Cass's other true paternal relatives had not received any payment from Bird. Big Insect ruled that Raggiana had a perfect right to the marriage payments, because Vine had put the baby Cass in her string bag and gone to Raggiana, who had brought up the girl as his own child. Stone Herb objected that Raggiana had married Vine by capturing her in an old fight, and he threatened that if Bird and Cass were to quarrel again he himself would take the case to the Court of Native Affairs. Big Insect, as *luluai*, ended the discussion as he had ended many others, by saying, 'It is better for Cass to stay married to Bird. That is the end of the matter.' But Bird grinned broadly and could not help commenting, 'If Cass actually goes to another man, we'll talk further.'

A month passed. One day, Cass had gone to the Government Station to sell some vegetables to the wife of a resident officer. She used to sell them for small quantities of coloured beads, which she hoarded to string together and hang about her neck and arms. Bird was talking to some other men in a public place when she rushed up to him and blurted out her story. She had been walking along the road, she told him, when a native who worked as a household servant at Minj had followed her and asked where she was going. 'I am going home,' she had answered. 'You're going to your lover, not to your house,' he had laughed, and dragged her into the bushes. A native policeman had come along the road, and they had sprung apart and fled their separate ways. Cass had come straight to Bird to tell him about it.

Bird discussed the incident with the other Koimamkup men, and concluded angrily that Cass had only told him about it because she had feared that he might hear of it from the policeman. He snatched her *lap-lap* cloak and the scarf she wore on her head, and tore at her string apron. He tried to pull off the beads she was wearing, but Cass protected them. Bird shouted that it was plain that she had a lover because she decorated herself with scarf and beads and *lap-lap* whenever she visited Minj. He did not mind his wife having a lover; what had offended him was that Cass had drawn public attention to her adulteries. Since everyone knew about the incident, he granted Cass's plea that it should be reported to the Court of Native Affairs. He and Cass told me later that the officer hearing the case had asked Bird whether he would prefer the offending native servant to be sent to jail or to be ordered to pay Bird two Australian pounds as a compensation for usurping his marital rights. Bird chose the money. He was convinced now that Cass's attempts to break up their marriage did not express a simple wish to sever relations with himself, but a desire to seek with some other man a variety of sexual experiences. Original said disgustedly, in conversation with me, that Cass was nothing but a 'wandering woman', a harlot.

Some months passed, and Cass's reputation for being an adulterous woman who enjoyed public arguments was more and more firmly established. During this time, she did in fact commit adultery on one occasion with a native policeman. The case was dealt with by the Court of Native Affairs, and Cass had to serve two months in jail. She worked with other prisoners on the Government Station, and had countless opportunities to meet and talk with the Kugika when they visited the Station. Original often went to see her. He told me that she was sad at the thought that she might still be in jail when the Kugika killed their pigs at the end of the ceremonial. In his view, she deserved to miss the pig-killing; Bird had given a large payment for her, so she should have been a good wife. Bird himself frequently predicted that Cass would desert him for another man as soon as she was free. His clansmen muttered that even the Government knew now that Cass was a harlot.

Her mother, Vine, was an old woman and did not visit Minj as the others did. Original and I found her one day going through the contents of a string bag Cass had left in her care. It contained all of her daughter's possessions. There were two similar net bags folded inside it; a blanket, a red *lap-lap*, a cake of soap, and a steel spoon; a parcel of beads which were strung together, and odd little parcels of beads still unstrung; four green snailshells strung on a greasy cord for wearing around her head; a rope of small cowrie shells and a glass jar containing *tambu* shells, which are smaller shells resembling cowries; a spare apron, and a bundle of home-made cord; a parcel of European salt. Vine opened each of the little parcels wrapped in newspaper and coarse bark-cloth, and examined its contents closely. She tasted the salt, and tried the green snailshells on her head. She told us she was sorry for Cass, who had been so long in jail. Then she asked Original to tell the European officer to let her daughter come back to Kondambi and look after my house and garden instead of doing similar work on the Government Station. I had to discourage the idea.

Eventually Cass came home, and she insisted on staying with Vine and Original. Raggiana told her that she must go back to her husband, and he cunningly encouraged Bird to take her back by force. The quarrels between Bird and Cass became more violent and more frequent. They culminated in a great public dispute when Raggiana and others demanded to know what grounds Cass had for thinking she was justified in leaving Bird. The examination grew fiercer as Cass recited all of Bird's trifling neglects—so fierce that I was expecting her to be goaded into mentioning the valuables her husband had taken from the bodies of their children. But finally, angered, humiliated, and obviously ashamed, Cass cried out to the assembled company, 'Bird did something evil. He tried to make me eat his penis.'

Cass referred to the crude insult which, spoken at the height of a serious private quarrel, may drive a man's wife to hang herself. The reciprocal insult, uttered by a woman, may lead her husband to beat her insensible. But if I understood Cass correctly, Bird had insulted her physically as well as verbally. I asked my interpreter from the other side of the valley, who was listening with me, to tell me exactly what Cass had said. He was a Mission boy, whose ideas of propriety were commendable but inconvenient. He gazed steadfastly at the ground and curled the splayed toes of one foot against the great toe of the other in embarrassed silence.

Konangil—Original's closest age-mate, and (like Original himself) an unfailing source of information—came over to us. He told me simply that Bird had uttered the forbidden words and then, hurling his wife roughly to the ground, had tried to force her to comply with the insulting demand. Konangil echoed Cass's judgment that Bird had done something bad, and added that he himself had never heard of the practice before. Bird, he explained, had a friend who was a policeman from the coast; perhaps he had learned it from him.

Bird was plainly astonished by his wife's revelation. The men of Penkup subclan, who had been supporting him earlier in the dispute, suddenly agreed with a suggestion from Big Insect that they should take the case to the Court of Native Affairs and let the administrative officer decide whether or not the marriage should be dissolved.

The Court decided that Cass should leave Bird and live with Raggiana and Original, and that they should settle amicably between themselves the ownership of the pigs Cass had tended. It ruled quite clearly that her stepfather and half-brother must not contemplate giving her to another man. Ugly Mouth had been looking after all the pigs Bird himself had owned. Some had died, and Raggiana and Big Insect had given him others for Cass to care for so that he would have plenty to kill at the end of the Pig Ceremonial. Raggiana seized these pigs as soon as Cass's marriage was dissolved, but Bird sought the advice of his friend the policeman and sued for them successfully in court. The Court's decision that Bird should keep the pigs required that he should make no further claim on Penkup subclan for the valuables he had given in marriage payments. Raggiana had had no intention of surrendering the valuables, and when he found that he had no chance of regaining the pigs, he decided that Cass must go back to Bird, despite the decision of the Court. He and Original took Cass's bag of belongings back to the house she had occupied as a wife of Bird.

Raggiana and Big Insect—blood brothers, one the traditional leader and the other the Government-appointed headman—had lately had many differences. Raggiana had been urging that the pig-killing should be hurried on before the clan's existing stock was further depleted through illness, whereas Big Insect had been trying to meet the Government's increasing demands for labour as the programme of road-building was intensified. Now Big Insect insisted that Cass was no longer Bird's wife because the Court at Minj had officially dissolved the marriage. He recovered Cass's belongings and deposited them with the widow Guardian, whose son was his staunch supporter. Bird interpreted this action as evidence that Big Insect wanted to give Cass to another man.

Cass was concerned about one of her pigs. She had once earned a great quantity of beads by doing some work on the Government Station, and had given them to a relative in exchange for two piglets. One she had cooked and shared with her husband; the other she had continued to tend. She still had a few of the beads left, and she showed them to the Government interpreter, Arrow.

'The administrative officer knows all about your case,' Arrow advised her. 'Keep the rest of the beads. If Bird doesn't give you the pig, tell the Court how you obtained it, and show the beads as proof.'

Bird kept the pig with the others and continued his efforts to make Cass go back to him. She was staying with Guardian, but spent much of her time with Vine and Original. One day she went off with the other women of the Kugika to carry firewood to Minj. The women drifted back at their leisure. Cass stayed behind to have further words with the interpreter Arrow about Bird's refusal to give her the pig she had claimed. Then she set off for Kondambi with two Konumbuga men who wanted to visit their Kugika relatives on their way home.

Bird hid in a tangle of wild sugarcane at the shallow river crossing, waiting for her. He seized her and tried to throw her into the river, but she struggled to free herself and the other men held him off until she escaped. He chased her, dragged her to the house she had lived in as his wife, and ordered her to cook him some food. Cass refused, and fled to Kondambi as soon as she managed to get away from him. Bird pursued and tried to drag her back, striking her savagely and shouting at her. He stopped when he realized that a crowd had gathered to watch them.

It was getting late. A mist of rain had gathered between the mountains up the river and would soon be coming to Kondambi. Guardian took the steamed spinach and asparagus out of her earth oven and walked towards her house. Bird called out, asking her to take Cass's belongings down to his house. But Guardian pretended not to hear him and continued preparing her meal. The rain swept down, and the people dispersed. Bird went to the men's house he shared with other members of his subdivision of Koimamkup subclan . Cass slept with one of Guardian's daughters-in-law. The next day a Kugika woman asked me whether I had any news of Cass that morning. She wanted to know whether Cass had escaped, or whether Bird had succeeded in killing her.

Months passed, and the Kugika were nearly ready, after countless delays, to hold the final ceremonies and kill their pigs. More and more friends and relatives were staying at Kondambi to view the dances, and the women had to go to more distant gardens to find enough vegetables to feed them. Cass had gone back to live with Vine and Original, and was busy helping Raggiana's womenfolk to feed his guests. One day she took Spinach's young daughter to gather asparagus near the Wahgi River. They returned to find three of the Koimamkup women angry with them for taking asparagus from Koimamkup gardens.

Big Insect said that Cass must give the Koimamkup women some beads to compensate them for the theft of asparagus. Raggiana disagreed; the Koimamkup women, he said, had already taken banana leaves from Penkup gardens. A crowd had gathered, and a Koimamkup man who was leader of Bird's subdivision said that if Penkup and Koimamkup stole from each other they must pay indemnities.

Cass protested that she had not stolen the asparagus, because the Koimamkup had given her the gardens. One of Bird's age-mates said that if this were so Cass should cook the asparagus and give it to her husband to eat. She must not stay any longer with her mother and stepfather.

There was a lot of muddled discussion about the extent to which women of the two subclans had been helping themselves to the produce of each other's gardens. Then suddenly Bird seized Cass and dragged her towards one of the Koimamkup houses. A man and three women helped him— two of the women whose gardens Cass had robbed, the husband of the third, and this man's brother's wife. Big Insect, as *luluai*, ordered the women to desist.

'Get a rope and tie her up!' Bird cried to the Koimamkup people. 'Throw her into my house so that I can copulate with her and show her she is married to me.'

Most of the people had built fences around their houses in the temporary village to discourage pigs, dogs, and human thieves. Bird, dragged Cass inside the enclosure he had made around his houses. Cass struggled. The Penkup would not help her, because they did not want to come to blows with the Koimamkup, their 'brothers'—at least until they had all killed their pigs. Cass was trapped inside the enclosure, with three of Bird's age-mates guarding the entrance and onlookers swarming around the fence.

'Are you a girl who attends courting ceremonies?' Bird demanded of Cass.

'She's a woman afflicted with mushroom madness,' one of his age-mates mocked.

'The *luluai* says not,' Cass stated bravely.

Although Big Insect wanted to see that the Court order for Cass to stay with her stepfather was obeyed, he did not intervene when he saw that the Koimamkup were unanimously insistent on keeping her. Cass stayed as a prisoner in Bird's house, but managed to escape during the night.

The next morning Spinach offered the Koimamkup women some beads as compensation for the asparagus Cass and her own little daughter had stolen. They rejected them as being inadequate. But the husband of one of these women (Love, Chapter 6) had just taken a new bride, and they were preoccupied with the older wife's efforts to drive her away. The theft was temporarily forgotten, to be remembered about a week later when Bird made a further attempt to take Cass back by force. Big Insect referred the case to the Court of Native Affairs and Cass went to jail for a short term, this time for stealing.

Cass went across the Wahgi River to Banz as soon as she was released. A policeman named Eating, whom she and Original had known at Minj, was now stationed there, and he had invited them to visit him whenever they wished to get some produce from his garden. Cass went to get some. Banz was only a few hours' walk away, and normally she would have returned the same day or the next, but four days passed and Original began to worry. He told me that he did not know whether Cass had decided to stay with Eating as his wife, whether she had gone to another man, or whether she had drowned in the Wahgi River. He thought it unlikely that she would have drowned by accident, but wondered whether Bird had followed her and pushed her into the strongly flowing stream. If she did not come back tomorrow, Original said, he would go and look for her body in the river. But he did not go; he thought he would wait a little longer. Then Cass came back, carrying a great load of vegetables she herself had dug from Eating's garden, and bearing presents from her brother, Stone Herb, whom she had visited on the way.

The men of Penkup subclan, led by Raggiana, were in further strife with the Koimamkup, whose pigs had been ravaging their gardens. Raggiana threatened them, 'If you don't give us compensation for the damage your pigs have done, and tie up the animals so that they can't do more, you will regret it. When Cass goes to another man, I shall play no part in adjusting the marriage payments. You yourselves can go and persuade the new husband to pay you.'

Cass chose the time when Raggiana had a grudge against the Koimamkup to go to the Government Station and complain that Bird had not yet returned to her the pig she had bought with her hard-earned beads. A policeman arrived with orders to escort Bird and the pig to the Court of Native Affairs. Bird was reluctant to go, and he kept the policeman waiting for half an hour while he went to fetch the pig. Then he came back and said that he could not find the animal: Ugly Mouth was in hospital at Minj, and he did not know where his pigs were. Cass interrupted to say that Ugly Mouth was not in hospital but had been seen visiting her brothers on the other side of Minj two days before.

The native policeman grew impatient. Raggiana had told him that he would accompany him to Minj in order to complain about the pigs that had been destroying his gardens. The policeman turned to the crowd now gathered on the ceremonial ground, and demanded that *all* the Kugika women should round up *all* their pigs and lead them to Minj. Once there, he said, they could sort out Cass's pigs and the animals that had been breaking into Penkup gardens.

The Koimamkup had been murmuring resentfully among themselves. Now three of them spoke out loudly, each reiterating what the other two had said—that Cass's marriage payments had never been adjusted, and that this question should be settled before a decision could be made about one particular pig. The *luluai* Big Insect, made bold by the presence of the policeman, commanded the Koimamkup to find the pigs immediately.

The Koimamkup drifted away, but the Penkup remained on the ceremonial ground to discuss Smoking, the girl they had given to the Konumbuga Taukanim several years ago as a substitute for Cass. She had come back to them with various complaints, and they were trying to decide whether to take her back to her husband or give her to another man. It was a lively issue, likely to involve them in several hours' discussion for several successive days. The policeman had arrived with Cass at about eight o'clock in the morning; at eleven, he was still at Kondambi and the pig had not yet been found. Bird had gone off saying that he did not know where the pig Cass wanted was likely to be, and the policeman had pushed another Koimamkup man in the direction Bird had taken. It was three o'clock when Bird appeared with the pigs Cass had formerly tended and the policeman was able to depart for Minj. The Court decreed that Cass should have the pig she herself had bought, and that Bird should keep the others.

Raggiana was planning the programme of the final ceremonies before the pig-killing and holding public meetings to make sure that everyone concurred. The women were busier than ever, bringing more loads of green vegetables from the Wozna and the Wahgi. Some had already brought their pigs to Kondambi, ready for the slaughter.

I scarcely saw Cass during this period. Once, when I encountered her briefly, she told me with relish: 'As soon as the pigs are killed, Ugly Mouth is going back to the man she was married to before, because Bird is always hitting her without cause. Not even an ugly woman no man will look at wants to stay with Bird.'

I did not know whether Ugly Mouth would in fact go back to her first husband. Whether she did or not, Bird would undoubtedly renew his efforts to take Cass back. Cass's divorce was still not final when I left Kondambi. The matter of marriage payments had never been satisfactorily adjusted, and inevitably the question of her remarrying would sooner or later arise.

Cass's life would have been different in many details if the Australians had not come to the Wahgi Valley and established control there during her lifetime. Her separation from Bird would have been even more tenuous an arrangement than it was if she had not had the support of the Court of Native Affairs and of her family's friends among the interpreters and native police.

Cass never referred publicly to Bird removing the valuables from the bodies of their children—because, she told me, he might be put in jail if this were known, and the clan needed all its men to demonstrate its strength in the dances of the Pig Ceremonial. Cass never identified herself with the subclan of her husband, but she was Kugika by informal adoption and long association, since her mother had married Raggiana.

* * * *

When the Court of Native Affairs dissolved the marriage of Cass and Bird in 1955, the Acting District Officer commented that 'the litigation has been over a period and the story appears to alter on each occasion'. Three years later the court heard a claim by an ex-constable named Dure of Chimbu for the custody of a child of his, Cooking, a two-year-old boy who was living with his mother, Cass. Raggiana testified that Dure did not go to see the child when he was born and had not previously shown any interest in him. The patrol officer who heard the case ruled that because Dure had made no payment for Cass he had never married her 'by local custom' and therefore had no claim on the child of their union.

In 1963–64 Cass's brother, Original, who had one daughter but no sons, was acting as father to Cooking. He was confident that the real father would never come back and get the boy, and he was determined that the lad would grow up as a Kugika. Other Penkup people told me that as Cooking did not know his father he would think of Original as his own parent. Being a Kugika, he would not be able to marry Kugika girls, for he would regard them as sisters. Original explained that this arrangement was possible because Cass herself was Kugika by adoption, not by birth. If strangers were to tell Cooking later that his father was a Chimbu man, he would not believe them. 'But my father is here,' he would say, referring to Original. Original would have named his real son, if he had had one, Raggiana, to perpetuate the name of the lad's grandfather; similarly, when Cooking grew up and married he would call his son Original after the man he knew as 'father'.

Cass heard that I was intending to drive to Goroka, and she pleaded with me to take her as far as Chimbu so that she could see Dure and go back to being his wife. I consulted Original, who forbade me to take her along.

'Cooking has to stay here,' he said. 'The Chimbu man doesn't want Cass. When he left Minj to go back to Chimbu, Cass wanted to go with him but he said he already had a wife and children at home and didn't want any more. If you were to take her to Chimbu and leave her there, Cooking's father would give Cass to someone else. She and Cooking would be too far away for us to watch their interests. The Chimbu has never looked upon me as a brother-in-law, and it is better that Cass doesn't see him.'

I did not take Cass to Chimbu, though she asked me to do so on other occasions as well.

Bird had acquired another wife, Goldlip, and had built a 'women's house' for her at Gwaip, the Burikup place, though he himself was Koimamkup. He told me he had built it there because Ugly Mouth, who was still with him, had caused quarrels between him and Cass when they had lived as co-wives in the same locality. Bird's version of how his marriage to Cass was dissolved was that she had been adulterous and he himself had sent her away. She had wanted to come back to him, he said, but he had been adamant. He did not want a wandering woman for a wife.

10

The Witch-Girl and the Shrew

[This chapter of Reay's manuscript is missing.]

11

True Cousin[1]

In 1963–64 a precarious marriage took place between the girl Close River and the boy Jacob Sitting. Sitting was the son of the mild-mannered Burikup orator, You Ate, and his more impulsive wife, You Did. When I had known him during my first visit, he had been an undistinguished little boy who had acquiesced in all the mischief of the other lads of his subclan and had eagerly enjoyed the more brutal pleasures of the Buri-Penkup gang when they joined forces against the Koimamkup. He had taken part in all the formalized kicking matches of traditional pattern and in games of the newly introduced football, and had managed to hold his own in the undisciplined brawling that always resulted because competition between the two teams was too great to be contained within the rules. But he had never displayed any particular intelligence or initiative. Only the accident of good looks had made him, by the time I came back to Kondambi, a youth who was a model for his age-mates to follow.

My little companion, Banana, had developed from an engaging child into a awkward adolescent—big for his age, angular in stance, shy and tongue-tied in the presence of strangers, and always conscious of his prematurely thick moustache. Jacob Sitting, on the other hand, had blossomed into a youth of unusual beauty by local standards. He was already so used to girls of the neighbouring Konumbuga and Ngeni-Muruka clans fighting for possession of him that his manner was habitually smug and swaggering. He already had one wife, Ancestral

---

1   This chapter is incomplete.

Woman, who had come to him from Ngen-Apka clan just before I arrived back in New Guinea, and already he was neglecting her in favour of the girls who were still unmarried.

Close River was one of the Konumbuga girls who summoned him to carry leg with them. When he complied, as he had to, she repeated her invitation and soon they were constantly being seen together holding hands and whispering, with their legs entwined. The Kugika spent some weeks dancing in preparation for a ceremony in which a large clan west of Minj was presenting them with food. This was a clan they themselves had presented with food sometime before. As the day of the presentation grew closer, the men danced a little further along the main south road, returning home in the evening and dancing yet further the next day. By the time they had reached their destination, all had seen Sitting and Close River huddled with other couples in patches of grass and sweet potato gardens by the side of the road wherever they had had a spell from the dancing. After the food presentation Close River went to Mangi, the neighbourhood near Kondambi where You Ate and his family had gardens and also houses where they slept sometimes in preference to their usual abode at Gwaip.

I had heard little comment on this couple carrying leg, but when Close River went to live with Sitting the Konumbuga remembered that the two were related to each other through Sitting's mother. You Did was by birth a Konumbuga woman of Wogum subdivision. It was well known, when Close River went to live with Jacob Sitting, that she intended to marry him. Her parents and brothers tried to bring her back, but she was adamant. Her father was an old man who had been an important leader, executive officer for the great Konumbuga *luluai* who had died during my previous visit, and himself often called 'Luluai'. His word still carried great weight with the Konumbuga people of Konmil, though he was too reactionary for their councillors to heed. The Swiss missionaries had persuaded Close River's mother to become a Christian, and whenever she had to encounter people of other clans she wore a long mauve woollen dress. Her springy grey hair was clipped close to her head in the manner of converts. Her manner towards the pagans of Kondambi was gracious as a queen's. The European dress and her conviction that as a clothed Christian she was superior to these naked savages gave her confidence in oratory. Whenever she came to Kondambi to dispute her daughter's right to marry Jacob, the air was heavy with her vituperations. She used the rich resources of the vernacular to make puns with obscene and abusive overtones, and her anger was formidable. But she always cut short her most violent outburst when she noticed that it was time to go home and cook her husband's evening meal; then she would stride forward and, grasping the limp hand of each of the persons she had just vilified, murmur graciously 'We shall talk again tomorrow. God bless you.' She did not seem to see any incongruity in being a nominal member of a sect that saw Minj culture as wholly evil and her strenuous defence of a traditional marriage prohibition.

For Jacob Sitting was marrying his 'true cousin'. If she had belonged to a different subclan from his mother, they would have been nominally 'cousins' but no one would have minded their setting aside this 'distant' relationship. But Close River belonged to the very subdivision of his mother's subclan from which You Did herself had come, so marrying her was viewed by many as a serious transgression. The relationship did not bother You Did, who saw her son's acquisition of a wife as an opportunity to gain a help-mate in tending gardens and coffee and looking after You Ate's pigs. She saw getting a Konumbuga wife for him, a girl from her very own clan, as a personal triumph: her own brothers would benefit from any payments You Ate and Jacob Sitting had to make. The closer the relationship between her son's bride and her own brothers, the more they would benefit. If the girl had come from another clan she would ultimately be competing with You Did for appropriating Burikup food and pigs and wealth for their respective groups of origin.

Many years ago You Did had caused the death of another woman. An age-mate of her, from the same subdivision of her subclan, was disturbed because her Penkup husband was acquiring a new wife and she had rallied all her Konumbuga age-mates who were married to Kugika men to help her chase away the new bride. You Did, who was something of a ringleader, went with the other young women to the house where her age-mate's husband kept his new bride. They stalked silently to the house in the evening gloom, all armed with spears, sticks, and whatever weapons they could improvise. They crept into the house while the girl was sleeping, and You Did speared her fatally in the neck. This must have happened twenty years ago, but You Did was worrying about the incident now. Her daughter, South River, was urging her to be baptized as a Lutheran. 'When you have been baptized,' South River told her, 'my father will not have to wait until you die before giving my uncles compensation for your death. Remember how Westerly and his brothers gave you and You Ate a payment when I was baptized? They gave fifty pounds. They could not wait for me to die before giving his payment because I am going to live forever and I shall never die. When a marriage payment or a death payment is for a person who has been baptized, they cannot give shells and plumes but have to give money and clothes. My uncles want plenty of money to pay their tax. If you care for your brothers and do not want them to go to jail for not being able to pay their tax, you will get baptized and make You Ate give them a payment for you.'

You Did pondered the idea of getting baptized. She did not like the idea of living forever: beyond the lifetime of her pagan relatives she would be lonely for her old associates; also, a Konumbuga convert had recently boasted in a quarrel that he would be inheriting all the gardens and coffee belonging to his subclan because the other members were all mortal and he would outlive them, and there had been talk of his carrying out illicit magic in order to make this happen. But the temptation to secure a premature death compensation for her brothers, especially in the form of money, was great. Also, South River reminded her that she had once killed a woman.

'Be baptized and you will never die,' she urged her mother. 'All the enemies of the Konumbuga and the Kugika can pierce you with spears and arrows and they cannot kill you. But you have done a great wrong; you have killed a woman. God has not forgotten this. If you are not baptized you will die, and as soon as you die God will hold a court just like the councillors' court of the Court of Native Affairs and he will throw you into the big fire. The big fire eats all wicked people, and not even your bones will be left.'

You Did came to my house secretly one evening and asked me to tell her the truth about the big fire. The Lutherans and the Catholics and the Swiss missionaries all insisted, she said, that people were evil and that when they died the big fire would consume them. Murder was evil and she herself was wicked because she had killed a woman. Where was this big fire? Was there really a fire under the ground that consumed dead people as soon as they were buried? She had been having nightmares and insomnia ever since South River had told her that she could not hope to escape being burnt because she had killed the new bride so long ago. White people, she said, always came back from the dead; what had my parents told me when they came back to visit me? Had they seen the big fire?

Later she asked me whether I had some magic I could give her to help her win the court case about her son's marriage. if I had some, she said, she would buy it from me for ten shillings or whatever price I wanted.

Man Pit-Pit, Close River's old father, was suing in the councillors' court for the return of his daughter. He had already expressed some reasons why he did not want the girl to marry Jacob Sitting. Close River was Jacob's 'true cousin' through You Did belonging to the same subdivision as Man Pit-Pit. The old man had given his two sisters to the Kugika Penkup and the Kugika Koimamkup; the Koimamkup had given him a bride in exchange, and the Penkup had given him As If's younger daughter, Grass Woman, for his son. The Burikup had given him a girl for another son to marry, but she had soon left so he was under no obligation to give them his daughter. Both the Penkup and the Koimamkup had given him women, and if Close River had to marry a Kugika he would not object to her going to them. But he would prefer to give her to another clan. He recalled peevishly that the Koimamkup did not simply offer him a woman in exchange for his sister: they had given the girl to a Konumbuga man of a different subdivision and when it became clear that she did not like him they agreed to her marrying Man Pit-Pit. He had also exchanged women with the Kugika's traditional enemies, the Kondika. Close River could not marry a Kondika man, because her father could not insult the Kondika by giving them rejects from their old enemies. One of his sons wanted to marry a particular girl of Ngeni-Muruka clan, and Man Pit-Pit was aiming to exchange Close River for this girl.

The councillors' court heard Man Pit-Pit's plea. Three of the Konumbuga 'big' councillors sat in judgment. The Kugika councillor was present, but he refrained from intervening: Man Pit-Pit was his own brother-in-law and he could not have spoken without supporting the claimant. The councillors ascertained that Close River wished to marry Jacob Sitting, and they asked Man Pit-Pit why he opposed the marriage. The angry father, aware that the councillors were already familiar with some of the reasons for his objection, blurted out that he did not want Close River to marry yet but wished her to stay at home and look after him. He advanced no other arguments. The councillors ruled that the government's law, 'what a girl wants' (*laik bilong meri*), should prevail and Close River was free to marry whom she liked. They commanded Jacob Sitting to get a marriage payment together within the next few days and give it to Man Pit-Pit.

The parties to the dispute were leaving the councillor's house at Minj when Man Pit-Pit attacked Jacob Sitting and You Ate angrily. He told them he had no intention of accepting a marriage payment from them. The councillors separated the brawling men. As it was plain that the dispute was not resolved, the case went to the Court of Native Affairs. The two cadet patrol officers who heard the case confirmed the councillors' judgment that Close River was free to marry any man she liked and that as she wanted to marry Jacob he must get together a marriage payment within the next few days. They specified further that Close River must go home to her parents until Jacob brought the payment to them. The parties to the dispute left Minj in an orderly manner and adjourned to Kondambi to continue their quarrel.

I drew Banana's attention to Close River and Jacob Sitting who were quietly drifting away from the stormy scene and going towards Mangi, hand in hand.

'Close River is not a fool,' Banana whispered. 'She knows very well that if she were to go home and wait for the marriage payment as the *kiaps* said she should her mother and father would keep her a prisoner and give her to another man.'

You Ate gathered together a marriage payment for Jacob Sitting to give to Man Pit-Pit. Banana and his father were saving up to buy a machine for skinning their coffee, which was going to cost them over thirty pounds. They had explained to me that they would let the other Burikup people use it freely but they intended to charge Koimamkup ten shillings for using it to skin one bag of coffee. The Penkup man, Head, had set an example in this, but he had cannily been charging even Penkup people who belonged to other subdivisions besides his own and he was growing rich at the expense of the rest of his subclan. Burikup was only a small group, so Forest Tree and Banana could not differentiate between the people of their own subdivision and the other Burikup; but the garden where they skinned their coffee was midway between the territory of the two larger subclans and they were hoping that some of the Penkup who had their coffee some distance from Head's gardens might decide to hire the Burikup machine. They had saved eighteen pounds by diligent work and careful hoarding. Forest Tree cut firewood regularly to sell to the government; Banana's mother, Courting Ceremony, carried loads of vegetables to Minj and gave her husband the paltry shillings she earned when Europeans bought them; Banana had been one of the first of the

Kugika to plant coffee and already it had returned him a few pounds. But they were obliged to help You Ate with his marriage payment for Jacob Sitting's new wife, and their savings were diminished by two thirds. Banana did not grumble at this, though he was bitterly disappointed at having to delay yet further the purchase of the machine. This machine had become for him a symbol of a successful future in the modern world. He was planning to invest the greater returns he would get from his own coffee and the rent he would get from others who used the machine in buying cattle. One of his plans was to build himself a European-style house close to Kondambi which would have a special room where I could stay and be his guest whenever I visited my clan. He did not approve of Jacob Sitting's marriage to his 'true cousin', but he acknowledged the obligation of himself and his father to contribute towards the payment.

You Ate offered Man Pit-Pit the marriage payment, but the old 'Luluai' refused to accept it. Close River's Christian mother supported him and went to some trouble to assure the Kugika that this refusal was not a signal that warfare was imminent between their two clans as it would have been in the days before the government had taught them to live in peace. Jacob Sitting gave the pigs to Ancestral Woman to care for and he hid the money and the shells in his house until Close River's parents could be persuaded to accept them. When You Ate and the rest of the Burikup gave a party for his daughter's Konumbuga husband, Westerly, Man Pit-Pit and his wife had still declined to receive the payment.

When the party was over, a Konumbuga *tultul* accompanied Jacob Sitting and Close River to their house at Mangi. The *tultul* and his wife were planning to stay the night with their kinswoman before going home. Darkness had fallen when the *tultul*'s wife asked Close River whether she had any water and Close River admitted that she had not brought any to the house.

'Light a flare,' Jacob Sitting suggested, 'and both of you go back to the party house at Gwaip and bring back some water.'

The *tultul*'s wife let Close River go alone. Before she arrive at the party house, she saw the doorway of Banana's house illumined by the glow of the fire inside. She approached the house and asked Banana for a tin or other container to hold water.

'You haven't got a lamp,' Banana reproved her with surprise. 'You shouldn't be walking about in the dark without a light.'

'I have this flare,' Close River answered, showing him the smouldering bunch of dry kunai she had dropped outside the doorway.

Forest Tree gathered a more adequate torch of twigs and lit it from the fire. Banana's little sister, a girl of eleven, went with Close River to get the water.

A little boy who had been wandering about since the party went inside the party house where some of the Burikup and some of the Konumbuga were still sitting around talking. He told You Did eagerly that Close River had taken a flare and gone to Banana's house. You Did told Ancestral Woman to go to Banana's house and report what she saw. Forest Tree and Banana told her that Close River had gone with the little girl to get some water.

Jacob, alarmed because Close River had gone alone and had not come back promptly, went in search of her. He went straight to Banana's house when he heard his father, You Ate, calling from the party house 'Ancestral Woman! Ancestral Woman!'

'Is Ancestral Woman here?' he asked Banana.

'Yes, she is here,' Banana replied. Jacob was about to address Ancestral Woman when You Ate's voice came again clearly from the party house: 'Ancestral Woman! South River wants to go home. Light a flare and go with her.'

Jacob, annoyed with his father at giving orders to his wife, gave a counter command.

'This girl Close River has a pain in her stomach. Ancestral Woman, it would be better if you went and got the water and let Close Rover stay inside.'

'Ancestral Woman!' You Ate called again. 'Get a light and hurry up and come!'

Ancestral Woman, confused at the conflicting commands from her husband and her father-in-law, lit a flare and took it outside. Jacob, standing in the doorway, vented his anger by kicking her on the buttocks. Ancestral Woman screamed shrilly, but her husband kicked her twice more before Banana separated them.

'Who is hitting Ancestral Woman?' You Ate demanded.

'No, Jacob is giving her a beating,' Courting Ceremony called back. You Ate dashed from the party house and ran quickly to Banana's house. He slapped his son hard.

'I'm not a woman, I'm a man,' Jacob objected. 'If I were a girl you could hit me and bring blood. Let us fight.'

'All right,' You Ate agreed. 'If you're a man I am one too. If we die, we die.'

Father and son struggled for awhile. Banana tried to intervene but was not able to part them until Apron, who had rushed over from the party house with You Did at the sound of fighting, helped him.

'Why did you hit Ancestral Woman?' You Did demanded.

'Why do you ask?' Jacob said jeeringly, striking his mother. Banana and Apron held his arms to prevent him from hitting her again. Several young men had come over from the party house, but they watched with interest without trying to intervene.

'It is too dark now,' You Ate said. 'Some boys have come to watch, and there are some old women here too. We shall be involved in a great court case if some boy takes a stick and injures someone.'

Nevertheless, the squabbling continued.

'Ancestral Woman,' said Jacob coldly, 'tomorrow you go. I am sending you away.'

You Ate lashed out angrily at his son. 'You yourself obtained this woman, Close River, and you yourself can pay her mother and father. When Close River came I gave three fat pigs and some good goldlip shells and fifty pounds. We are continually having disputes with Close River's father and mother. Now I shall take back what I gave you and you yourself can find the payment to give them.'

'All right,' Jacob said angrily, 'we can straighten this out early tomorrow morning. It is too dark now.'

You Ate had not finished speaking.

'This woman Ancestral Woman,' he said, 'knows how to care for pigs well. You scold Ancestral Woman and she doesn't answer you back. When we tell her to dig sweet potatoes or do something else she just does what we tell her. She stays in the house and acts with propriety. When we are absent she looks after the garden and the pigs and the house and the fowls very well. She is a good Woman. You didn't beat Close River and Ancestral Woman jointly. You left Close River alone and beat Ancestral Woman. Now I am angry and we have been fighting.'

'When I slept with my sister at Minj,' You Did added, 'she told me Close River had told her sister that she intended to go back to her parents. I told her brother Whitewood and discussed it with him, but we didn't tell You Ate and Jacob because we didn't know whether it was true.'

'Tomorrow we'll ask Whitewood,' You Ate suggested. 'We'll send a little boy to get Close River's sister and also Whitewood and early tomorrow we'll hear what they have to say.'

'We shan't wait for tomorrow,' Jacob objected. 'This very night Close River and I shall go and see what words come out of Whitewood's mouth.'

Jacob and Close River left together. Banana followed them quietly without carrying a light, for he feared that they might be intending to kill themselves by throwing themselves in the river or by hanging themselves in a burial ground. But they went straight to Whitewood's house. On the way, Jacob asked Close River whether she had indeed said that she was intending to go back to her parents. She replied that he could hear her version from her sister and from Whitewood. She herself declined to tell him what she had said. But Whitewood was away from his house playing Lucky and the matter was dropped.

Some weeks later Jacob's gardens at Mangi needed attention so he and Close River took to sleeping at Gwaip while Ancestral Woman and her mother-in-law slept at Mangi. You Did still visited Gwaip to attend to her work there in the mornings, returning via Kondambi at noon. Jacob had asked me whether I had any medicine for stomach pains and I had suggested that he should take Close River to Minj for a medical examination.

Bluebell, a young Konumbuga woman who was the wife of my former servant, Spinning Top, had accompanied me to Kondambi and helped me when her husband could not leave Goroka. She went to Gwaip one day to help an age-mate who lived near Jacob cook a pig to send by air to Spinning Top. She saw Close River lying on her stomach and asked her whether she had a pain that made her lie like that. Close River said she did.

[Chapter ends here.]

12

One Family[1]

Kombuk, the son of Tultul Tai and his oldest wife, Mai, married soon after he began to attend courting ceremonies. His bride, Mandigl, was a girl Tultul Tai had secured for him from his own brother-in-law, and the marriage had been his father's idea, not his own. He told me that he envied boys who were older than he and still unmarried, for his work had multiplied. He had to build a separate house for Mandigl at the ceremonial village and chop firewood for her every day, but his father expected him to continue to act as unpaid servant for him. Tai never tired of reminding him that he had found him a bride and provided the marriage payment, and Kombuk was constantly humiliated by having to depend on his father for the loan of plumes to wear in the dances of the Pig Ceremonial. Mai had no further children after Muru and later Kombuk, so the boy was never formally weaned. Even at fifteen, when he was already married, he sucked his mother's breasts occasionally for comfort. His father was aware of this and warned him that his association with his mother would weaken him. Tai urged him to have children, and laughed when his son told him he was impotent: that was what happened, he said, when a man associated closely with women and depended too long upon his mother. I suspect Tai himself may have impregnated Mandigl on his son's behalf, for Tai made several references to Kombuk's unmanliness and referred to his son still sleeping with his mother and leaving other men to sleep with his wife, making his father do things he himself should be doing. When the child arrived everyone accepted her as Kombuk's daughter.

---

1   This chapter is incomplete.

When I met Kombuk again in 1963 he was a young man of consequence, no longer ineffectual, fearful, and effeminate as he had been earlier. Now he went confidently to Garu Wiro ceremonies at the opening of new houses, and at every public gathering a girl summoned him to carry leg. For the most important dances in a Wubalt food presentation he wore his father's *tultul* badge proudly on his forehead. His father had died in 1961 and although he had chafed at the old Tultul's autocratic ways he now remembered him with deep respect and was clearly proud of having been the son of an important man.

Kombuk had acquired a second wife, Waiya, a girl of Konumbuga Pipikanim Kumngakanim. She had summoned him several times to carry leg with her and eventually she had arrived at his house saying that she intended to marry him. He gave her family the marriage payment they demanded. He was pleased with his new wife, his only complaint being that she was continuing to associate with her unmarried Konumbuga age-mates instead of settling down to finding friends among the married women in the Kugika Penkup group.

In early 1964 Kombuk's sister, Omngar, disappeared and was rumoured to be staying with the Ngeni-Muruka. A girl goes away secretly only when she is intending to marry against her relatives' wishes, and Wamdi and Kombuk soon discovered that the man Omngar was intending to marry was a young man with the same name as the old Tultul. Tai II was Kugika Penkup by descent. His father, Tabindam, had gone to live with maternal relatives many years ago, taking his whole family with him, and Tai II had grown up as a Ngeni-Muruka man. Wamdi and Kombuk were shocked at Omngar wanting to marry her 'brother'. Wamdi declared that if Omngar married Tai II she would never be able to visit the Kugika again and if she had children these would be without the useful mothers' brothers all other people had.

Wamdi and Kombuk had a further objection to Omngar marrying a man of her own choice, for they had been hoping to give her to the Konumbuga Taukanim. Wamdi had planned to give Omngar's sister, Kommun, to the Konumbuga Taukanim, but she had rebelliously insisted on marrying a Konumbuga Tausekanim man. A young man of Konumbuga Pipikanim Kumngakanim had given a betrothal payment for Omngar, but the young man had died and Wamdi was proposing to give Omngar to the Taukanim to take the place of her sister. The Taukanim had given Wamdi his two senior wives, and although he had secured brides for the Taukanim from other divisions of his subclan he wished to …

[Chapter ends here.]

13

Laik Bilong Man[1]

In October 1963 Konangil and his wife were talking together. She was a girl the late Raggiana had procured for him from his own brothers-in-law in Dingekup clan. Raggiana's Dingekup wife was lamenting that none of her clanswomen was with her among the Penkup. 'Plenty of Konumbuga girls have come to Kondambi,' she complained, 'but I am the only Dingekup woman here.' Konangil agreed that the Dingekup should be encouraged to send more wives to the Kugika Penkup.

'But you know what happens these days,' he said. 'A man betrothes a girl and when the time comes for marriage the girl says "No, I want to marry someone else", and the *kiaps* and the councillors tell her "All right, what a girl wants is the rule of marriage now." It would be better for you to ask the Dingekup girls to come to Kondambi to visit you. We could hold courting ceremonies for them, and they can find Penkup men they themselves want to marry.'

Several Dingekup girls arrived, and a courting ceremony was held for them. Some of the young men of Penkup subclan, urged on by Konangil, had been hoping that they might acquire wives from among these girls, but the only girl who stayed after the others went home a week later was Gibbis. She had not chosen a Penkup boy, nor even a Kugika boy of one of the other subclans, but she wanted to marry a Konumbuga youth, Hardwood. Hardwood's family had long settled with the Kugika Penkup, for his mother was Bluebell, a woman of that group, and his

---

1 This chapter has been put together by the editor from fragments which Reay clearly intended to go into the chapter 'Laik Bilong Man'. Three major fragments comprise the chapter, and related writing from Reay's notes is included as Appendices.

father was Strong House In-Law, the man who had betrothed her for another Konumbuga man and stolen her from him so long ago. He was accustomed to attending the courting ceremonies the Penkup arranged.

Hardwood was an alert and ambitious lad with an engaging disposition. I had employed him in various ways: he helped me efficiently and enthusiastically in some enquiries I was making, and he proved himself an excellent carpenter. When the recruiting officer for the Pacific Islands Regiment visited the area, Hardwood tried to enlist, for he realized that the Army offered its trainees a good education, but he had not gone far enough in his schooling to be accepted as a recruit. I was aware that he gambled his wages at Lucky, and for some months he seemed unable to lose at the game, but a sudden run of bad luck led him to steal from me so I dismissed him, explaining that I could not employ anyone I could not trust. Hardwood took his dismissal philosophically and we remained friendly.

Gibbis told her age-mates to inform her parents that she was staying at Kondambi and wanted to marry Hardwood. She moved from the house of Konangil's wife to that of Hardwood's mother, and the young people walked about together holding hands and whispering to each other. The Dingekup agreed to give Gibbis to Hardwood on receipt of £2/10/- and a few valuables, provided he agreed to give them a large payment later. When he had given this initial payment, he took to sleeping with Gibbis in the living room of his mother's house instead of in his father's house. He was hoping that I would employ him again and that his luck at gambling would change so that he could quickly amass enough money to satisfy Gibbis's relatives. When she had been living with him for three months, messengers came from the Dingekup reminding him that he should be gathering together his marriage payment and bringing it to them.

Gibbis was a plump, attractive young woman with the pale tawny skin the Minj people admire. Her attentions had flattered Hardwood, who had had some success in the courting ceremonies and was a popular choice with girls who liked to carry leg with different youths in succession but he had had little experience with women. This was the first girl who had marked him as her own by announcing publicly that she wished to marry him. Despite Gibbis's attractions, which were obvious to all, my impression was that he was no more firmly attached to her than he would have been to any girl who had chosen him. Gibbis herself, however, was genuinely fond of Hardwood.

Hardwood killed a pig and sold cooked portions of it for money. He did this, he said, to raise money for his marriage payment. When it yielded him nearly ten pounds, he decided that he could multiply this sum by gambling. He deserted Gibbis for the Lucky schools, and there fell in with other lads of his own age (he was now about eighteen) who were thinking a lot of girls and courting ceremonies. At this time several Penkup and Koimamkup men had built new 'women's houses' for their wives' pigs, and Hardwood slipped easily into the habit of going to the opening ceremonies at night and carrying leg with girls who had his name called. They called his name unfailingly, for everyone knew that this was the youth on whose account a Dingekup girl had stayed at Kondambi instead of returning home.

Gibbis herself wanted to be with Hardwood, and she spent the evenings sitting in Strong House In-Law's 'men's house' waiting for her bridegroom to arrive home from the gambling school or the courting ceremony. She found herself thrown more and more into the company of Bluebell, Hardwood's mother. Gibbis was an intelligent girl, and when she first stayed in Bluebell's house she tried to ingratiate herself with the older woman. But Bluebell was plainly irritated by her presence.

Bluebell was a woman of strong character. Settled among her own relatives instead of with her relatives by marriage, she had a compliant husband. Her sons, Go Insect and Hardwood, had always defended her in her battles with other women. Go Insect had tactfully built houses for his wives some distance from his mother's house, but Hardwood had not yet built a house for Gibbis. I knew Bluebell as a vocal and obstinate woman who dominated her family. Gibbis was not the kind of girl who could stay subservient to an older woman, and Bluebell was disinclined to tolerate a young woman who would not bend to her will, particularly when this young woman was responsible for diverting her beloved younger son's affection from herself. Inevitably there were arguments.

Bluebell accused Gibbis of being lazy and failing to help her with the pigs and gardens, hanging around the men's house instead of settling down to the life of a married woman. Gibbis was a paltry kind of woman, she said, a real rubbish woman. Several times she suggested to Gibbis that she should go back to her father. Indeed the girl did go back to the Dingekup four or five times, but each time she came back.

I asked Hardwood why he did not follow Go Insect's example and build a house for Gibbis far from Bluebell's home, but the suggestion did not please him.

'I like being near my mother,' he replied, 'and I like to think of her having Gibbis to help her. I know they quarrel, but Gibbis will learn to live contentedly with Bluebell.'

Noticing the quarrels between the two women becoming more intense, and noticing also Gibbis's unhappiness, I asked Gibbis whether she had ever suggested to Hardwood that he should build a separate house for her.

'No,' she replied sadly. 'It would be better if he did build a house for me where I need not see Bluebell all the time, but if I suggest it to him he will think I am criticizing his mother.'

One day Bluebell directed an intolerable insult at her daughter-in-law.

'You're a rubbish woman,' she said as usual, but continued, 'you're supposed to be married to my son, but it would be better if you went back to your father and let him marry you himself.'

Gibbis was deeply shocked at Bluebell's words. They were much worse than anything else Bluebell had said to her. She went home to her father and shocked him also by telling him how the older woman had insulted her. She told him she could not go back to Hardwood this time, for plainly his mother had sent her home for good. Her father and his clansmen discussed the matter and decided to sue the Konumbuga for compensation and also for termination of the marriage.

Five months had gone by between the time Gibbis came to visit Konangil's wife in company with her age-mates and the morning the prominent Konumbuga councillors held a court to grant her a divorce. A few people gathered on the lawn beside the Sub-district Office at Minj. Three councillors heard the case. Casuarina, the president of the Council, was present and watched the proceedings but only made occasional comments. Of the other two, I was glad to see that Councillor T-, dominated the court, for he had a reputation for being just and impartial, whereas Councillor B-, who had little to say on this occasion, had recently heard a case in which he had awarded himself generous compensation for a trumped-up wrong. This morning, however, T- was inclined to hurry through the case without hearing both sides. He had already heard the girl's story second-hand from her father, and he assured me that Hardwood's version (which, he said, was the one I would have heard) was a pack of lies. Hardwood and his mother had not yet arrived. T- suggested to the people who had already gathered that as the outcome of the case was clear and the Dingekup had a long way to go home he and Casuarina should settle the business immediately, without waiting for Hardwood and other witnesses to arrive. The Dingekup, he pointed out, lived just outside the Minj Council area and had their local disputes heard by the Court of Native Affairs at Kerowagi. It was important for the reputation of the Minj Council, he said, that the Dingekup should be awarded a large payment for compensation in the form of plenty of money, pigs, and goldlip shells. Casuarina said he understood that T- was satisfied that the Dingekup had a good case, but he said further that neither he nor T- had heard the other side and that it would be fair to do so. He would listen to what had happened from the very beginning, he said.

An interpreter and a policeman suggested that the court should be held at Councillor B-'s house, out of sight of the Sub-district Office, and Councillor T- and the Dingekup plaintiffs went there immediately, soon to be joined by the other principal witnesses. Casuarina and B- stayed behind to resolve a minor court before following.

This minor court seemed a trivial business to occupy the time of two important councillors. A big courting ceremony had been held to open a new 'women's house' the night before, and 21 men had attended. One man stripped off his old and dilapidated sweater before sleeping, and when he awoke it had disappeared. He could not discover which of the other 20 men had stolen the garment, so he tried to get compensation for the theft. He called on all the men who had been at the ceremony and asked them to give him 3 shillings each towards the cost of a new sweater. Some gave him the money readily, but others refused to do so without an explicit ruling from the councillors' court.

'If they all paid him,' whispered Original, who was listening with me, 'he would get 3 pounds. I have seen that "cold-singlet" of his; it is the kind you can buy at the trade store for 15 shillings. Even after paying his two pounds for tax and getting another "cold-singlet" he would have enough to play Lucky.'

Councillor B- confessed that he did not know what to decide about the case. Casuarina, however, suggested that each man who had attended the courting ceremony should contribute one shilling towards the cost of the sweater, since the complainant would be able to buy himself a serviceable garment to replace it for fifteen shillings and have a few extra shillings to compensate him for the trouble the theft had caused him. The plaintiff was clearly displeased at this verdict, and I thought Original's interpretation of the case was probably right.

Meantime, the principals in the dispute about Hardwood's marriage had been assembling on a lawn, partly shaded by bamboos beside the road outside B-'s house. Hardwood and Bluebell had arrived, and Go Insect and Gibbis's sister came with Original and myself.

Gibbis gave her version of events in a strong, independent voice. Then Bluebell told her story. Her compliant husband punctuated her speech with approving comments, confirming her statement that Gibbis had spent most of her time in the men's house and elaborating on the laziness Bluebell had discerned in the new wife. Bluebell's story was not as comprehensive as the younger woman's, for whenever she came to events which were hard to explain to her own credit she would say: 'Let us deal with this particular matter briefly, for there is much more to talk about.' At last she finished, and Gibbis spoke again. She had gone back to her parents five times, she said, after quarrels with Bluebell and had always returned of her own volition because she was fond of Hardwood and wanted to marry him. The sixth time, after Bluebell's dreadful words to her, Luluai Big Namesake and Original and Konangil had brought her back. They did not have to 'pull' her, she explained, as she herself wanted to go with him: her only objection to being with Hardwood was the trouble his mother was causing her. On this occasion her father's brother had told her that she must not let Bluebell abuse her further; if the old woman continued to insult her, he advised, she should go back to her parents for good.

Gibbis was plainly regretful that everything she said made the dissolution of her marriage to Hardwood more certain, but she spoke frankly as ever and as a Dingekup girl she had to watch the interests of her fathers and brothers. At one stage tears trembled on her lashes. Hardwood was not similarly affected. He had liked Gibbis, but as soon as she announced publicly that under the circumstances as she had described them she had no alternative to going back to her parents he decided that his marriage was over and began immediately to calculate how little extra pay he could get away with giving.

Councillor T- came to a decision, gave his verdict, and left. He said that the marriage had not broken up through Hardwood's own fault but through that of his mother. He therefore charged her with giving some pigs and perhaps some money as well, whatever they settled on between themselves, as compensation for her obscene insult to Gibbis. He also charged her with the duty of finding another wife for Hardwood. The judgment sounded simple. T- had transferred responsibility from Hardwood to Bluebell, but there was no way of making this distinction in practice, for the pigs and pay she had to give the Dingekup were the property of Hardwood and his father, not her own. Already Konumbuga and Kugika were disputing over whether Bluebell's husband and son should be responsible for her debt or whether the burden should be borne by her brothers and their families. Casuarina and B- tried to sort out the issues to be decided. The disputing became heated: at one point, Bluebell swung her net bag on to her head and strode off angrily down the road; at another, Gibbis's father took out his hatchet and buried it into the ground. This action was a means of 'pulling' money or valuables: a man would only do it when he was so offended that only a substantial payment could placate him. What had offended him was Bluebell's insulting suggestion that he should undertake an incestuous marriage with his daughter. Casuarina waited patiently until tempers were spent, and soon the litigants were talking reasonably to each other. He echoed T-'s judgment that Bluebell should give some compensation of some kind to Gibbis's clansmen and that Gibbis herself should go home to them with her marriage dissolved. The little councillor of Kugika clan undertook to determine the amount of the compensation. Gibbis was asked again whether she wanted to go home to her parents or stay with her husband. The question did not allow her to indicate her choice to stay with Hardwood so long as his mother stopped victimizing her, so she repeated, 'I shall go east', back to the Dingekup.

Returning to Kondambi, the Kugika Penkup gathered near Big Namesake's house, together with the Koimamkup councillor and the Dingekup. Hardwood and his father and brother were the only Konumbuga present. The boy had already prepared a substantial part of the final marriage payment, including £33 in cash, 18 goldlip shells, and 5 bailer shells, and the Penkup enumerated each item and checked on who had contributed it. They decided to award the Dingekup £3, and one shell of each kind, but soon revised this to include two shells of each kind. They spread the entire amount of cash and goods on banana leaves on the ground where Gibbis and the Dingekup could see it. Gibbis eyed it regretfully and tears trembled again on her lashes, but when Big Namesake asked her whether she would stay or go back she had to repeat what she had said in the hearing of the big councillors. Her father was looking at the partial marriage payment admiringly. I could not help thinking that if the Dingekup had to pay tax like the people closer to Minj his eyes would have been hungry and he might have persuaded his daughter to remain so that he could collect the entire payment with the promise of more to follow.

Bluebell gave a short and gracious speech. She told Gibbis's father that if his daughter were staying with Hardwood he would be receiving the entire payment that was laid upon the ground, but now he was receiving £3 and a few shells because she herself had been cross with his daughter and had spoken ill of him. This was her apology in the true Minj manner: she admitted being in the wrong, and proceeded to pay for it.

Bluebell was notorious as a trouble-maker among the Kugika and the Konumbuga who lived with them. Soon after the dissolution of Hardwood's marriage she met her match in one of Go Insect's wives, who turned upon her and accused her husband and his mother of incest, but this did not change her.

Hardwood watched Gibbis swing her net bag on to her head and disappear along the track.

'It is a pity she has to go,' he said, 'but she is only a woman, and I shall get another wife in time. I'm too young to settle down with a wife, anyway.'

The Penkup told me that Gibbis would stay with the Dingekup for awhile, attending courting ceremonies as before, just as if she had never been married. Later her father would give her to another man. Hardwood's next wife would not be a Dingekup girl.[2]

---

2   See Appendix C, a letter by Reay describing some of the events depicted in the preceding.

The Marriage of Buda and Gibbis[3] (19/3/64[4])

Five months ago some girls of Dingekup clan (in the east) visited Kondambi at the invitation of a clan sister who is married to Konangil. They stayed in her house for a few days and Penkup subclan of Kugika clan turned on a *kanant* courting ceremony for them. Some of the young men of Penkup subclan thought they might acquire wives from among these Dingekup girls, but the only Dingekup girl who stayed after the others went home was Gibbis, a plump and attractive young woman with the fashionable pale skin who fell in love with a Konumbuga boy, not even a Kugika boy, let alone a Kugika Penkup boy. Gibbis is clearly an intelligent young woman. She is also outspoken when need be. As well, she has an affectionate disposition. She met the man of her choice at the courting ceremony the Kugika Penkup had arranged; he is one of a group of Konumbuga who live close to Kondambi among the Kugika Penkup, and this explains how he happened to attend the courting ceremony.

The Konumbuga boy is Buda. He is an alert lad with a winning nature. I employed him for awhile in various capacities. He helped me substantially with some enquiries I was making, and he proved himself an excellent carpenter. At one stage he tried to enlist with the Army, but he was knocked back because his education (begun rather late) was insufficient. He went as far as Standard 4 (which I would judge to be comparable to the first year of primary school in New South Wales) and was then dismissed from school because of his age. I had to dismiss him from my service when his luck at Lucky (*kanaka poker*) turned and he himself became somewhat light-fingered. He was very good natured about it, however, and we remain friendly.

Buda was very coy when Gibbis decided that she wanted to marry him. She was his very first wife, and she lived with him near Kondambi in his mother's house. It is really only about three months since she definitely came to live with him as his wife with the consent of her parents and other relatives. There was some negotiation about marriage payments, but everything was settled amicably. The Dingekup agreed to give Gibbis to

---

3   This is a version of Chapter 13, presumably somewhat earlier than the other and with some references to persons and to Marie Reay herself not contained in the other version.
4   The dates on this and the following section evidently represent an editing process in March 1964.

Buda on receipt of £2/10/- and a few valuables and wait for him to prepare a larger payment later. At the very beginning they went about holding hands like a very uninhibited honeymoon couple, but soon Buda began to seek means of finding the payment to seal his conquest. He killed a pig and sold cooked portions of it for money. He deserted Gibbis for the Lucky schools, and there fell in with other lads of his own age who were thinking a lot of courting ceremonies (Kanant and Garu-Wiro). At this time quite a few new houses were built and Buda slipped into the habit of going along to a Garu-Wiro ceremony at night, when he carried leg with all the girls. Gibbis was thrown into the company of Buda's mother, Omngar, and forced to sleep a lot in Omngar's house. Gibbis herself wanted to be with Buda, and spent a lot of time sitting around in the men's house where Buda and his father, Kendji Winggar, sleep—just waiting for her new husband to come home. Early in the marriage Gibbis tried to get Omngar to warm to her but Omngar was irritated by the presence of a young woman she did not know so well. Also Omngar is a very 'strong' (vocal and obstinate) woman who has a compliant husband and a couple of sons who have always defended her in her battles with other women, and she had additional cause for resenting the interference of a strong-willed girl. Omngar must have realized, from Gibbis's manner, that soon the younger woman would be the dominant figure in the household. There were a few rows between the two women. Omngar would accuse Gibbis of being lazy and not helping as she should with the pigs and gardens and hanging around the men's house instead of settling down to the life of a married woman. Several times Omngar called Gibbis a 'rubbish *meri*' a moderate insult. Several times, too, she made it plain to Gibbis that she ought to go home to her father. Indeed Gibbis did go back to the Dingekup four or five times, but each time she came back. By this time it was obvious (at least to an impartial observer) that Gibbis's feeling for Buda was not simply the fly-by-night infatuation that young girls get and soon slough off in favour of a new attachment. Gibbis, who has more character than most girls of her age, was deeply in love with Buda. Buda liked Gibbis, recognized her attractions and was flattered by her devotion to him, but he is still too deeply attached to his mother to develop a mature regard for a sweetheart or a wife.

In my opinion the marriage could have been saved from dissolution at any phase if Buda had been man enough to build a new house some distance from where Omngar lives. He himself was too much of a mother's boy to think of this, and Gibbis herself did not like to suggest it to him in case he should take this as a criticism of his mother. One day Omngar went too far. 'You're a rubbish *meri*,' she said as usual, but continued, 'you're supposed to be married to my son, but it would be better if you went back to your father and let him marry you himself.' Gibbis, a child of her culture, was deeply shocked at this mention of incest in connection with her father and herself—an unspeakable kind of incest that never occurs because it is too horrible to think about. This was infinitely worse than the moderate insults Omngar had been hurling at her ever since she arrived. She went home to Daddy and told him about it and shocked him too. Gibbis said she could not go back this time; she had been sent home for good. Thereupon her father and brothers decided to sue the Konumbuga (in the Konumbuga-dominated Councillors' Court) for compensation and for termination of the marriage. The case was timed for today.

This morning, when I went to Minj, I saw a crowd gathered on the lawn outside the Sub-district Office. With the whole of the Wahgi Valley and all its side valleys to hold their courts in, the Kuma choose to hold them right under the windows of the Assistant District Officer. My main purpose in going to Minj this morning was to go down to Jimbin's house and see the six model houses he had built for use in the projective test. But I could not broadcast this, as I wish the models to be a surprise to the people who see them in the test, and I had other legitimate business in Minj. We called for my mail, which included a bundle of newspaper clippings from you with John Ellard's comments on the useful nature of neuroses and your own hurtful marginal notes. We called for the two torches I had left behind in the schoolhouse when the first count of the election results finished at 1.30 this morning. Then we went to the Sub-district Office so that I could give moral support to Mek (Tagba's son) while he got his signature checked so that henceforth he can operate his savings bank account here instead of merely at Kainantu, where he worked with the Swiss Mission for awhile and to Kombuk, who charged me with the sacred duty of helping him to open a savings bank account and deposit the £14 I have been hanging on to for him for weeks. Kombuk added £1 to his savings this morning, and now I have the sacred duty of caring for his passbook (as well as Mek's) with £15 in it. I am hoping to get a few more of my brothers and friends to open savings accounts, as this seems to me the only sure way of reducing their participation in Lucky.

Gibbis's father and father's brother and some other Dingekup people were sitting on the lawn, with Councillor Tumun dominating proceedings and my friend Nop looking on and making occasional comments. Tumun has the reputation of being an excellent judge of court cases and being very fair and just, but this is in comparison with the run of the councillors. (Mbagl, for instance, heard the case the other day in which he himself was complainant, and brought in a verdict in favour of himself!) Tumun had heard the girl Gibbis's story, mostly second-hand from her father, and he assured me that Buda's version, which I had heard, was a pack of lies. The Dingekup, he pointed out, are not in the Minj Council area and in fact their local disputes go to the Court of Native Affairs at Kerowagi, not Minj. It was important, he pointed out, for the sake of the Sub-district, that we show the Dingekup that we are fair-minded and award them a large payment for compensation in the form of plenty of money, pigs, goldlip shells, and so forth. I pointed out to him that he should not prejudge the case until he had heard both sides of the story and certainly not before Buda and Omngar had even arrived. He agreed to wait to hear what they had to say before making a definite judgment. Buda and Omngar were a long time coming, and at my suggestion Tumun sent a man to yodel from the airstrip a command to them to hurry up and come. (Tumun had already suggested that as the case was cut and dried and the Dingekup had a long way to go home he and Nop should settle the business immediately, even in the absence of Buda and witnesses.)

Nop is my friend Nopnop, the president of the Minj Council and one of the candidates in the election. I think Kaibelt (who polled the most first votes) is going to win the election on preferences; but David Bettison told me in Moresby the other day that the Administration would almost certainly send the unsuccessful native candidates on a kind of educational tour of Australia (Sydney and Canberra) and if this happens we MUST have Nop to stay. You will like him enormously. He is so typically Kuma.

(On this subject, by the way, a sobering thought is that my 'father', Luluai Wamdi, is quite determined that I take one of his children south with me for a few years and send him back. We have the choice of Mek, aged 12, and Tai, aged seven. Mek is a sweetie, but at 12 he has never attended school and perhaps a seven-year-old would be a better bet from the point of view of crash literacy and general education? NO, I am not thinking of taking one of them to live with us for the whole period of three to four years, but I AM thinking of putting one in a school somewhere or placing him with someone interested and having him occasionally with us for holidays. I haven't learned yet either the official attitude about this kind of thing or the cost of an airfare for a child, which I would have to pay if the scheme proved feasible. Both kids are adorable. I don't see how you could fail to love them both. Wamdi's idea is one I go along with wholeheartedly, which is why I would indeed like to help him in this. He recognizes that the up and coming Kuma need literacy and education, but two things prevent him from encouraging his clansmen's children to go to school. He sees that the Education Department's accent on youth takes the child away from the 'village' culture during the formative years and produces a near-adult who has a veneer of white men's education and no understanding of the education traditional to his own culture. Secondly, he has the nous to see that the cluey people like the District Commissioner and his daughter the anthropologist didn't pick up their clues in a local kanaka school: Australia is the place to get education in the white man's way, but if one of his own sons is to go there it must be somehow under the tutelage of the daughter-anthropologist who is one of the rare people who understand that the lad must also acquire education in his paternal culture for him to turn out to be a complete person and not just an imitation white. Thanks for the clipping of P. Croft in the Canberra Day Play: she is a person who has always wanted to adopt a child and has been thwarted by the legal restrictions on spinsters adopting children. I wonder whether she might be induced to provide a home for one of these lads? No one would be better suited to giving Mek a crash education programme with a bit of mother love thrown in; if something like that could be arranged I could see him often to talk Pidgin and Yuwi and see that he retains knowledge of his parental culture and continued to acquire more. Little Tai might be more of a problem; if Wamdi could be induced to part with them both at once—and they are his only sons—they would give each other support when they met if we could arrange for them to meet regularly. Any ideas you have on this subject would be appreciated. When I find out the official position, if the whole thing is legally feasible, I shall put it to Wamdi that I might provide the fares for one and he might dream up the fares for the other. With substantial help from his interested supporters, we might manage this.)

The circumstances of our life is such that it is just not convenient for us to have anyone else besides us threefella Pippy in the house all the time, though occasional guests are good. But if we had the kids or one of them handy we could see them regularly. But this is a digression, by the way, when I mentioned that it is quite on the cards that Nop may be visiting us for a short time in Canberra.

I mentioned Nop originally because as President of the Minj Council I suppose he OUGHT to be the ultimate model for councillors conducting court cases. In fact this is an aspect of councillorship that does not interest him all that much and he tends to leave a lot to Tumun and Mbagl, who are both Konumbuga like himself. He is reasonable and fair-minded, so long as he does not have to prod too far for the facts. He tends, in fact, to come in on court cases at the last when the other councillors have already made up their minds what is what. This morning heeding something I had said about councillors' tendencies to hear one side of a story only, he listened in to the thing from the beginning.

Another friend of mine, Obo (the only decent interpreter employed by the government and indeed he is really superb in his job: I got a bit exasperated when I found an electoral officer using an inferior interpreter while he detailed Obo to collect the ballot papers and put them himself in the box) and also a policeman Toimba (originally Chimbu, but he has been here a long time) advised the councillors that the case might be heard out of sight down at Mbagl's house—presumably their way of suggesting that the environs of the Sub-district Office were not an appropriate place to hold a court involving many witnesses and also a court that could flare up into substantial differences and angers. Tumun went down immediately to Mbagl's house with some of the key figures of the case, while Nop and Mbagl stayed to hear a very minor court before departing.

This minor court was something that seemed to me laughable as an excuse for taking up the councillors' time. Last night a very big Garu-Wiro ceremony was held for a new house. One participant took off his old and dilapidated sweater before sleeping, and when he awoke it had disappeared. It was established quite early that 21 men had attended the Garu-Wiro ceremony. The complainant had started on his own campaign of recovery of the stolen goods. Since it was impossible to find out who exactly had stolen the sweater he had solicited some of the Garu-Wiro participants to give him 3/- each to enable him to buy a new sweater, but he had struck trouble when some had refused to give him their contributions without an explicit ruling from the councillors' court. I perceived quite early that if he succeeded in his object he would end up with 3 guineas; the price of a new sweater of the kind lost is less than one guinea, and he would still have more than the £2 he will be needing soon to pay his tax. The idea of the tax is almost certainly uppermost in his mind and the very cause of the court case. Mbagl, a bit of a dolt as always, was not sure what verdict he should bring in about this, but I was pleased to observe that

Nop suggested that since there were 21 men who MIGHT have stolen the sweater they should each contribute 1/- towards the cost of a new one. The complainant will probably be able to buy himself a serviceable and new-looking sloppy joe for 16/- and still be a few shillings in pocket (if he doesn't gamble the entire guinea away on Lucky), but he was clearly displeased because this arrangement would not give him a free amount for his tax.

The 'tax' is the local government tax fixed by the Minj Council last year, under considerable pressure from the *kiap*s, at £2 per head for adult (17 and over) males. The AMOUNT of the tax is something to be determined by the councillors themselves (theoretically), but in fact the *kiap* looking after council business last year tried for months to raise the tax and at last confessed to me that he had 'managed to push it through'. Previously it had been £1/10/-, which is bad enough as a compulsory levy to pay for something the Councillors themselves have to decide on. The law requires a Council to levy a tax, of an amount to be determined by itself, to be spent on such matters as it sees fit. This means that a council here has to dream up purposes to which they can put a compulsory levy which it was not their own idea in the first place to impose.

Just now, as intermittently it happens, the people are very conscious of Tax. The Acting District Officer seems to have told the councillors, or some of them, that now that the elections are over they must collect the annual tax. However Barry phrased this, it came to the kanakas (via their councillors) as: on Friday the 20th March the Council meets at Tombil to decide that on Monday the 23rd March the tax collection will begin at Begbe. This means that the tax is to be collected here on Thursday the 26th March, and all the kanakas take this as already decided. The true facts are as follows: when the elections were looming, Philip Bow (the Papuan control officer who was last year in charge of council business and, being a Papuan, took as gospel every dictate of the *kiap*s) asked the councillors in meeting whether they wanted to collect the tax before or after the elections, and they decided to leave it until the elections were over. Well, the elections are over, but it is still the Council's own business to decide just when the tax is to be collected. And the councillors cannot be unaware of the rumblings from the kanakas who STILL think £1/10/- is plenty to throw away on something they do not understand. Pigs are carved up for sale; the game of Lucky has a burst of intensity; and friends and relations are solicited for financial help. Also, court cases that might yield some cash return are increasingly popular. The tax is for nothing in the kanakas' view, and it is appropriate that they should want to raise the money for their taxes by the least possible effort.

I haven't got very far, have I, with all these ramblings, with the story of Buda's marriage to Gibbis? While the minor court case about the sweater and the Garu-Wiro ceremony was going on, the principals were assembling at Mbagl's house, an appropriate place for hearing courts because there is a nice large lawn, well shaded by bamboos, right on the road. Buda and Omngar turned up, and we brought in the car Pundi (Buda's brother, much older), Gibbis's sister, and other essential witnesses.

Gibbis gave her version of things in a strong, independent voice. This behaviour was very different from the typical young girl's talk of 'I have nothing to say', meaning 'I am ashamed to say what I have to say in public but the people who need to know have already heard my story'. Gibbis really went to town on everything that had happened. Then Omngar gave her story, which surprised me a little, knowing Omngar, who always calls me 'daughter'. She spoke confidently but kept interspersing comments like 'Let us deal with this matter briefly; there is plenty more to talk about' (*Yu tingam pasim erim. Yu baim*), whenever something cropped up which she found difficult to explain to her own credit. Her poor little husband, Kendji-Winggar, punctuated her speech with approving and enlarging comments. Councillor Mbagl gave a crazy and immature judgment. Then Gibbis went on to recount the history of her running away to her father's place. She said that she had gone back five times and had always returned of her own volition. The sixth time (after Omngar's dreadful words to her) Luluai Wamdi and Kombuk and Konangil had brought her back. They had had no difficulty in doing this, since she herself really wanted to come back and had no objections to being near Kondambi with Buda except for the fact that her husband's mother was continually making it hot for her. Gibbis's father's brother told her on this occasion that she must watch out for Omngar wanting to abuse her: if the old woman continued to abuse her she should go home for good, but if not she ought to stay with her husband.

All the time Gibbis was talking she seemed regretful that her words always exaggerated the distance between herself and Buda, but she could not stop herself from telling the truth about the matter and also, as a good Dingekup girl, she had her fathers' and brothers' interests to watch. At one stage the poor girl had tears trembling on her lashes. Buda is not nearly so sensitive. He liked Gibbis but as soon as she announced publicly that under the circumstances she could only go home he immediately decided to cut his losses and got to calculating how little extra pay he could get away with giving.

Councillor Tumun, the Great Judiciary of the Kuma, came to an interesting decision, gave his verdict, and departed. He decided that the break-up of the marriage was not Buda's fault but the fault of his mother Omngar. He therefore charged her with giving some pigs and perhaps some pay as well, whatever they settled on between themselves, as compensation for her disgusting talk, and he also charged her with the duty of finding another wife for Buda. It was all as simple as that. But, looking at things coldly and logically, it is clear that if Omngar has to provide some pigs and stuff it is pigs and stuff that is not her personal property, strictly speaking, but property of Buda's father or even of Buda himself, since a woman has no rights of ownership in pigs and valuables. So, although the purpose of Tumun's judgment was to transfer responsibility from Buda to Omngar, there was actually no mechanism for doing this (short of giving Omngar a gaol sentence as I would myself have done). After Tumun left, Nop and Mbagl tried to straighten things out between them. Things got heated at one stage; Omngar swung her string bag on to her head and set off down the road, to be called back by the councillors, and Gibbis's father took out his hatchet and angrily buried it into the ground. This action, ironically known by the term for 'play' (*deimagl*), is a means of 'pulling' money or valuables. You only do this when you are so offended that only a substantial payment will placate you. This was in reference to what Omngar had said, suggesting that he undertake an incestuous marriage with his daughter. Nop, however, has a facility for waiting patiently until tempers are exhausted, and soon the litigants were talking reasonably enough. He echoed Tumun's judgment that Omngar should give some pay of some kind to Gibbis's clansmen and that Gibbis herself should go back home with the marriage dissolved. Little Councillor Mani undertook to determine the nature and amount of the pay back at Kondambi. At one stage Gibbis was asked whether she wanted to go back home or stay with her husband. Unfortunately it was phrased in such a way that she could not indicate her choice to stay with Buda so long as his mother kept out of the way and stopped picking fights with her, so, as the councillors had already heard her say that she was going home she just repeated '*Ag punal*' = I shall go eastward.

Before we got back to Kondambi I found an opportunity to ask Buda what chance there might be of Gibbis coming back to him. He said absolutely none, since she had committed herself to the decision to go back home in front of all the councillors and would not retract that decision. Pity.

Back at Kondambi I had to attend Konangil's feast (*mong'nya mbil*) for his marriage. The feast was at Aiyang's house, Aiyang being Wamdi's youngest wife. Konangil is Wamdi's deceased brother's son and the nearest Konangil has to a true father, and this is why Wamdi held the 'reception' for Konangil's marriage. There were 39 people present, including me and the principals and interested spectators including some who had attended to get some small return for helping with the marriage payments. Aiyang's house is at Kuzibil. Wamdi's other two wives, who are living on the Wahgi flats, quite a distance from Kondambi and Kuzibil, did not attend, although Kaing's two little boys were there.

Because of Buda's group's association with Kugika Penkup, and the fact that Kugika Penkup were gathering together to celebrate Konangil's marriage, the settlement of payments in the Buda-Gibbis divorce was held at Kuzibil. Buda had already prepared a substantial part of the final marriage payment, including £33 in cash and 18 goldlip shells and 5 bailer shells, and first there was a preliminary checking on who had contributed which article or which amount. They decided to award the Dingekup £3, one goldlip shell, and one bailer shell. They spread the entire marriage payment out on the ground on banana leaves and let Gibbis and the Dingekup see it. Gibbis eyed it regretfully and her eyes brimmed with tears again, but when she was asked whether she would stay or go back she had to stand by what she had said in the hearing of all the big councillors. If the Dingekup lived in the region where the Council applies and taxes are due I have no doubt at all that at this stage they would have persuaded Gibbis to remain so that they could collect the entire payment with some more to follow. Omngar graciously told Gibbis's father that he was getting this part payment (which had swelled to £3 plus two goldlip shells plus two bailer shells) because she had been cross with his daughter and spoken ill of him. This is the nearest the Kuma get to apologizing for a mistake; they pay for it.

Among the Konumbuga and the Kugika, Omngar is well known to be a woman who quarrels and insults other women and as a mischief maker on this account. But there was no attempt to discipline her in any way. Gibbis swung her string bar on to her head and disappeared along the track with the Dingekup.

Buda regretted that Gibbis had to go, but said she was only a woman after all and he would get another wife in time. He was a bit young for marriage anyway. Gibbis will stay with the Dingekup for awhile, as if she had never been married at all, and her father will later give her to another man. Buda's next wife will not be a Dingekup girl.

The Marriage of Nere and Walump (26/3/64)

Nere, aged about 18, has two wives, Batri (Ngeniga) and Walump (Konumbuga Taukanim). For at least a month I have heard complaints from the Koimamkup that Nere never visits Walump but devotes all his attentions to Batri. Batri lives with Kabi and his family, and Walump lives with Nere's parents, Kauga and his wife.

Koimamkup used to consist of four sub-subclans: Bomungdam, Kissukanim, Tunambauoldam, and Entskizinga. But Entskizinga sub-subclan died out, with only two remaining. One, Konangil's father, joined Penkup Baimankanim for some reason I do not know, and Konangil is thoroughly identified with this group. Youths of Penkup Baimankanim accounted for him in their genealogies in 1954. The other man, Ogunbenga, stayed with Koimamkup subclan and became known as a member of Tunambauoldam sub-subclan. Ogunbenga is well known to be a *yi rom* ('man no-good') or, more usually, a *yi komugl* ('long-long man'). He has not married, though he is old enough to have several wives. He is a short, scrubby-looking, unattractive man of the type known as *yi rom*. He is also somewhat deaf. One has to raise one's voice and stand close to him to ensure that he hears. He appears to be of normal intelligence and without any mental disorder, so far as I can judge. People tell me, however, that sometimes his conversation is normal and sometimes it is peculiar. He has pigs and gardens of his own, and his work seems to be adequate.

There was a good deal of discussion in 1954 within Koimamkup subclan as to whether the division into sub-subclans should continue or whether they should join together simply under the one name 'Koimamkup', now that their numbers had shrunk. Kubun (Koimamkup Kissukanim) expressed himself strongly, saying that they were all Koimamkup plain and simple; he was very annoyed with the Komungdam people for deciding to celebrate the Pig Ceremony on a separate ceremonial ground at Bomung. He thought they should share a single longhouse at Kondambi. Kauga (also Koimamkup Kissukanim) disagreed strongly. He said that his ancestors had been Kissukanim and he also was Kissukanim. To demonstrate his conviction on this point, Kauga built his houses at Bomung. Kauga is a short-tempered man, much given to drama and tears. He announced that members of Kissukanim who decided to celebrate the Pig Ceremonial at Kondambi would henceforth be Tunambauoldam, not Kissukanim. More Kissukanim celebrated the Pig Ceremonial with Kubun at Kondambi than with Kauga at Bomung. As a result, the Kissukanim people as a whole began to be known as Tunambauoldam. Now they consider themselves the one group. The only real distinction seems to be that in reckoning relationships a person who is, say, cross-cousin to someone in the original Tunambauoldam group is known as 'real cross-cousin' of people in this group and 'distant cross-cousin' of people who used to be Kissukanim. In fact there are more ex-Kissukanim men (13) than original Tunambauoldam (10), but no one has suggested that they should all be known as Kissukanim.

Kauga and Nere are ex-Kissukanim, and Kabi is original Tunambauoldam. Walump is 'real cross-cousin' to the ex-Kissukanim, and Batri's father is 'real cross-cousin' to the original Tunambauoldam.

Although the marriage of 'real cross-cousins' is frowned upon (and used to be absolutely forbidden before the law of '*laik bilong meri*' assumed importance) a really ideal and preferred marriage is between the children of 'real cross-cousins'. Both of Nere's marriages are excellent from this point of view. His father is ex-Kissukanim and 'real cross-cousin' of Walump. He himself is becoming increasingly identified with the original Tunambauoldam. Kauga has five sons, with only enough land to divide between three. Kabi has no sons but has two daughters who need to visit and be given food. Kabi has suggested to Nere that he should take the place of the son he never had and inherit his land in return for providing Mbogl and Kunt with pandanus fruit and other food they need.

Walump was originally betrothed to another Koimamkup youth, Tunga's son Fundi (ex-Kissukanim). But she and Nere became lovers and in November 1963 she told Nere she wanted to marry him. She came to live with Kauga and his wife, Nere's mother. They welcomed her warmly, and Kauga was very glad indeed to have his 'real cross-cousin' with him. It is customary for a man and his wives to live with his parents if they are living. For the first month Nere divided his attentions between Batri and Walump, both of whom were living with his parents. Then a dispute arose between Kauga and Nere. There had already been disputes of a minor kind between Kauga and Nere. Now Kauga alleged that Nere was favouring Batri in the allocation of gardens between the two wives. This was a misunderstanding, as Nere had sent for both his wives when he wanted to allocate the gardens and although Batri had come Walump had been away doing some work Kauga had given her to do. Nere became angry and told his father that he was always cross with Batri for no reason so he was going to take Batri to live with Kabi and if Kauga wanted to give Walump to his older son Kolyam or to any other man he was welcome to do so. Nere regretted this angry talk later, and he compensated both Kaugan and Walump for the words he had spoken. So far as he was concerned, they might just as well never have been uttered. Nevertheless he refrained from visiting Walump from this time forward because he would have to encounter his father and he did not want any more arguments.

Nere came to work for me, and during the elections he came with me to obtain extra information I was unable to get. A week ago Nere head someone say that when I went to Canberra I was intending to take Nere and Batri. Yesterday Non went with Walump to Councillor Mani and told him that Walump was going home to her parents and Nere would have to give her about five pigs and some money and shells to take with her. Nere has already given the marriage payment for Batri, but has not given it for Walump yet. This morning Mani sent a lad with a message for Nere to come to his house immediately to attend a court. Nere told me he had to go. I said that Mani should have notified me that Nere was required to attend court at a certain time on a certain day, since Nere was working for me, instead of assuming that Nere could leave his work without any notice at all. I told Nere he could attend the court at 'belo bek' (1 pm), and he sent the boy Lukas to tell Mani this. Mani himself came down to Kondambi at 12 noon and insisted on hearing the court immediately. He was very angry with Nere, as he admitted, for what he interpreted as an insult to his 'cross-cousin'. I told Mani that he was not qualified to judge the case if he himself was angry on behalf of the complainant. I said a councillor or a committee man of some other group should hear the case, or else he should take it to the Court of Native Affairs. Mani agreed verbally, but began to hold the court inside my house.

Mani began by assuming that what Walump had heard about my proposal to take Nere and Batri to Canberra was true. I assured him it was not, and asked Walump who had told her this. She said Non had told her. Non (wife of Wom, Koimamkup Bomungdam) is another Taukanim woman married to Kugika. I asked Non who had told her, and she said Ogunbenga had done so. Nere said that no one should take any notice of what a Komugl man said. He told me further that the version he himself had heard was that I was proposing to take Nere and Batri to *nambis* (the coast), not to Canberra. In Tok Bokis,[5] a favourite way of saying that someone is going to die through witchcraft is that he is 'going to the coast'. It was possible that Ogunbenga had heard someone hint that Nere and Batri were going to die from witchcraft and had interpreted that as meaning that I was going to take them to Canberra with me. I insisted on hearing what Ogunbenga had to say about who had said what, and he was summoned but was a long time coming. Much later Ogunbenga arrived and was questioned closely by Mani and Wamdi in concert. Wamdi has two wives from Taukanim himself (Karu-uk and Kaing), so he has a special interest in the marriage of Nere and Walump. Ogunbenga said that Kubun's wife Man had told him this yesterday, when he had met her on the track. I insisted on Man being summoned and after much waiting she eventually arrived. At first Kubun arrived, somewhat put out that Mani had been summoned for a court case which did not concede them directly when she was busy cooking a pig to give to her brothers. Man is from Kambilika, a clan traditionally hostile to the Konumbuga, and it is possible that Man might have a certain interest in getting rid of one of the Konumbuga women. She seemed reluctantly to say who had told her but eventually admitted that she had heard the story from Aine, who had had it from Batri. Neither of these women was available to give her version.

Walump has been a willing worker, on the accounts of Kauga, Nere, Mani, Non, and others. She is offended and clearly hurt by being denied her marital rights when she herself had insisted on marrying Nere, but when I asked her whether she wanted to stay married to Nere or go home to her

5   Tok Bokis corresponds to 'talk bogus', a common Tok Pisin expression for allusive language which refers to an important matter not freely discussed.

parents she refused to answer. Since women in such circumstances have no hesitation in saying *Keg punal* ('I want to go') but are never heard to say that they want to stay, I interpret this as meaning that she really wants to stay married to Nere. Nere himself told me privately that he himself could not bring himself to sleep with Walump again after the fact that he had neglected her for nearly three months had been discussed publicly. I told Mani that marriages should not be broken lightly, and suggested that they wait one week before deciding. Mani agreed, and suggested that he hear the court again one week from today. I suggested that he should not hear a further court about the marriage unless wither Nere or Walump asked him to dissolve the marriage.

A dispute arose immediately between Gubukets (wife of Kai, original Tunambauoldam) and Kauga about some pigs. Gubukets is Berebuga by birth, but she gave Batri a sow because Batri is 'true cross-cousin' to her husband. Batri was living with Kauga and his wife at the time, and Nere's mother cared for the sow The sow bore three piglets. Gubukets insists that the pigs, which are still cared for by Nere's mother, should be returned to Batri now that Batri is living with Kabi's family. Kauga insists that as Nere's mother has been looking after the pigs she should keep them. A suggestion of mine that Nere's mother should be given one piglet to compensate her for looking after the sow and its litter was agreed upon as being just, even Kauga admitting that that used to be the law and one piglet would be better than none.

I asked Nere why he had not built women's houses for his two wives instead of letting them sleep in other people's houses. He replied that while a man's father is alive it is customary for him and his wives to share the father's premises. This is true, but when a man's wife is constantly in strife with his father it is customary for him to build her a house some distance away, and Batri and Kauga had crossed swords many times. Nere pointed out that so far as he personally was concerned he had two fathers, Kauga and Kabi. Since Kabi wished him to inherit his land, he was entitled to have his son's wife living on his premises and helping him. He insisted that Walump could not go to stay on Kabi's land too. Both he and Batri were threatened with witchcraft, as well as Kabi himself, so long as Kauil remained with Kabi, and at least one of his wives ought to be protected.

Kauil is the former wife of Kun (Penkup). She came from Kup. She was always a person who sees ghosts, and she brought the cargo cult to Kondambi and Kuzibil in 1949. She was the only real cult leader in

Kugika clan. She is periodically subject to *komugl tai*[6] in the mushroom season. When Tultul Tai died in 1961 she was one of the witches held responsible. She was banished by the Kugika, and went briefly in marriage to a man of another group on the northern side of the Wahgi, but soon she returned to marry Kabi. Kabi gave her to Yeu (original Tunambauoldam), and both Yeu and Kabi's own wife died. Kabi then married her himself, despite the danger of marrying a known witch who had probably caused the two recent deaths in his own group as well as the death of Tultul Tai. He said he would take the risk, as Kauil was so keen on marrying him and he was now a widower, and if he became ill he would send her away. He grew thin and somewhat sickly and blamed this on to Kauil's witchcraft. Also she directed a lot of obscene abuse at him on many occasions, and once removed her pubic strings in front of his very eyes. He told her to go home to her birth clan but she refused. He reported his wish for a divorce, and the grounds for it, to Mani and Kaa, and Kaa told Kauil to go back to her birth clan. She seemed willing to go when Kaa told her to, and was on her way from Kondambi when Kaman (Koimamkup Bomungdam) grasped her hand and took her to his house.

Kaman's wife Danga is Konumbuga Pipikanim. She is the sister of Kobia. Kabi's mother was Kobia's father's sister. Shortly before the divorce case concerning Kabi and Kauil, Kauil's brother's son was raising a marriage payment and Kauil was soliciting contributions towards it in Kugika clan. Since Danga is Kabi's true cross-cousin, Kauil asked Kaman for a contribution. He gave her some shells. When Kaa commanded Kauil to go home to her brothers for good, Kaman could see his shells vanishing to no good purpose, so he prevented Kauil from leaving with his shells. Kauil gave him back his shells, but did not immediately go back to her birth clan. She stayed at Kaman's house.

Danga resented Kauil staying with Kaman. 'Do you intend to marry Kauil yourself?' she asked her husband. 'Is that why you keep her here?' Kauil overheard what Danga said, and she said she was going back to Kabi. Kaman persuaded her not to go back to Kabi, and she remained. Some men were playing cards in Danga's house at night and some of them pulled Kauil outside and raped her, treating her as a *pamuk*. Kauil ran away and went to Kabi's house.

---

6   Mushroom madness (see Reay, M.O. 1960. 'Mushroom madness in the New Guinea Highlands', *Oceania*, 31(2): 137–139).

When Kauil returned, all the people sleeping at Kabi's place ran away. Nere, Batri, Kabi's daughter Kunt, and old Obo went to the house of Batri's father, where they are still living, because they did not want Kauil to kill them. Kunt has since gone to live with her sister Bogl in Minj. Kabi refused to sleep in his own house while Kauil was there, so he sleeps in men's houses at Kumbuku and Kondambi. Kauil sleeps alone in Kabi's house and gets her own firewood from the bush.

14

'Wandering Women' and 'Good Women'[1]

Everyone wanted to participate in the Pig Ceremonial—the men and girls to decorate themselves and dance, and the married women to watch the spectacular proceedings and be present at the final mass slaughter of pigs. It was especially important for the men to take part. Failure to do so would deprive them of the rewards of fertility in their wives and pigs and gardens.

At any other time, the prospect of going to gaol for some offence against good order would not have worried them. Imprisonment may be a temporary inconvenience, but no stigma attaches to it. Indeed, people imprisoned for major crimes and sent to Goroka and other places return with heightened prestige; they impress their more provincial kinsmen as tourists coming back with first-hand knowledge of the great world. Even in the more modest gaol at Minj, a man meets and becomes familiar with natives from all over the Wahgi Valley, and he makes useful contacts among the sophisticated coastal policemen. Imprisonment offers an unparalleled opportunity to learn Pidgin English and generally widen the social horizon. The Kuma regard imprisonment less as a punishment for wrong-doing than as a result of action of which the Administration disapproves. Erstwhile warriors complain that pacification has made them soft and weak like women.

---

1   This chapter version evidently dates from an earlier form of the manuscript, prior to Reay's having changed indigenous names to English.

When a woman neglects her duties towards her husband or is reluctant to obey his commands, she invites a beating. He is likely to attack her with a hatchet or a stout stick and inflict visible wounds. But she is well aware that the Administration has banned violence, and she may seek redress by displaying her wounds to the Court of Native Affairs. Some of the women were quick to take advantage of the men's well known fear of going to gaol while the Pig Ceremonial was in progress. They flouted the authority of their husbands on numerous occasions, knowing that their husbands were afraid to strike them.

I know of no other woman who went to the lengths that Wozna did, deliberately taunting her husband and even delivering physical blows. But Wozna was a strong young woman, whereas her husband, Wuzig, was both naturally peaceable and physically weak. Wozna would not have dared to defy Wuzig to the same extent if she had been living with his clansmen. She was assured of protection by the presence of her parents and her own clans people. Wuzig, riled beyond endurance, eventually raised his arm to strike her, but his wife's clans people restrained him. They were acting in the interests of their brother-in-law in preventing him from going to gaol during the Pig Ceremonial.

Yagumam was also exceptional. She had been a strong and determined woman, so active in women's fights that in her youth she had caused the death of Kommun's mother. She was exceptional in being a desirable widow who was free to choose whom she would marry and, indeed, whether she would marry at all. Normally, widows are either inherited by their husbands' brothers or given to members of their husbands' subclan. Yagumam had already taken her husband's brother, Tai, as a lover, and he was willing to have her as his fifth wife. But Yagumam knew that she could not settle down peaceably with Tai's other wives, and she preferred to remain a widow. Tai and Wamdi had two reasons for allowing this. Yagumam was not past the age of child-bearing, but she had two sons and so had already contributed to the strength of the clan into which she had married. A woman who had not yet borne sons would have been given promptly to a new husband. Secondly, it was well known that Yagumam was a vigorous and independent person who had killed another woman in a fight, and they hesitated to give her to a man who already had wives with whom she might disagree.

I have been concerned in this book with some of the more dramatic aspects of the women's behaviour: their protests at marriage, their rebellions against the authority of their menfolk, and the fate of 'wandering women'. The protests at marriage are usual. Even if a girl has not developed an attachment to a youth she cannot marry, she tries to prolong her period of adolescent freedom. There are two ways of stating in the Kuma's language that a girl marries: she 'goes to' a particular man, or he and his clan 'take' her. The first expression implies that she has chosen a particular man who is willing to accept her as his wife, and that both her relatives and his are agreeable to the match. This is most unusual. It is much more common for a girl to be 'taken' (i.e. captured) by the clansmen of a man who has formally betrothed her.

A girl who is 'taken' makes many attempts to escape from the marriage that has been arranged for her. She runs away to her parents; she tries to hurl herself into the river; she seeks the protection of her mother's brother; she runs away to a lover. Her new husband and his clansmen guard her jealously and try to prevent her from escaping. The bridegroom makes rough attempts to consummate the marriage in order that she may bear him a child and so be forced to stay with him. Children in Kuma society belong to their father and add to the strength of his clan, so a woman who has children cannot leave her husband without deserting her children.

I have related how the woman named Man tried to make her husband discard his new wife and was herself discarded. An established wife is expected to try to get rid of a new co-wife. Thus Man told her husband, Kubun, that she had attacked Yere because the other woman had told her not to tolerate the newcomer. The only kind of new co-wife a woman welcomes is one she can regard as a sister or a daughter—normally someone from her own clan of origin. Amp-Damba was acceptable to Mai and Kunig because she was their daughter by adoption.

A woman cannot drive away a new co-wife without the help of at least one other woman. Manamp's co-wife had her mother to support her, but it is unusual for widowed mothers to live with their married daughters. Tai's various wives joined forces to drive away new women he acquired. Non's wife, Onim, was one of many Konumbuga women who had married into Kugika clan, and whenever her husband brought home a new wife she enlisted the help of her clanswomen to drive away the newcomer.

253

The worst that can be said of a women of the Kuma is that she is a 'wandering woman' (*amp wabure*). The stereotype is a harlot who wanders from man to man, from clan to clan, without ever settling down to raise children and gardens and pigs. Women who conform to this stereotype are rare. I met only two actual 'wandering women', Kolyai and one other, and I received accounts of about half a dozen, including Tolmag. Various people referred to both Manamp and Muru as 'wanderers', for they could only explain the behaviour of these women in terms of such a stereotype.

The Kuma interpret women's behaviour in terms of two extremes, 'wandering women' and 'good women' (*amp duma*). 'Good women' are nearly as rare as 'wandering women'. A 'good woman' is one who consistently obeys her husband and never quarrels with other women. When someone makes a complaint to her, she refers the matter to her husband and lets him deal with it. This requires a measure of self-control that is lacking in most of the Kuma women. One woman greets another with a flood of abuse, accusing her of negligence in letting her pigs enter other people's gardens. If the second is a 'good woman', she turns on her heel, disdaining to answer, and goes to find her husband. But more commonly she takes this opportunity to shout back loud complaints that the injured woman's husband should have fenced the garden if he did not want pigs to ravage it. The pigs are her concern, and she resents the charge of negligence.

Wamdi's wife, Kaing, was a 'good woman', subservient to her husband. She never participated in women's quarrels, but quietly tended her gardens and her pigs and cared tenderly for her little son. Konumbuga by birth, she managed to serve the interests of both her husband and her brothers. In helping to force the girl Gele to go to the Konumbuga, Kaing was helping her own clan of origin to gain a bride and she was also helping her husband's clan to implement the arrangements they had made. The only other violent behaviour I saw her display was the assistance she gave the other Kugika women in restraining her young clanswoman Pin from running away. Here again she was helping to enforce the marriage arrangements her menfolk had made.

Tai's senior wife, Mai, and Ka's young wife, Yuamp, were the only other 'good women' among the Kugika wives.

'Women are nothing,' the men of the Kuma say. Women play no part in political life, and when the men were obsessed with warfare in the days before pacification women had no role in this important activity. Women play no part in the complicated exchanges between clans, excepting the passive part of being exchanged along with pigs and plumes and shells. Women play no part in the spectacular Pig Ceremonial: they watch the dances from the edge of the ceremonial ground and unobtrusively cook food for feasts. But they are discontented with the subordinate role the men assign to them.

Male-dominated societies are common in Melanesia, but the standard accounts do not tell us how the women react to their treatment by the men. 'Compulsory marriage was resented by the women even in the old days', Mrs Hilde Thurnwald wrote of the people of Bougainville in 1934 (1934: 146).[2] In former times, 'a girl who was not willing to submit to her father's arrangements was flogged or fastened to a tree and allowed to stand in the full blast of the sun's rays for hours'. But most accounts of primitive societies seem to imply that women submit uncomplainingly to the arrangements the men make for them.

Kidnapping a person on the high road, as Yuaga kidnapped Nimbil, then dragging her over jagged fences to a place where she could be imprisoned under guard, would seem to people reared in our own society an unwarranted interference with personal liberty. Nimbil's family could have reported the kidnapping to a Government officer, and she would have been restored to them with little trouble. But they recognized Yuaga's claim to compensation for his brother's death, despite the edict that such claims relating to happenings before the advent of the Government should be forgotten, and agreed that he could keep the girl in lieu of payment in pigs and plumes and shells.

We can predict some of the changes that would come about if Kuma marriage depended upon the consent of both parties, as it would have to if all were to enjoy freedom and justice. The age of marriage for females (now 13 to 17) would rise: girls would wait until their breasts had dropped before going to men of their own choosing. Some women would never marry, and there would be more bachelors. Polygyny would disappear, for no girl goes willingly to a man who is already married. Actual and clan

---

2   See Thurnwald, Hilde 1934. 'Women's status in Buin society', *Oceania*, 5: 145–170.

sister exchange would no longer be possible, for men could not dispose of their sisters with a view to gaining brides for themselves. Men could no longer use women to satisfy their obligations to each other.

Perhaps the most serious consequences would be the men's inability to enforce their ideas of reciprocity between clans. Marriage is essentially an exchange of women between clans, and the system would break down if the completion of each transaction were left to the will of individual women. Further, the circulation of valuables in betrothal and marriage payments would be upset: a man would no longer be able to establish his right to marry a particular woman by presenting her relatives with a handsome betrothal payment, and a bride's clan would have no means of exacting a marriage payment from her bridegroom. The granting of a simple human right would have endless complications.

If liberty and equality are among the values an independent, self-governing Papua New Guinea will attain, the women of the Kuma will in time be able to choose their own partners in marriage in their own time. They will marry men of their own choice when they feel like marrying, instead of being forced prematurely into uncongenial and hostile relationships with men selected by relatives whose motives are mercenary. This would seem to be the granting of a fundamental human right. But anyone who reads this book must realize that granting this right involves not merely the dispersal of ignorance and ill will but also the dissolution of Kuma society. If men are no longer dominant, and women no longer submissive, the male ego will have to be reconstituted so that the integrity of men does not depend upon exchanges of women, pigs, and wealth.

Appendix A

The capacity of any anthropologist to observe exactly what occurs is limited and I have made a generalization about sexual behaviour among the Minj Agamp which is not based on direct observation at all but on information just casually given by the people concerned and not even systematically solicited. The generalization is: 'Their men had to achieve dominance, not simply take it for granted, in the sexual act, and the women themselves had to fight for the right to submit to them by putting up a losing struggle.' I base this interpretation on retrospective accounts of particular experiences given the next day either directly to me or to age-mates of the speakers in my hearing. Most of these accounts of sexual adventures were boastful reminiscences by young men aged about 16 to 26, often explaining wounds plainly inflicted by partners of the previous evening biting or scratching their torsos and arms. The few accounts girls gave to their age-mates (never specifically to me) placed as much emphasis on the fierceness of the struggle before consummation as male versions did.

I have no means of judging how often girls made assignations with men. It was inconceivable for a man to refuse an invitation to 'carry leg' in public or meet a girl privately, so girls were never shamed by a rejection. It is reasonable to suppose, however, that a man's command performance in the bushes might sometimes prove disappointing when he attempted it several hours after the sexually stimulating 'carrying leg'. Two girls I know of had developed the practice of inviting their chosen lovers to 'carry leg' with them again in private as soon as they met by arrangement.

The obstacles to a man achieving satisfactory sexual expression in these encounters would seem to be formidable. The places of assignation were not notorious haunts of bush demons, but the strong folk belief in these creatures provided part of the environment in which the encounter took place. After an assignation which seemed to have been unsatisfactory, a young man expressed concern as to whether the girl he had been trying to give love to was really the girl herself or whether it had been a bush demon masquerading in her form. The sexual act seems always to have been preceded by joking, which often began playfully but soon became competitive and scathing and led to physical struggle. I heard several accounts of a man trying to slap a girl who eluded him playfully until he chased her and, catching her, threw her to the ground where she struggled against him, biting and scratching, until he overcame her. According to one girl, a youth who was particularly inexperienced responded to her invitation to meet him by pounding upon her from behind the bushes and trying to rape her. A number of girls taunted their lovers during their mutual joking in such terms as 'I don't think you are a man; you are another kind of creature. I shall know you are a man when I see your penis'. Nevertheless, the young man who was supremely successful with girls and had great prestige among the other men on that account (Good was the only young man of this type in Penkup subclan) seemed to develop satisfactory relationships with the girls who summoned him.

Appendix B

Lothario Gains a Bride

14.10.54

Muga (Kambiliga);

Muga's Sr., married to a Komenka man, has run away to a Tuimukup man. Tomorrow, Muga is going to Minj for the court.

A Ngeniga woman married to a Kumnga man commented on this saying 'She is just like my mother, but she walks about like a long-long (*tai*) woman.' She disapproves of the woman going off to the Tuimukup and leaving her husband.

16.10.54

Kis had a dream two nights ago after he had been at a *kanant* c.c. (This while the Kumnga etc. were busy talking about and preparing for the Komenka-Ngeniga *wubagl*.)

Kis dreamed that he went to a sing-sing (*kanant*), where he saw two girls. One of them took his tomahawk, and they joked with him. They saw a *garuka* (pandanus nut) tree. The girls said, 'Is it ripe or not?' He went to have a look at it. Half the nuts were overripe, but some were just right. 'It is ripe,' he said. 'I'll cut and give it to the two of you.' One of the girls said, 'No, I'll cut it myself.' She took Kis's tomahawk and cut the *garuka*. He snatched his tomahawk back, and he himself tried to cut the *garuka* with it, but one of the girls had her arm raised and accidentally he cut her arm with the tomahawk. 'Why did you cut my arm?' she complained. Kis wanted to see some of the Kugika men with whom he had gone to the sing-sing. The Kugika men came up, but they were cross with him; they hit him and he could not see them and he was angry.

It was fortunate that he had cut the girl's arm instead of the *garuka*, although it was an accident, because Kis thinks that if he dreams of cutting *garuka* or *marita* his mother and his brothers will die. The Kugika should not have been cross with him, because it was only an accident.

Kis's second dream (the following night, i.e. last night):

Kis saw a crowd of men gathered together, crying for a man who had died. They said to him, 'You are not crying,' but Kis replied, 'He wasn't a friend of mine; I did not know him'. Kis went into a women's house, and his mother came to him. 'Where did you come from?' she asked him. 'I came from Kondambi,' he said. He heard the men say that they were going to bury the dead man. When he approached them, they told him they had already buried the body. They said that they had buried him deeply, put a smoked pig on top of him and earth on the top. Kis asked them, 'the men who buried him – have they gone back to their houses, or are they still there?' 'They are still there,' he was told. 'I'll go and see.' He approached the burial ground and met the men coming back. 'We have finished burying him,' they told him. Kis walked around a tree that had a very thick trunk. When he came back, he saw the dead man lying on the ground. The body was decomposing. He ran away. His friend Tultul Kontswol of the Antsbang joined him, Kis' half-brother came too, and together they went down a hill. There were a lot of pandanus of both varieties, all of them ripe. Kis said, 'There is some good ripe *marita*. The *garuka* I saw before; is it ripe yet or not? If it is ripe, I'll cut it.' He looked, but the *garuka* had already been cut. So Kis and his two companions went away. Then it was light and he awoke.

26.10.54

Kimp has gone to the Pingya. She and Gele went to stay with the Pingya (northern Wahgi) to 'carry leg' and be washed with grease. Gele came back when Kongangil II and the other young Kugika men went to bring them back. But Kimp stayed, and the Kugika were told that she wanted to stay as the Pingya man's wife.

Kis and Konangil II said of Kimp: 'She is like a casuarina in the wind. The wind blows and she stays where she is blown. The wind blows again and she stays where she is blown.' She was carrying leg met Kolyam (Kugika Koimamkup) and wanted to marry him. The Kugika intended to report the matter to the Court of Native Affairs but interpreter Tuan (Konumbuga Pipikanim) told Wamdi to wait until the *'bigpela kot'* (against a European) at present taking place is over.

13.11.54

Garipens eloped to Pengem. There was much discussion about whether the Kugika should insist on keeping her or whether the Konumbuga should be allowed to pull her back. It was known that her brothers do not want to give her to the Kugika. Konga particularly wants to give her to the Danga-Djegga in exchange for a bride for himself.

Ngambal's husband (Pingya clan) had a lot to say, although the issue did not concern him. He said the Kugika must help the Konumbuga to pull her back, so that Konga can get a girl in exchange for her. Alim repeated this, parrot-fashion. But Wamdi was against giving Garipens back, and when Ndu suggested that when the Konumbuga tried to pull her back the Kugika should let them get as far as the strong bamboo then resist them, Wamdi approved.

Tumba (Pengem's 'Father') and Pengem did not take an active part in the discussion, as their views were well known. They want Garipens to remain but will not do anything to ensure this against the wishes of (the rest of) the strong Penkup group.

Kaa and Tai said that they would not hold Garipens fast, as they did not want the Konumbuga to get the impression that the Kugika were determined to keep her. At the same time, they said that Pengem had lost Nggol because the Kugika did not watch her so that the Ngeniga could not capture her back, and they were in favour of Garipens staying and marrying Pengem.

O = NDUM = Nggoigan

O

Kumbun = KONGA   GUAN   Garipens   WUZIGL

14.11.54

Konumbuga arrived to settle the fate of Garipens. Guan, their respective mothers, plus Konga's wife came.

Guan: 'We have come to take Garipens back.'

(Garipens, who slept last night with Onim, came on to the ceremonial ground.)

Nggoigan: 'Are you cross, that you have run away from us?'

Garipens: 'No, I am not cross. I want to get married, that is all. I am tired at staying at Pagnga and have come here.'

Kumbun: 'Your stomach is swollen, and your nose is so close to your eyes that it looks as though you only have eyes. We have looked after you well and you have grown up to be big. So think think well. Do you want to be with your Abap and Arap, that you come here?'

Garipens: 'My Abap and Arap may die, but I shall (want to) stay here. (*ya moral*).'

Guan: 'We have brought back the dog, tomahawk and kinas the Kugika gave us when you stayed with Pengem last time. The Kugika can take these things back and you can come back with us.'

Kumbun: 'Did your mother tell you to come?'

Garipens: 'This woman (i.e. her mother) and I do not hold hands and sleep together. I came myself because I wanted to.'

Kumbun: 'Well, if Pengem gives his sister to Konga to marry, you can marry Pengem.'

Nggoigan: 'We came here early in the morning. Now the sun has come up strongly, so come with us and let us go.'

Kumbun: 'Garipens only sleeps in men's houses (*yi-nggar*). She never sleeps in women's houses (*am-nggar*).'

Guan: 'You Kugika haven't put grease on Garipens. So I am waiting for you to do this.'

Garipens: 'I don't want to be washed with grease. I want to be married.'

Kabi: 'We have nothing to say. If you have anything to say to Garipens, Garipens can answer you. We are just waiting.'

Guan: 'Did you come to eat peanuts?'

Garipens: 'If they are eating peanuts, I can eat with them.'

(At the Penkup end of ceremonial ground, Garipens, Alim, Kaa, Ka, Wulye, Azip, Pengem, Kombukun, Kun, Kuru, Tai. Guan, accompanied by Garipens's younger brother, *aetatis* 10, crossed to the Penkup. Guan carrying 2 tomahawks, the boy carrying the dog. Guan put them on the ground and pulled Garipens, with no resistance from the Kugika. Nggoigan and Guan's mother. and Kumbun helped Guan to lead the struggling Garipens. When they came up near the strong bamboo in the centre of the ceremonial ground, Ndu grasped Garipens and wrestled her from Guan etc. with the aid of Komp. When Guan first began to lead Garipens away, Nggoigan held up her bush knife and struck her daughter's head with it'—the blade turned a little and the blow glanced off without cutting Garipens. Garipens went with the Kugika down to Mangindam's house, where she has been staying.)

Kumbun: 'I made you a nice *pul-pul*, and I want it back.'

Guan: 'No, not now. Tomorrow, Ndu and Komp can bring Garipens back to us. If they don't, we'll take the matter to the *kiap*.'

Two of Omngar clan were passing through Kondambi and were greeted by Tai and Konts, who said to them, 'See the young girls we have brought back with us! And Garipens has come to marry Pengem.' The two men were duly impressed and went to meet the girls.

This morning Pengem and Alim went to Minj to interview Luluai Konangil (Konumbuga) to ascertain his attitude to Garipens marrying the Kugika. Konangil said that although Konga and Guan don't want her to marry the Kugika, in his own view it is perfectly all right for her to do so, as the Kugika had just given the Konumbuga some girls who had been 'humbugging' and wanting to marry men of other groups.

(Kugika was Konangil's maternal clan.)

Appendix C

Tonight began the marriage ceremony of my 'brother' Konangil, who was one of my good friends back in 1953–55 and has always remained so. (He is my 'own' father's brother's son and the *di*, namesake, of Jimbin's father, the much admired Nambawan Konangil, the great *luluai* of Konumbuga clan who died in 1955.) I gave him £2/10/- towards his marriage payments, acted as banker while he was accumulating his money, and he followed my advice to set aside £2 to pay his tax without expending ALL his money on 'buying' Ondugl.

We went to Tubnogl (the creek called Tub, pronounced Toob as in 'book'); nearly all the men of Konangil's sub-subclan (excepting those who are busy with death payments elsewhere in Konumbuga territory), plus several women married to men of the sub-subclan plus Tunamp (member of another subclan, who came along for the heck of it and to wait upon me), plus myself. The houses belonging to Ondugl's family are quite close to the creek, on the far side of it. At the creek I noticed three long white things in the water, and they turned out to be tapeworms out of the pig Ondugl's family had killed and cooked for us to eat, so I began to pray that the meat was well cooked. At my 'true brother''s marriage ceremony I could not possibly refuse to eat pork! I had visions of visiting the European Medical Assistant tomorrow in search of a strong purge or emetic. The Konumbuga relatives of Ondugl greeted us warmly, the men shaking hands and the women embracing, and we sat with them around a fire in a hole where a saucepan of some kind of 'stew' was cooking. We sat on logs which we had to move back from the excessive heat of the fire. Nearby was a tall fine fence of split bush paling set close together. This was the fence Ondugl's family had built to keep the chooks and ducks and turkeys a former European schoolteacher had given them (along with £200) as marriage payment for Tup, one of Ondugl's sisters. Tup was a pupil of his, and his downfall. I am not clear whether it was the affair with Tup or his affair or involvement with another girl pupil that occasioned his removal from the district when it became public. The family think it is Lucky, however, that they managed to bleed him for the livestock and fence (constructed by his schoolboys) and still retain their daughter. The Kugika presented a cooked pig, and the Konumbuga presented a cooked pig in return. With the memory of the three tapeworms sharp and fresh in my mind, I found it hard to swallow the pork I was given. Nevertheless we all ate with enjoyment, even myself when I managed to blot out the memory of the tapeworms. Then Konangil stayed with his hosts while we went to find Ondugl and 'pull' her inside the house to be prepared for her marriage. I have seen lots of these Wailik ceremonies, and did not stay for the Wailik singing but just to witness the 'pulling'.

Ondugl was in a classificatory mother's house in company with her age-mates—girls who develop a close bond between them largely through giving each other support in fights against girls of other clans (over boys). They all looked sadly at Ondugl, a couple of them crying sentimentally because they were going to lose their mate, and some reminiscing about the times they had all combined to fight against the Ngeniga girls and so forth. Ondugl has long been a lover of Konangil and the marriage was initiated by herself going to stay with him with marital intent. Any protests she would make at this stage of proceedings would be purely ritual. The girls did, however, get her whipped up into some regret at leaving her single life.

Women married to men of Konangil's sub-subclan went inside the house and asked Ondugl to come with them. She said she was happy where she was. They held her arms and tried to persuade her to come outside, but her age-mates attacked the Kugika women with thumps and scratches. Ondugl and her age-mates were all robust young women, and they proved too much for the Kugika ladies, so the men had to enter the house and drag her out. She and her age-mates treated them to a few blows and scratches, which they proudly examined by the light of my lamp later.

The defeated women were old Yagumam, Ka's mother; Wamdi's youngest wife Aiyang; Kombuk's half-sister, the unmarried mother Muru; and one of Ka' wives, Komdilamp. Yagumam and Komdilamp are both from the bride's sub-subclan.

The men who brought Ondugl outside were Kabakl, who belongs to a different sub-subclan from Konangil but who has a wife from Ondugl's sub-subclan; Ka, the chap who was falsely reported drowned and has been something of a hero since his safe return; Kombuk and his younger brother Yuants; Pigip, an age-mate of Konangil's belonging to Kabakl's sub-subclan.

The men took Ondugl to her father's house, where the Wailik was to take place. They had to go through a fence on the way, and I was interested to watch this. Ten years ago men pulling a bride used to ignore the presence of a pig-fence and just drag her ruthlessly over the sharp palings, tearing her flesh. But this time Kabakl held Ondugl firmly while the other men pulled out a few palings to let her pass through without getting injured. She herself was twisting dramatically in Kabakl's grip, but when he got her to the fence she took care to edge herself through before she wriggled very hard again. It was plain that her protest was largely ritual.

Appendix D

2nd March 1964

My Very Dear Twofella,

Well all is right with the world again and without any private doubts I can preface my prayers with 'Thank you God for the gift of life because it is good'.

I think I told you how sick at heart I got at the wretched attacks in the South Pacific Post. It was my reference to 'boy scouts' that did it. This was headlined as if it had been meant to be jeering and critical, whereas I had no quarrel with the 'boy scouts' themselves. The correspondence columns of the Post were full of abuse and comment, the worst sample being a perfectly filthy libellous diatribe for which I think I could have claimed substantial damages if I had wished to remain in the public eye. I kept quiet, but it did make me sick. This unfortunately was happening concurrently with attempts to discredit my study of the group hysteria the Kuma associate with eating mushrooms. Don't think I am getting paranoid because I am alleging 'attacks' and 'attempts to discredit'. I was keeping an open mind on this aspect of things until people starting lining up very definitely FOR and AGAINST me and the FORS all warned me that certain persons were interested, mostly for professional reasons, in discrediting my study of the hysteria. It makes sense. But I must say that I had a somewhat lonely couple of weeks while the AGAINSTS were being distant and I had to alienate some of the FORS by telling them straight out that they were mistaken in thinking I was meaning to criticize the *kiap*s. My criticism is simply that the Administration, in the form of the central body based in Moresby, has really messed things up—despite the generally intelligent and well-intentioned attempts of the 'boy scouts'. When McCarthy, Director of Native Affairs, asked John to supply him with a transcript of my paper, and when John asked me to write to McCarthy, I really threw the ball back into McCarthy's own court by telling him straight that I was not criticizing his field officers but only the (his own) Administration. I stuck to my guns, though it made me sick to do it. After I had sent the letter off, I showed a copy to Brian Corrigan and he said that McCarthy, being a reasonable man, would appreciate the points I made and would be satisfied. I hope it is all over now.

Today I played hookey from the elections to follow a marriage dispute, really in the hope that I might get the picture Pat Croft wants of a girl being pulled over pig-fences and generally treated roughly because she is going against her men folk's wishes. I still may get the picture on Saturday, but I hope not. Thereby hangs a story. My father Wamdi and my father's brother's son Kombuk were very concerned because Kombuk's young sister Omngar went off yesterday and was rumoured to be with the Ngeni-Muruka group. Going off without telling anyone could only mean that she had gone off to a man intending marriage against her relatives' wishes. We set off for Pugmail this morning, I with my cameras and Wamdi and Kombuk and some others with the intent to capture Omngar and bring her back. At Pugamil we found that she was supposed to be at Kobung, so we proceeded to Kobung. There we found that Omngar had slept with a married clan sister last night and that a Ngeni-Muruka leader Tagba had sent for her this morning and urged her to stay and marry a young man Tai. The Ngeni-Muruka councillor Mugap held a kind of court at which Omngar was asked what she wanted to do. She stated firmly that she intended to marry Tai and had no wish to return to her relatives. Mugap promised to bring her down to Kolya, where the Kugika councillor Mani lives, so that a fresh court could be held by Mugap in collaboration with Mani, Wamdi, and *Komisi* (Committee Man) Kaa. We waited at Kolya but the Ngeni-Muruka did not turn up. Late in the afternoon they came, but without Omngar, and expressed their firm intention of keeping her with them as the wife of Tai. The background of Wamdi and Kombuk's objections is complicated. For one thing they had been intending to give Omngar to a particular subclan of a different neighbouring clan. But their main objection is that Tai is really Ngeni-Muruka by long association, whereas he is Kugika Penkup by descent. His father Tabindam went to live with the Ngeni-Muruka, his mother's clansmen, many years ago taking his whole family with him. Wamdi and Kombuk are also Kugika Penkup, and a marriage between Tai and Omngar is like brother–sister incest. The only 'native custom' the *kiaps*' court recognizes is the payment of marriage payments: and they interpret this as payment for the woman (as if she were a sack of potatoes that can be haggled over), not (as in true native custom) a gift to reward the woman's group for the donation of her child-bearing capacities. The courts do not recognize marriage prohibitions, and a girl can marry whom she likes. The Ngeni-Murukas are well aware that so far as the courts are concerned they can retain Omngar just because it happens to be her fancy to marry Tai. If the Kugika attempt to capture Omngar against her will, a complaint to the court by the Ngeni-Muruka will land my father and brothers in goal. Poised on this dilemma, the resourceful Wamdi let the Ngeni-Murukas negotiate with him over the marriage payment required and he stuck out for a colossal payment which must be paid on Saturday. He intends to capture Omngar if the payment is not made on Saturday. This is really just staving off the dilemma, since I doubt very much whether the Ngeni-Muruka could rustle up the required payment in a few days. Then we shall see what happens and I shall have my cameras ready, but I certainly do not want to see Wamdi and Kombuk of all people in gaol. What I am tentatively hoping to do is to let them capture Omngar and when I have got the required photographs persuade them to let her go back to Tai. Wamdi says definitively that if Omngar marries Tai she will never be welcome to visit Kondambi again. If she and Tai have children, these will be without the useful mothers' brothers all other people have.

Last night *Komisi* Kaa came to my house at midnight bursting with the news that Konga had killed his wife. We drove down to get her, as anyone described as killed is generally injured badly enough to need hospital treatment. She looked out to it, a bit bruised but nothing startling. She was breathing regularly but appeared to be unconscious. In fact she looked dead at first sight. Konga is the man I used to put in my notebooks as Pithecanthropus before I got used to his real name, because his profile looks so primitive, jutting in all the right places for a perfect illustration of Stone Age Man. He is big for a Kuma, at least 5'9" with bulging musculature and a great deal of strength. If a child or a dog were to get in the way of his great ham of a hand as he brushes a fly away it would be instantly killed. Konga is a simple man and would not hurt a fly deliberately, but he is quick-tempered and does not know his own strength. He was very concerned about his wife. He said they had quarrelled about a pig he had been searching for all night. I had private thoughts about this, particularly when I learned that she had already been off-colour with what might have been malaria. Dire giggled into my ear that a man and his wife only quarrel about one thing at that time of night, when the man wants to do something his wife does not want him to do, but of course Konga could not tell us that. My diagnosis (admittedly unskilled) was that she would recover easily but probably had a bit of concussion. All the lights in Minj were out when we went to the hospital and delivered the poor woman to the doctor boy. He made an examination but decided he needed the opinion of the European Medical Assistant, Frank, and he and Jimbin went to get him. By this time it was raining heavily. There is a nasty little bridge, far too narrow, over a ditch at the beginning of Frank's drive. When Jimbin drove on to it one plank was broken, another missing, and all the rest slippery from the rain. He landed the car in the ditch with a broken shock absorber and a bolt off a back spring. Poor Jimbin had to get the car out of the ditch single-handed while Frank returned to the hospital. When Frank arrived it was obvious that he had been on the Scotch all night; his eyes were blurred and his gait unsteady and his speech muffled. But he leaned against the bench the woman was lying on and straightened himself up immediately. Afterwards he was pretty hopeless again, but during the examination he was admirably controlled. Clearly he had his wits about him because, finding Konga's wife's temperature, pulse, and breathing normal he moved her head slightly to see whether it would flop right over, as the head of an unconscious woman must do, but there was muscular resistance and also a lamp held in her face made her eyes screw up a bit.

6th March

The next morning Konga's wife still appeared to be unconscious, but I would back Frank's judgment on this and obviously she has not died yet.

Councillor Mugap of the Ngeni-Muruka is Jimbin's maternal relative, so he has gone to visit him tonight to find out whether that clan intends to produce the payment for the girl Omngar tomorrow.

Just before Jimbin left, he told me how he had acquired his second wife. He had been visiting the Ngeni-Kuzilka up the Minj River at the time of their pig-killing and he was going home when a girl came up to him and held his wrist.

'Why do you grasp me?' he asked.

'I want to marry you,' she replied.

Jimbin was surprised, because he did not know the girl from a bar of soap, except for recognizing her as a Ngeni-Kuzilka girl. Nevertheless, he asked her, 'Will the Ngeniga bring a court case if you marry me?' 'No,' she answered. 'It is perfectly all right. There will be no court case.' He therefore slept with her that night and the next morning brought her home to Minj. But the same day the Ngeniga arrived and took him and the girl to the District Office.

The *kiap* (Phil Bow, a Papuan) asked Jimbin whether he wanted to marry the girl and Jimbin replied, 'We were not lovers until she followed me and told me she wanted to marry me. I am not fussy. If she wants to marry me she can.'

'Can you prepare a marriage payment by tomorrow?' Phil asked him.

'No,' said Jimbin. 'I have no money. It would take me a week to gather the money together.'

'Then the girl must go home and sleep with her parents until you have the pay ready,' Phil told him.

Jimbin went to Amban, a member of his subclan, who promptly gave him £40. He gave this to the Ngeni-Kuzilka and they took the lot, without returning part of the payment as has always been customary. Now he has two wives. He tells me two are quite enough and next time a girl approaches him with an 'offer' of marriage he would be strong and—not knock it back, because he could not shame the girl and himself, but tell her he could not afford the money to marry her.

7th March

Now it is Saturday, the day the Ngeni-Muruka are due to bring the fabulous pay for Omngar—£100 cash, 15 live pigs, 40 Princess of Stephanie Birds of Paradise (worth a fiver or so each), 15 goldlip shells. Wamdi has just called in to keep me up to date what is happening. 'We'll wait and learn whether they give the pay today' he told me. 'Then tomorrow we shall go and bring Omngar back.'

In the meantime the women of the Konumbuga, mostly married women but the unmarried girls too, of the little Kumngakanim group to which an affianced bride of Tai's belongs, have taken the initiative in an attempt to get rid of Omngar. It seems that Omngar flew off to Tai in order to beat the Konumbuga Kumngakanim girl to him, and the Konumbuga women are incensed. They went to Kobung at least two days running and gave Omngar a good thrashing. Dire (who is also Konumbuga) gave me her opinion that if the Konumbuga women are persistent enough and belt up Omngar enough she will come home of her own accord without the men having to pull her. I agree, and think that so long as the women just indulge in punching and hair-pulling and a bit of wrestling they are likely to win their point, but the women in fact are much more likely to lose their tempers and seize 'sticks' (anything from a hunk of wood to the ridge-pole of a house) and probably spill blood. Once blood is spilt the Ngeniga have a case for the Court of Native Affairs. The first day they went to Kobung they tore apart the house Omngar was sleeping in. This was the house belonging to Mau, the daughter of Kumbang, my neighbour who died last year. You may remember my mentioning that the Ngeniga gave a handsome payment for Mau when Kumbang was dying; she is now firmly married to the Ngeniga man. Now the Konumbuga women have literally pulled the grass roof off Mau's house.

You say that I am not observant, and I have to agree with you excepting in regard to things I have been trained to observe. Going up the Minj River the other day I suddenly noticed that some of the firewood stacked by the side of the road for the government to collect was in piles much larger than my own two piles of firewood. The system is to plant four sticks known as a 'mark' for the firewood and these enclose £1's worth. The government has to check continually on the position of the 'mark' because the sticks gradually creep closer together until the natives are getting £1 for about ten bobs' worth of firewood. I stopped the car and measured the 'mark' the Kondikas (our traditional enemies) had filled for the government, and found on returning home that I had been paying £1 for about 15/-'s worth. So we have had to change our 'mark' to conform with govt. practice and save myself a few bob here and there.

Nere, the semi-literate Kugika Koimamkup lad who has been helping me lately, is walking around very proudly this morning in brand-new khaki shorts and a nice blue-flecked sloppy joe I bought him. It would be easy (and perhaps desirable) to pay one's helpers more and let them buy their own clothes, but their taste is unformed. Nere was with me in the trade store where I bought his sloppy joe, and it was plain that if he had been left to choose it himself he would have settled for a gaudy and relatively flimsy cardigan, zipped up the front and costing twice as much. He is very happy with the one I helped him choose, and he looks really nice in it. Last night he wrote a letter to his former teacher (who had to leave the district when scandal broke about his relations with his female pupils) telling him how happy he is at Kondambi.

The 'mushroom madness' has evidently received notice abroad. Yesterday I had a letter from a Dayak in Sarawak telling me about a somewhat comparable mushroom complex among his own people.

(Later) Dire and Jimbin and Nere have gone for a swim. I wanted to send a note to Minj to a Papuan girl dental assistant who is coming to lunch with me tomorrow so when Jimbin told me that we did not have enough water for him to wash the mud out of the floor of the car properly I jumped at the opportunity to tell him to take the car down to the Minj River and wash it, and incidentally take the note to the station. Soon afterwards Dire told me that she was going for a swim in the Minj River with Jimbin, just the two of them. That sounded all right, but two thoughts sprang to my mind. One was that it is a wretchedly cold day with a bitting wind that would make it most uncomfortable for swimming. The other was that when Wau, Dire's husband, had written to her he had expressed slight concern that Dire and Jimbin were the only partners in the store venture besides myself and he advised her strongly to bring in someone else who could chaperone her, and when I read this out to her she blushed. So I asked Nere whether he would accompany them and chaperone them, and he has gladly gone off to do so. After they had all left Tunamp told me he felt rather out of things being left and I told him that it was really just Jimbin and Dire going for a swim and that I myself had sent Nere along to chaperone them because otherwise Wau might hear that Dire and Jimbin were walking about together and he would be cross.

Tunamp nodded wisely and thought this was excellent. He told me that Wau had charged him and Tugu (and also Tuan whom I have discarded because he had no work to do) with the sacred duty of chaperoning Dire. So everyone is satisfied—perhaps with the exception of Dire and Jimbin themselves. Even I can see that Jimbin is jolly attractive, and though they both belong to the same clan, Konumbuga, it is a very big clan indeed and secretive relations could easily take place between members of different subclans, as these two are.

Dire has made a perfect mess of herself lately. When I first knew her she had peroxided hair which looked very attractive with her brown skin and gave it a golden glow. When I came back last year she still (or rather again) had peroxided hair, but while I was here she dyed it black. It still looked good when one got over the shock of seeing her change overnight. But this time she has experimented with red (sic) hair dye and I suddenly noticed that the top of her hair was bright auburn and the sides still black. It looked ghastly and I told her so. As a consequence of my comments (as I thought, but perhaps it was to attract Jimbin) she dyed her hair black again today. Generally Maria, her step-daughter, does it for her, but Maria is away visiting relatives for a few days so Dire did the dirty deed herself. As well as staining a blouse and laplap irreparably, she got mucky black dye on her neck, face, shoulders, and running down her back. When eventually I noticed what a mess she had got herself into I insisted on taking her to the bathhouse and scrubbing her myself. It was a bit like scrubbing a more docile Pippy, or an unprotesting baby. The excuse for the 'swim' is that I have ordered her to rinse her hair because it is matted with the black dye.

Dire has been dripping black dye all round Kondambi with a shocking lack of reticence. And this reminds me that when we were at Kobung on Monday we saw a truly shocking sight. You will never, of course, forget the sight of those old ladies dancing at night at Borroloola in their brassieres and pink bloomers, but at least they were apart from the men when they were wearing that horrible garb. But at Kobung I was shocked to see *one* woman walking around wearing an uplift brassiere in conjunction with her pubic strings and nothing else. It is the only case I have seen here of this ghastly use of female underclothes as public apparel. I wish now that I had spoken to the woman, as I nearly did, telling her plainly that brassieres are something hidden which should never be revealed in the presence of men. At the time I did not know quite how to phrase this, but it was an opportunity lost. At least I intend to give Dire a good talking to on the subject of dyeing her hair in public. On one occasion last year I had to tell her firmly to wear a slip under a semi-transparent shirt I had grown out of and given to her. Unlike the woman at Kobung, she has girlish breasts that point slightly upwards with the coloured parts around the nipples as big as chestnuts. I think you would find the physiognomy of the people here decidedly interesting. The breasts of the young girls have to be seen to be believed, and a well-built man almost invariably looks completely muscle-bound as if he had been taking body-building courses. When a woman has suckled a child for awhile she usually has one breast three or four inches longer than the other.

The conduct of the elections has shown that Native Affairs officers need some instruction in two spheres: estimation of age, and recording of vernacular names. A certain amount has been written here and there on the estimation of age among non-literate populations, and I am hoping to draw these sources together in a short article. Girls whose ages I would estimate as 16 or 17 have sometimes turned up to vote and often the electoral officer has found their names well and truly on the roll. But the business of finding the names is a time-consuming one. It would help enormously if the names recorded were intelligible when read out. So that is meat for a further short article.

* * * *

Tai's son, Kombuk, has just come back from visiting the Konumbuga, with his second wife, Waiya, in tow. You will remember that Kombuk has been concerned about his sister Omngar, who has eloped to the young man of Ngeni-Muruka who bears the same name as Kombuk's father and in fact is called after him. Kombuk's first wife, Mandigl, is the mother of Marie, the little girl who was born during my first visit and called after me. Mandigl's marriage to Kombuk was arranged according to traditional practice when Kombuk was an adolescent. It has been a happy marriage, though Mandigl has borne Kombuk only one daughter. (I am inclined to suspect that Marie is really the daughter of the virile old Tultul himself, though I have no firm evidence for thinking this. At the time of conception, Kombuk was still finding pleasure in sucking his old mother's breasts, though he was already 15. He told me at about that time that he was impotent, and certainly he behaved as an impotent man would. Tultul Tai despised his son for being unmanly and referred in my hearing to Kombuk still sleeping with his mother and leaving other men to sleep with his wife and making his father 'do things he himself should be doing'. Certainly the family resemblance between Tai, Kombuk, and Marie is very strong; and if it is true that Kombuk had to get someone else to impregnate Mandigl it MUST have been his father.) Early last year, or at least before August, this Konumbuga girl Waiya came to Kombuk with marital intent and he rustled up the pay and formalized the union. When I arrived last August I was amazed to see the change in Kombuk. He is no longer ineffectual and somewhat effeminate. He has a 'muscle-bound' stature and is a young man of consequence. In really special sing-sings he proudly wears his father's Tultul badge on his forehead. His father died a couple of years ago and I would guess that Kombuk's development and maturity came with the decease of his father, who was a most important man and a good deal too directive for a boy like Kombuk to have as father and model. Ten years ago it seemed that Kombuk's younger brother Yuants might succeed his father. And certainly Yuants was Tai's favourite. But now that the old Tultul has departed this life, Kombuk's personality has come into full flower. He is no longer shy about attending *Garu-wiros* (the formal opening of brand-new women' houses at which the men have to wait in the ante-room until a girl sitting in one of the pig-stalls gets the crier to call his name to come and carry leg with her). On days when there are public gatherings he always (or nearly always) has to excuse himself to go and carry leg with some girl who has summoned him. He did not 'mark' (put down a betrothal payment for) Waiya. She carried leg with him until she could live without him no longer and she came, parked herself in his house and said 'I am marrying you.' Now Waiya has been married long enough to know that she is no longer a free and easy young girl, but she has continued to associate more with her age-mates who are still unmarried than with the married women of Kombuk's clan, as her own group lives very close. When Omngar's elopement took place, Waiya had a row with Kombuk and packed up (i.e. put her empty string bag on her head) and went home to her family. Her grievance was that Kombuk had given his sisters Omngar and Komun to other groups instead of giving them to her own group and thus making exchange for the gift of herself. Kombuk objected that Komun herself had run away to Obo, a man belonging to a different division of Konumbuga from Waiya herself, and that he himself had had no part in arranging Komun's marriage. Further, he argued, he himself had planned to give Omngar to the Konumbuga but she herself had run away to the Ngeni-Muruka. Waiya was extremely angry and went home to her family. The Councillors' court was to hear the case this morning.

In the meantime, the elections have been going on and I have been deliberately getting to know Nopnop better. Nop is one of the three native candidates for the Minj Open Electorate and is also President of the Minj Local Government Council. At present he seems very likely indeed to win the election. He has a special interest in visiting the polling places, so I have encouraged him to come with me when I myself visit them. He and Jimbin and myself are planning to do a grand tour of the far western highlands when the election is over, whether Nop wins or not. We have become good friends, so when Kombuk (who is known to him to be the father of my namesake and like a brother to me) approached him about the court Waiya was getting up he lent a sympathetic ear and promised to be present himself.

This morning, before he went to the court, Kombuk called in to collect the £10 he had deposited in my care over the last few weeks. He said that he needed it to give pay to Waiya's family. Why? To bribe them to let Waiya come back to him, as he had already paid for her. He was certain that she would 'talk strong', i.e. be determined and persistent in her arguments, and that he would not be able to talk her out of her obsession about his falling down on the exchange of women. I suggested to him that the case of Omngar was not yet resolved and that it would be wise to wait until it was before throwing away £10, perhaps for nothing. Kombuk protested that it was Kuma fashion to use money in this way when a woman was so determined that the men could not persuade her to their viewpoint. I asked him whether this was native fashion before money had come and he said no in those days the women were not so determined and the men could control them. In a case like Waiya's he and some of his brothers would have simply gone and dragged her back. I said that he was throwing his money away to no good purpose. He could not agree, but when I suggested that if he were to go with the money in his hot little hand the Konumbuga would get it from him whereas they just might not if he left it behind. He was easily persuaded to leave his £10 in my care until he actually needed it.

Nop heard the court and told Waiya that she was acting as if she were still an unmarried girl. He ruled that *laik bilong meri* ('like belong mary', i.e. the wishes of a woman) prevails only when a girl is still unmarried and must be allowed to choose whether or not she wants to marry a particular man. Once she is married to the man of her choice she has no choice at all about staying with him or leaving him unless he does something very wrong to justify breaking the marriage. This had not happened in Kombuk's case. Nop is highly respected, and Waiya went back with Kombuk at Nop's bidding.

You may remember my discussion of suicide in *The Kuma*. At the time of my first visit the government was still trying to stamp out the custom of suiciding in various specific circumstances. Certainly suicide and attempted suicide seem to be very much rarer now; but an interesting development has been the modern use of the *threat* of suicide as a feminist weapon. The girl who waylaid Jimbin up the Minj River *forced* him to marry her by threatening that if he did not she would hang herself on a tree or throw herself into the river. This is not at all uncommon.

A case that cropped up last year when I was here is a delicious example. The precarious marriage of the girl called Minj to Paulus Mambugi is fraught with lively issues: she is the girl who belongs to the same subclan as the mother of the boy she chose. At the time she was cavorting with Mambugi, before the question of marriage arose, his mother and other people tried to discourage him from getting too involved. His father kept trying to find excuses for keeping Mambugi at home. But Minj proved to be hypochondriac and also threatening. Whenever Mambugi failed to visit her she developed headaches. The headaches she gets seem to be a kind of migraine; she gets them now whenever things do not go her way. But also she told Mambugi when he eventually did come to her that the next time he absented himself she would commit suicide. This really brought him to heel.

I have learned of yet another issue in the Minj-Mambugi alliance. Minj's father, ex-Luluai Timanga, has always been strongly allied with the Kugika, so strongly indeed that he has used his powerful war sorcery against the Kugika's traditional enemies the Kondiga, although his own clan, Konumbuga, has friendly relations with the Kondika and intermarries with them. His war sorcery caused the death of a particular Kondika man, whose name eludes me, just about the time one of his own children married a Kondika against his wishes. A young son of his, an unmarried youth, visited Kondika territory for courting ceremonies the night after the Kondika had killed a pig in the burial ground in honour of the dead man's spirit. The people in whose house the boy slept that night had a bundle of the cooked pork hanging up in a basket. They wanted to eat the pork but could not do so without offering some to him so they did not tell him that this was the pig they had killed in the burial ground. He ate it, and the very next day his stomach swelled up and he soon died. As a result of his son's death and the events that led up to it, Yimanga resolved that those of his daughters who were still unmarried must not get involved in this particular warfare complex but must marry into any other clan besides Kondika or Kugika. Mambugi has prepared the marriage payment for Minj, but Yimanga refuses to accept it. Minj's brothers, including Mont, whom I know well, want very much to accept the marriage payment but they are afraid to do so because their father threatens that when the marriage payment is given he intends to kill a Kugika. He says they may accept the payment after he is dead but not in his lifetime if they wish to avoid death and disaster. He has forbidden his sons to visit Minj; Mont is the only one who sneaks down to visit her sometimes without his father knowing. An unmarried sister of Minj, a big strapping girl called Man, was one of the ring-leaders in the Konumbuga women's forays to Kobung to destroy Mau's house and attack Omngar.

The psychologists in Moresby have found a projective (personality) test which they think is genuinely cross-cultural in application and suitable for New Guinea. I want to administer this test to all the Kugika who experienced the so-called 'mushroom madness' and an exactly matched control group of people of the same clan who did not. All told, about 60 people. The test takes about one hour to administer to one person. The psychologists want me to visit Moresby for a couple of days to familiarize myself with the test, which is a very good idea. If I am going to spend all this time on the test, I think I should also administer it to a sample of young women (perhaps also to young men, to get at sex-differentiation in personality here). But at the moment I cannot see myself getting to Moresby until the elections are over. They end on the 18th of this month, but then I am heavily committed to this projected tour of the far western highlands with Nop and Jimbin, which will take up to a week.

* * * *

I have bought a new transistor wireless and a record-playing pick-up. The latter is magnificent. The wireless is a National Transistor 8, not so powerful as the transistor 10 we have in Canberra but with a wonderfully big speaker which compensates a lot of the slight lessening of power. The speaker makes it superb for attaching the pick-up to it.

To go with the pick-up I bought a few records. Two are records of Maori music, partly to amuse the Kuma and partly to get myself into thinking in terms of Maoris and it does both beautifully. One is a Groucho Marx recording of *The Mikado*, which is helping me with my comic opera or musical comedy or whatever it turns out to be. The Kuma adore *The Mikado* and the story of it makes real sense to them. Another is an omnibus record of Beautiful Melodies from the Operas or some such title, which includes many of my favourite operatic themes. The remaining record is a thing called *Seven Cities* (musical moods of Australia's capital cities) by Bruce Finlay, with your favourite theme for strings running through it. I think you will enjoy this little collection.

Well, I have so much work to do that I have written you much that I want you to keep since I have had no time to record it in my notebooks. It is 7.30 on Sunday morning. If the weather is like this in Canberra, you and Mine Boy will be up and out in the garden. It is a perfect morning. Last night I felt like an orgy of film so went to the European Club and saw *Rob Roy*: a pictorial demonstration that the Scottish Highlanders of a few centuries ago were pretty similar to the New Guinea Highlanders on the 20th century. Much fun, and all my love to you twofella.

Marie

Appendix E

Obituary: Marie Olive Reay, Born Maitland, NSW, Died Booragul, NSW, 16 September 2004, Aged 82[1]

Michael W. Young

It is a painful task to record the death of Marie Reay, who for almost thirty years was a member of the Department of Anthropology, in what was at the time of her appointment the Research School of Pacific Studies (now Pacific and Asian Studies) at The Australian National University. While perhaps best known for her research in the highlands of Papua New Guinea, most notably among the Kuma, Marie will be remembered as a pioneering ethnographer whose work was at the forefront of expanding fields in twentieth-century Australian anthropology, including the anthropology of women and the study of race relations in the small towns of western NSW. She was a significant figure in the founding and growth of the Australian Anthropology Society (AAS), a role which was acknowledged by her peers when she was made the first life member of that Association. Marie's career in anthropology began at Sydney University, where she studied for an MA (graduated 1948) under the dictatorial A.P. Elkin who directed her fieldwork among fringedwelling Aborigines in western NSW. This fieldwork initiated an important strand in Marie's career. She became part of a new pioneering wave of fieldworkers in Indigenous communities, comprising Bill Stanner, Nancy Munn, Mervyn Meggitt, Les Hiatt, Jeremy Beckett and Diane Barwick (all of whom, at

1   This obituary was originally published in *The Asia Pacific Journal of Anthropology*: Michael W. Young 2005. 'Marie Olive Reay, Born Maitland, NSW, Died Booragul, NSW, 16 September 2004, Aged 82', *The Asia Pacific Journal of Anthropology*, 6:1, 81–84.

one time or another, held positions in the Anthropology Department in RSPacS at ANU). Marie also conducted fieldwork among Aborigines of Borroloola in the Northern Territory, and from the time of its founding in the mid-1960s she was closely associated with the Australian Institute of Aboriginal Studies in Canberra.

In 1951 Marie took up what would become the second prominent strand in her career. She travelled to Papua to study social change among the Orokaiva of Northern Province, intending to follow up F.E. Williams's research in the 1920s. She was there when the catastrophic eruption of Mt Lamington occurred, killing over 3,000 people. Evacuated along with other survivors, Marie subsequently wrote a report on the social consequences of the disaster. During 1950–51, Marie also lectured at the Australian School of Pacific Administration in Sydney, where she was a junior colleague of notable ethnographers of Papua New Guinea including Mick Read, Ian Hogbin and Camilla Wedgwood.

Having won a scholarship to the newly established The Australian National University in 1953, Marie was one of the first research scholars in what was then the Department of Anthropology and Sociology in the Research School of Pacific Studies. Directed by S.F. Nadel and supervised by W. E. Stanner, in 1953 Marie was sent to the Wahgi Valley in the central highlands of New Guinea where she did pioneering fieldwork among the Kuma. She belonged to that heroic first wave of anthropologists to work intensively in the vast, relatively unknown Highlands, along with Ronald and Catherine Berndt, Mick Read, Richard Salisbury, Ralph Bulmer, Mervyn Meggitt, Robert Glasse and D'Arcy Ryan. Marie was again ahead of her times, as she was the first ethnographer to investigate in depth the position of women in a Highlands society, a topic that became fashionable as anthropology responded to the critiques of second-wave feminism in the 1970s. She keenly followed political developments in Papua New Guinea as the country moved to independence and parliamentary elections.

The travel writer Colin Simpson met Marie in Minj as she was about to begin her fieldwork and he wondered about her survival prospects among the misogynous warriors of the Wahgi. 'She appeared diffident and "soft"' to Simpson (1954: 232). Few who knew Marie in later life would call her diffident: she held some radical opinions and was never afraid to express them forcefully. As for being 'soft', the Kuma would have been the first to disagree. Her students and junior colleagues, too, learned that Marie could be intimidating and abrasive, though she tempered her sharpness with sly, dry humour.

Embarking on the writing of her thesis, she became even more scornful of the 'God-Professor' Nadel and her authoritarian supervisor Stanner. To both of them 'PhD students were a lesser species'. She had to 'tone down' her field reports on the Kuma because her findings concerning family life and the position of women did not conform to her advisers' preconceptions. When she planned to take a short holiday from her thesis, Nadel had sneered: 'Anthropologists don't need holidays.' She took one any way, and noted with a twinkle that Nadel died while she was away (Reay 1992: 158).

In the Wahgi she also defied the god-administrator who disapproved of female anthropologists, especially ones who broke the White Women's Protection law by wearing shorts. 'Modified Bombay bloomers', Marie called them, 'equipped with five generous pockets' for her custom-made notebooks. These capacious khaki shorts, she wrote dryly, 'looked terrible and would be certain to discourage any sexual passion that happened to be present'. Kuma, in any case, treated her as an honorary male and even allowed her to witness boys' initiation rites (Reay 1992: 166).

'Shorn of verbiage', Marie's PhD thesis was published as *The Kuma: Freedom and Conformity in the New Guinea Highlands* in 1959, the same year that she was appointed to a research fellowship in the Anthropology Department. During the next thirty years, Marie observed a succession of male chairs and different styles of academic leadership: namely, those of John Barnes, Bill Epstein, Derek Freeman and Roger Keesing. She did not much care for any of them, and took delight in privately puncturing their pretensions. As a graduate student she had been exploited by Elkin, bullied by Nadel, and patronized by Stanner, so she took a dim view of god-professors in general, and tended to remain aloof from departmental politics. But Marie was politically and administratively active elsewhere; she served as a Justice of the Peace in Canberra for many years and was elected a Fellow of the Academy of Social Sciences in Australia in 1977. She had been the secretary of the Australian branch of the Association of Social Anthropologists in 1963 and served on the executive of its successor organization, the Australian Anthropological Society. Marie viewed with alarm the push within the AAS to establish it as a professional organization, to provide accreditation, especially for anthropologists working outside the university. Her strongly held view was that the AAS was established as a 'learned society' to promote anthropological knowledge and understanding. In 1995, although in poor health, she determined to attend the annual conference in Adelaide to do some 'quiet lobbying' for her point of view.

From the early 1960s until after her retirement in 1988 Marie revisited the Kuma regularly, and for this purpose she maintained a house at Minj. Her long-term association with the district allowed her to pursue an abiding interest in political and social change, about which she wrote innumerable articles. A graceful writer (of poetry and short stories as well as anthropological essays), Marie succeeded in making her academic writings accessible to a non-specialist readership. While she read carefully and engaged critically with theoretical developments in anthropology, she was no lover of grand theory and her essays invariably had a sharp ethnographic focus. She wrote on every conceivable aspect of Kuma life. Books that she edited or co-edited include: *Aborigines Now: New Perspectives on the Study of Aboriginal Communities* (1964), *The Politics of Dependence* (1971) and *Metaphors of Interpretation* (1985).

In an autobiographical essay entitled 'An innocent in the Garden of Eden', Marie concluded an engaging account of her life among the Kuma:

> I associate my early fieldwork in the Highlands with three basic experiences: the place, incredibly beautiful and as yet unsullied by tin roofs, steel pylons, and the dust of vehicular traffic; the people, colorful and friendly and eager to share with me their joys and sorrows; and discovery, the recognition of a set or sequence of events clicking shut in my understanding like a poem satisfactorily resolved. (Reay 1992: 164)

Marie was a notable if somewhat eccentric fixture of the ANU anthropology department and many generations of students will remember her with respect and affection. Her academic standards were of the highest order, and, although she encouraged independence of mind in her students, she was alert to any suspicion of fudged data and was particularly harsh on sloppy writing.

Marie Reay was a consummate ethnographer of great sensitivity, imagination and—given the obstacles and hazards of her time— extraordinary persistence and courage. Her classic book on the Kuma, her path-breaking research on race and gender and her commitment to the development of the discipline have secured her a place in the posterity of Australian anthropology.

References

Reay, Marie 1992. 'An innocent in the Garden of Eden', in *Ethnographic Presents: Pioneering Anthropologists in the Papua New Guinea Highlands*, ed. Terence E. Hays. Berkeley: University of California, pp. 137–166.

Simpson, C. 1954. *Adam in Plumes*. Sydney: Angus and Robertson.

Index

Page numbers in bold are illustrations. Page numbers with 'n' indicate footnotes.

adoption 193, 208, 243
adultery 66, 79, 188, 200
   compensation for 188
   punishment 200
age-mates
   adolescent girls 79
   affection and relations between
      93, 95, 98, 112, 113, 114,
      125, 143, 144, 151, 194, 204,
      211, 222, 228, 266, 279
   pig ceremonial and garden fertility
      251
agnatic ideology 19
agriculture
   major resources 69
   motivation for adoption 71
   women's roles tending gardens 73,
      76, 195, 212–215, 219, 227,
      233, 245
antiquities
   volcanic stone mortars and
      pestles, 69
apology 232, 242
army (employment) 233
assistants 136, 171
attractiveness
   female attractiveness 15, 91, 97,
      139, 171, 181, 197, 211, 226,
      232, 276
   male attractiveness 87, 88, 137,
      152, 181, 243

bachelors 96, 255
banking 235
Barnes, J. 288
Barwick, D. 35, 285
Beckett, J. 5, 10, 35n11, 40, 285
Berndt, C. 35, 286
Berndt, R. 20n5, 35, 40
betrothal
   payment 26, 28, 55, 73, 74, 102,
      105, 114, 116, 118, 120, 137,
      144, 175, 180, 222, 256, 279
Bohannan, L. 76
Bolim (Red Spirit) 66
boredom 93
bosboi 164n1, 169
brassieres 277
breasts 126, 129, 163, 193, 255
   breast-feeding 163, 221, 278
bride 131, 134, 169, 175, 205, 213
   exchange 137, 143, 145, 154
   killing 214
   procured 221, 223
   reluctant 163
bridegroom 253, 256
bridewealth 26
   see also marriage—payment
brother 80, 81, 101, 102, 111, 120,
      122, 133, 198, 222, 270, 279
Brown, P. 35
Bulmer, R. 35, 36, 69, 71, 286
burial 30, 97, 107, 196, 260, 281
Burridge, K. 12, 40

cannibalism 108
capture (girl) 16, 109, 115, 134–140, 147–151, 171, 179, 181, 182, 184, 186, 191, 196, 253, 261, 266, 271
    kidnapping 255
cargo cult 19, 36, 247
carrying leg *see karim lek*
Chimbu 31 (first mention)
choice 1, 14, 24, 101, 105, 122, 145–147, 149, 151–152, 171, 186, 226, 231, 233, 241, 256, 280
    see also laik bilong man, laik bilong meri
Christianity 24, 163, 180, 201, 212, 212–214, 217
    see also Roman Catholic Mission
clan 9, 10, 29, 30, 31–32, 49, 50, 53, 54–55, 256
    see also groups named
    clanship 19
    sub-clan 243
    women's relation to 9
coffee 216
comparison 53n16
compensation *see also* death
    adultery 188
    damage by pigs 205
    slander 231
    theft 229
conception
    native theory 136, 182
conformity
    deviants *see* woman—wandering
    women's *see* woman—good woman
courting 13, 14, 50, 76, 101, 111, 112, 115
    see also karim lek, tanim het
Court of Native Affairs 31, 37, 49, 74, 136, 144, 148, 157, 181, 182, 199, 200, 201, 205, 207, 216, 229, 235, 236, 241, 246, 261
cousins
    cross-cousins 244

co-wives 175, 176, 181, 182, 185, 193, 253
damages (payment) 205, 213, 231, 236, 242, 246
    see also apology
dances 83, 94, 96, 97, 145, 153, 178, 207, 212, 221–222, 251
    decoration 80, 88, 148, 160, 198
    participation 93
    technique 88, 94, 99
    women's roles 83, 255
death
    by sorcery/witchcraft 246, 247, 280
    by women's fights 253
    compensation payment for 255, 281
    compensation to maternal uncle by husband's clan on death of child 82
debt 54n19, 55, 230, 231
    women given to repay 55, 121, 133
decorations 80, 83, 87, 100, 101, 105, 109, 118, 122, 148, 196
designs 92, 123
disputes 141, 147–157, 178, 201, 216, 229, 230, 236, 245, 247, 270
divorce 177, 207, 228, 242, 248
domestic group activities 66
drawing 92
dreams 106, 259–260

Eastern Highlands 27, 35
elections 3, 239, 270, 278, 280, 282
Elkin, A.P. 20n4, 285
elopement 261, 279
Emanuel, J. 59
encounter 48, 50
Epstein, B. 288
ethnography 46
event 48, 49, 50
exchange (marriage) 54–56, 102, 105, 143, 148, 154, 195, 198, 202, 215, 222, 256, 261

exchanges 13, 73, 195, 255
  sister exchange 54
exogamy 19

Feil, D. 37
fellatio 201
fertility
  pig ceremonial for 83, 251
  propitiate Great Spirits for 66
fighting 97, 101, 115, 116, 126, 160,
  266
  see also violence
food
  food-names, identity and
    substance 114n1
  food presentation 129
  food taboos, sorcerers 162
  former semi-nomadic food
    gatherers 70
  gardens 99
  ground *Nothofagus* beechnuts 71
  pigs and sweet potato 69
Fortune, R. 35
freedom 19–20, 38, 40, 82, 83, 255
  adolescent freedom 1, 253
  and conformity to subordination
    83
  girls' choice of courting partners
    14
Freeman, D. 4, 37, 288
friendship 93, 105, 198

Gale, F. 35
gambling, cards 225, 226, 230, 233,
  235, 238, 248
gaol (jail) 129, 162, 241, 251
garden *see* food—gardens
garden land 244
gender relations 2, 43, 44
  in the Southwestern Pacific 2,
    20n6, 21, 24, 38, 43, 44, 66
genealogy
  reckoning 19, 54n19, 243
Geru 66

Geru boards 66, 85, 160
ghosts 66, 97, 121, 247
gifts 79, 80, 109
girls
  girl child, valuation of 183
  unmarried girls 'work' 76, 77
Glasse, R. 36, 286
Gough, K. 76
government presence 24, 105, 134,
  140, 167
government station 92, 105, 119,
  133, 202
government work 91, 136, 162, 233,
  246
grief, expression of 122, 124, 197
groups named [first and main
  mentions]
  Aiikup 176, 178
  Baiman 91, 169, 171
  Baimankanim 133, 243
  Bambilngya 144–147, 154
  Berebuga 137, 183, 187, 247
  Burikup (subclan) 95, 96, 133
  Damba 91, 169, 193
  Dambakanim 143
  Dambilika 134
  Gaimakanim 121, 122
  Kambilika 136, 163, 246
  Koimamkup 90, 95, 119, 125,
    133, 169
    sub-clans: Bomungdam,
      Kissukanim,
      Tunambauoldam,
      Entskizinga 243
  Kondiga (Kondika) 126, 153,
    180n2, 281
  Konumbuga 180–183, 185
  Konumbuga Pipikanim 121, 248,
    261
  Konumbuga Pipikanim
    Kumngakanim 222
  Kugika 29, 30, 31–32, 83
  Kumnga 91, 259
  Kumngakanim 137, 191, 222

Ngeniga 93, 98
Ngeni-Muruka 126, 215
Penkup Kumnga 91
Pingya 134, 154
Tangilka 83, 133
Taukanim (Konumbuga) 195,
    243
Waga 104–107
guns 24

hatchet 81, 139, 145, 153, 154, 161,
    170, 241
    attack on women with 252
Hau'ofa, E. 37
haus man (lineage) 13
Hays, T.E. 40
Hiatt, L. 285
Hogbin, I. 9, 10, 12, 28, 28n8, 40,
    286
house 24, 31, 66, 70, 77, 235
    cult house **85**
    Geru's house 66
    long-house 91, 92
    man's house 248, 262
    tethering runaways to house 82
    war sorcery house 97
    woman's house 247, 262, 279
Huli 21
hunting 70

incest 232, 235, 241, 270
indebtedness 82
individualism 24
infant mortality
    neglect 31, 184
infertility 104, 239
informants
    relations with 233, 234–236, 244,
        246, 282
intermarriage
    Kugika and Konumbuga clans
        between 117
interpreters 238

jealousy 79, 89, 94, 100, 102, 181,
    197
Jolly, M. 21, 40
Josephides, L., 21, 40

Kaberry, P. 35
karim lek (carrying leg) 13–14, **15,
    16,** 78n7, 87, 88, 93, 94, 101,
    104, 112, 113, 114, 119, 120,
    143, 168, 169, 179, 212, 227,
    257, 260
    fights during 97–101
Keesing, R. 20n6, 288
kiaps 31, 49, 59, 62
killing
    avenge clansmen's death 116
    fighting 194
    resentment from marriage 117
Kubor mountains 65

laik bilong man 24, 225ff.
laik bilong meri 24, 26, 29, 31, 49,
    70, 225, 270, 280
languages
    Minj Agamp Yu 60
Latukefu, R. 36
Lawrence, F. **4**
Lawrence, P. **4**, 35
leaders
    ceremonial leader 103
    effect of colonial presence on local
        leaders (luluai and tultul to
        councillors) 49
    leader of young men of subclan
        112
    prospective leader 181
    ringleader, young women's 213
    secondary leader 189
    'strong' man judged by number of
        wives 104
    succession 101
    traditional leader versus
        government-appointed
        headman 201

lineage 13
longhouse 101
love 234
luluai liv, 92, 96, 135, 152, 171

Macintyre, M. 20–21, 20n6, 39, 40
magic 69, 82, 87, 162, 165, 214, 215
male
    anthropologists' handicaps 76
    dominance 75, 76, 256, 257
    freedom 76
    sexuality 258
marriage 26, 27, 80, 83
    arrangement 105, 106, 113, 121,
        131, 280
    disposition of women in marriage,
        structural centrality of 16–17
    forced 105, 108, 115, 121, 123,
        179, 205
    payment 80, 102, 173, 181, 198,
        207, 216, 226, 230, 241, 273,
        282
    prohibition 213
    protest 252
    rituals 80–82
    return 214
    transaction between groups 82,
        256
Mayer, A. **4**
McCall, G. 37
McCarthy 269
McConnell, U. 35
Mead, M. 35, 76
medical care 220, 272
Meggitt, M. 35, 285
Merlan, F. 49, 53n15
Minj 288, 289
Minj Agamp Yu 60
missionaries 162, 212, 214
money 214, 280
mortar and pestle 69, 71, 73
mourning 93
Munn, N. 35, 285

mushrooms 26, 38, 170, 204, 248,
    269, 276, 282
myth 4, 45n5, 70, 71, 107n3

Nadel, S.F. 3, 27, 37, 59, 59n1, 286,
    288
naming, system of 54, 62, 63, 77

obligations 17, 54, 126, 197, 217
O'Connor, P. 6n2
O'Hanlon, M. 36
orators 81, 103, 150, 212
origin myths 70, 71, 82

Papuans 239
parents-in-law
    'fathers-in-law' 124
    mother-in-law, abuse by 227
    predatory in-laws 82
Parsons, E. C. 36, 41
patrivirilocality 13
pearlshell 80, 88, 99
Penny, R. **4**
pig ceremonial 83, **84**, 96, 99, 244,
    249
    carrying leg and dancing during
        87, 88, 93, 208
    duration 119
    frequency 83
    marriages contracted during 80,
        113, 117, 118, 121
    pig killings for 201
    rationale of ceremony, fertility
        66, 83
    temporary ceremonial village 96
    threat of gaol liv, 139, 162, 165
    treatment of visitors 99
    two phases 99
    women taking advantage of men's
        fear of going to gaol during,
        251
pig exchanges 73, 80, 140
pig grease, bathe in **18**, 80, 88,
    101–104

pigs 65, 66, 74, 77, 83, 247
  arrival in the Highlands 69
  devaluation effects 65
  female relation to 74
  'like a wild pig' 70
  obsession 65, 66
Pink, O. 35
places mentioned [first mentions]
  Bomung 91, 243
  Gwaip 134, 162
  Kerowil 183
  Kondambi 33, 83
  Konmil 101, 119, 125
  Kumberag (near Kugmil, west of
    Minj) 70, 73n4
  Mangi 185, 186
  Nondugl 107
  Pugamil 144, 154
  Tunambauolg 187
  Wozna River 194
plumes 83, 87, 88, 90, 93, 94, 99,
    101, 102–05, 109, 119, 123, 126,
    128, 133, 143, 144, 149, 151, 154
  see also valuables
  as compensation 188
  as pig-wealth exchange 195
  loaned 221
poetry 4, 28, 45, 289
poison 13
politics 289
  see also leaders
  electoral politics 38
  female political leaders 24
  study of exploitation and
    oppression of women 43n1
  transaction as male political
    activity 21
pollution 21
polygamy 79, 101, 104, 163, 164,
    165, 168, 175, 182, 187, 196,
    213, 214, 222, 243, 249, 253, 256
pork 66, 80, 81, 128, 138, 151, 162,
    183, 198, 265, 281

power
  adolescent girl's power 125
  colonial power 35
  departmental 38
  understanding inequality and
    power difference in male-
    female relations 39
  war sorcery 281
prestation see gifts
prestige
  associated with adolescent girl
    favours 76, 181, 258
  competence in warfare and
    sorcery 97
  gaol time from 251
  polygyny from 104
  reward; power; sexual
    attractiveness 112
  'strong' man, headman, leader
    104, 181, 201
projective tests 121, 282
punishment see also Court of Native
    Affairs
  attitudes towards imprisonment
    251
  avenge death by compensation
    126, 134, 135
  by killing 117, 118
  compensation for adultery 188
  government bans 74
  runaway wife of 82, 129
  women's punishment 20, 31, 34,
    91, 120, 138, 193, 200, 251

Radcliffe Brown, A.R. 76
rape 31, 136, 139, 171, 191, 199,
    248, 258
Read, M. 27, 28n8, 44, 45
Reay, M.
  archives 5–7
  biography 2–4
  experimental ethnographic
    writing 24–28
  manuscript 5–12

reciprocity *see* exchange; sister exchange
Red Spirit *see* Bolim
Research School of Pacific Studies (RSPacS) 285
ritual
    children's death rituals 197
    courtship 13, 77–78
    death 93, 107
    ritual protest 266
    see also exchange; fertility—pig ceremonial for; *karim lek*; marriage; mourning
Roman Catholic Mission 180
rubbish man 96
run away 125, 128, 135, 138–39, 145, 182, 184
Ryan, D. 36

sacrifices *see* Bolim; pig ceremonial
Salisbury, R. 35, 286
school 226, 227, 233, 236, 237
seance 66
segmentation 8, 13, 19, 38, 57, 69
seniority 101, 104
sexuality 75, 79, 87, 257, 272, 276
    see also girls; *karim lek*; rape
shells *see* valuables
sister exchange 54
Sitlington, G. 35
solidarity *see* age-mates; brother
song 112, 120
sorcery 97
speech-making 104, 113, 123, 124
spirits
    ancestral, 69 *see also* Bolim; Geru
    bush demon, 106 *see also* witchcraft
Stanner, W.E.H. 37
Strathern, A. 35, 114n1
Strathern, M. 12
subclan *see* clan
suicide 119, 138, 200, 219, 281

Svoboda, W. 4
sweet potato 69, 160

taboos
    cooked food for distinguished war magicians 162
    pig taboos, affecting women 65
tanim het 14, 77n6
    see also courting; *karim lek*
taro 71
tax 238, 239, 242
thatch 99
theft 225, 229
tok bokis 246
trade 65, 69, 115, 143, 181
trading partners 62
traditional enemies 116, 126, 136, 163, 180, 182, 194, 214, 275
tribe 12, 13
    see also groups named
tultul liv, 103, 160, 173

Valentine, C.A. 4
valuables *see also* cargo cult; exchange; wealth acquisition
    adornments 88, 101, 170
    categories 73
    courting gifts 14
    disposal at death 196, 197
    marriage payments 128, 190, 201, 256
violence 16, 20–25, 34, 38, 43, 47, 53, 74, 82, 88–90, 120, 122, 126, 128, 134, 138, 143, 155, 167, 169, 172, 176, 177, 191, 193, 201, 202, 203, 204, 205, 218, 252, 254, 262, 270, 273

Wahgi Valley 49
wandering women *see* woman—wandering
Wardlow, H. 21
warfare 62, 69, 97, 121, 134, 195
    battle-cry 167

government ban 74
war magicians 162
wealth acquisition *see also* pig
   ceremonial; valuables
   accession of new wealth 83
   pig-wealth 195
   woman's contribution to
      husband's clan wealth 74, 83
weaning *see* breasts—breast-feeding
Wedgwood, C. 35
Weiner, J. 40
Wenner-Gren Foundation 5, 40
widowhood 172, 193
Williams, F.E. 286
Wilson, J. 5, 40, 56
witchcraft 97, 137, 246–248
witches 248
woman
   as mother, 227, 230
   as mother-in-law 241
   choice, by young women of
      partner 1, 101, 105, 122, 222,
      231, 232, 242, 256, 281
   good woman 74, 191, 220, 254,
      255
   independent 240
   male evaluation of 74, 75, 254
   querulous 243
   wandering 31, 51, 74, 75, 80, 82,
      83, 172, 175, 180, 183, 185,
      187, 190, 191, 208, 251, 253,
      254
   women's houses 78
   women's jealousy of male
      promiscuity 79
   women's protests 74
   women's structural position,
      Reay's and other views 12–25
Woodger, H. **4**
work
   paid 118, 137
Wubalt   **84**, 222
   see also food—food presentation

yams 71
yi rom (rubbish man) 243 (also *yi
   komugl*)
Young, M. 3, 12, 20n6, 36, 37, 39,
   44, 45n5, 285